Jay-Z

JAY-Z

*Essays on Hip Hop's
Philosopher King*

Edited by JULIUS BAILEY
Foreword by CORNEL WEST

McFarland & Company, Inc., Publishers
Jefferson, North Carolina, and London

Library of Congress Cataloguing-in-Publication Data

Jay-Z : essays on hip hop's philosopher king / edited by Julius Bailey ; foreword by Cornel West.
      p.   cm.
Includes bibliographical references and index.

ISBN 978-0-7864-6329-9
softcover : 50# alkaline paper ∞

1. Jay-Z, 1969– — Criticism and interpretation.   2. Rap (Music)— History and criticism.   3. Rap musicians— United States.   I. Bailey, Julius.
ML420.J29J39   2011
782.421649092 — dc22   2011002125

British Library cataloguing data are available

On the cover: Portrait of Shawn Corey Carter, also known as Jay-Z (Photofest)

Second printing, with corrections

Manufactured in the United States of America

McFarland & Company, Inc., Publishers
  Box 611, Jefferson, North Carolina 28640
    www.mcfarlandpub.com

Table of Contents

Acknowledgments   viii

Foreword: On Jay-Z and Hip Hop Studies
CORNEL WEST   1

Introduction: In Search of Meaning: Sign, Symbol, and Shawn
JULIUS BAILEY   3

Part I: The Groundwork

1. Jigga Speaks: The Tradition of Black Oratorical Genius
   TONI BLACKMAN   25

2. The Authentic Cultural Agent
   G. JAHWARA GIDDINGS   39

3. The Meeting with a President and a "King"
   DAVEY D   52

4. A Urban Singer of Tales: The Freestyle Remixing of an
   Afro-Homeric Oral Tradition
   NICOLE HODGES PERSLEY   67

5. The Prodigal God and the Legacy of Socially Responsible
   Hip Hop
   T. HASAN JOHNSON   84

Part II: The Challenges

6. Zen and the Art of Transcending the Status Quo: The Reach
   from the Hood to the Suburbs
   BAKARI KITWANA   99

7. Black Marketing Whiteness: From Hustler to HNIC
   STEPHANY ROSE   117

8. A Forty Million Slave's Moment of Clarity
   DAYLAN DUFELMEIER   132

9. Hip Hop's Prospects for Womanist Masculinity
   MELINA ABDULLAH   141

Part III: The Classroom Freestyles

10. Complicating Shawn Carter: Race, the Code, and the
    Politics of School
    DAVID STOVALL   159

11. Oedipus-Not-So-Complex: A Blueprint for Literary
    Education
    A.D. CARSON   172

12. The Culture Industry: Mainstream Success and Black
    Cultural Representation
    GIL COOK   180

13. The Self-Reliant Philosopher King: Shawn Carter
    Exonerated
    SHA'DAWN BATTLE   191

About the Contributors   211

Index   213

To hip hop,
a continued breath of fresh wind
that sustains life and culture

Acknowledgments

With much appreciation:

To my mentor, father, and friend Dr. Cornel West for everything you have meant to this project and to me personally for all of my adult life.

To my mentee and philosopher in training, Dalitzo "Alfresco" Ruwe, who never sleeps yet consistently served as both agitator and foundation of this project. It was you who said it could be done, and it was you who pushed me to ensure that this project reached the world.

To our contributors who have endured countless requests for edits and extractions but tirelessly endured.

To my external readers and copy editors: Drs. Padmore Agbemabiese, Jonathon Gray, Amy Hobbs-Harris, Kamasi Hill, Erin Moore, and James Walton. Additionally, to cultural critics and writers Lasana O'Hotep, April Silver, and Kellea Tibbs. Lastly, to Andrea Meale and Laura Musselman, graduate students in English at California State University, Fresno.

To my student assistants: Kendrick Jones (Central State University), Christopher Moore (Central State University), and Cherella Nicholson (California State Fresno). And much love to the spring 2010 Philosophy of Hip Hop class (Central State University).

To Dr. Nancy McHugh and my new Wittenberg University Family, thank you all for your encouragement and support during some trying emotional times.

To the guardian angel of this volume, Dr. Anne Carroll ... Thank God for you.

Foreword

On Jay-Z and Hip Hop Studies

CORNEL WEST

This profound and pioneering book — edited by the superb and serious scholar Julius Bailey — is predicated on an indisputable truth: Jay-Z is an unadulterated genius and the most popular figure in the hip hop world. Needless to say, the hip hop world is the most influential and lucrative cultural force among young people in the world. So, *critical* readings of Jay-Z the artist, the man, and the visionary take us to the very core of the culture industry — artistic creation, monopoly distribution, and mass consumption — of capitalist civilization.

These brilliant and often biting critical engagements with Jay-Z's magisterial corpus — eleven classic CDs in fourteen years — give us the best interpretations we have of not only Jay-Z's work but also the present moment in the rich tradition of hip hop. These seminal essays exemplify and enact the *hybrid* character and content of hip hop studies — the complex intersection of cultural studies, capitalist studies, and contemporary politics.

Cultural studies consists of structural analyses and existential narratives of why and how meanings are made and feelings are felt. These analyses and narratives explain and describe the uses (and abuses) of sound, language, gesture, posse, image, and symbol in the emergence, sustenance, and decline of cultural forms and personal styles. Cultural studies proceeds by subtle ways of historicizing, contextualizing, and pluralizing our catastrophic-laden moments in space and time. Capitalist studies focuses on the complicated forms of economic power and influence, of financial authority and seduction. Capitalist studies highlights the moods and manners that accompany power-laden commodification processes at particular historical moments. Capitalist studies also keeps track of the fetishizing of commodities — ascribing magical and messianic powers to material things, objectified bodies, or luxurious products — that hide and conceal social hierarchies and subordinations. Contemporary politics is not

1

simply the state of elections in government or legislative procedures or policies. More importantly, contemporary politics is the balance of forces between powerful forms of organized money — oligarchs, plutocrats, monopolies, and bosses — and less powerful, less organized everyday people hungry for financial success and thirsty for public reputation. Hip hop studies requires all three fields — cultural studies, capitalist studies, and contemporary politics. Yet, as the great KRS-One always reminds us, to engage hip hop is not to be spectator or bystander. One should *be* hip hop as one engages hip hop. One should try to shape and mold hip hop to make it better, to make it more liberating — full of creative genius, full of political courage, and connected to the best of those who came before, such as Grandmaster Flash, Chuck D., Lauren Hill, and Gil Scott-Heron, as well as the Last Poets, Nina Simone and Curtis Mayfield!

I was blessed to have Jay-Z visit my graduate course on the black intellectual tradition (taught with Professor Eddie Glaude) at Princeton a few years ago. We read classic works by W.E.B. Du Bois, E. Franklin Frazier, James Baldwin, Anna Julia Cooper, and Toni Morrison. Jay-Z attended the same session that included the literary genius Toni Morrison and the towering actress Phylicia Rashad. Jay-Z remained silent most of the night, deeply engrossed in the intense intellectual exchange. He was curious and humble. When I lovingly pushed him to make comments, he said, "I've tried to play Plato to Biggie's Socrates!" His awareness of and sensitivity to his calling, tradition, and the legacy he would like to bequeath to the younger generation was quite apparent.

Jay-Z's sounds and lyrics, career and life are ideal for hip hop studies because of his incredible scope, depth, and breath. In these powerful and poignant essays, we witness the triumphs and failures, the complexities and ambiguities, the candor and complacency of Jay-Z's genius. We see how Jay-Z holds on for dear life to the Socratic, prophetic, and tragicomic roots of his hood in Marcy projects (Brooklyn) in the face of success within capitalist processes. And we also see him grow, mature, and try to shed his earlier sexist, parochial, and provincial outlooks. In short, this book is hip hop studies at its best.

I hope Julius Bailey's marvelous volume not only deepens our understanding of Jay-Z's precious presence among us, but also sheds more light on the catastrophic realities of the hoods in our midst — from the new Jim Crow caste system of the prison-industrial complex to the decrepit school systems, chronic unemployment, and gang violence, and to the patriarchal and homophobic practices. As Jay-Z reminds us, we all need more moments of clarity in order to leave deeper Blueprints for a better future!

Cornel West is the Class of 1943 University Professor in the Center for African American Studies at Princeton. He has published 20 books and has edited 13 texts, and The New York Times *has praised his "ferocious moral vision."*

Introduction

In Search of Meaning:
Sign, Symbol, and Shawn

Julius Bailey

"There's the gift, there's the spirit, and there's the work — all three have to come together. If one of those things is off, it can stop you from becoming who you were meant to be."
— Jay-Z in *O Magazine*, October 2009

In April 2008, presidential candidate Barack Obama gave a speech in which he acknowledged that he had received a number of sharp critiques from his main competitor, Hillary Clinton. He derided her personal attacks focused on what he called trivial issues and "textbook Washington" tactics. He also seemed fairly nonplussed by them. They're just part of politics, he told his audience; when you take hits like that, he said, you just have to ... and rather than finishing his sentence, he reached up and brushed the dirt off his shoulders. As the crowd leapt to its feet, Senator Obama laughed and repeated the gesture.

While the audience at the speech — including the young people behind Senator Obama onstage — seemed to love the gesture and understood its significance, others were confused by it. For example, MSNBC host Joe Scarborough admitted he and another commentator "looked at each other and said, 'What's he *doing?*'"[1] In both cases, the moment made one thing vividly clear: the immense impact of the rapper Jay-Z, one of the most successful hip hop artists and entrepreneurs in America. Senator Obama's gesture confirmed that the influence of Jay-Z — whose song "Dirt Off Your Shoulder" and its accompanying video popularized the gesture with millions of fans — stretches beyond the music world into popular culture and even politics.

This collection of essays is meant to help scholars and teachers more fully understand Jay-Z's influence and significance, and it is meant to offer tools for bringing this remarkable figure into the study and teaching of contemporary music and, indeed, contemporary culture. The range of his accomplishments suggests the varied contexts in which he can be studied: He has sold more than 40 million albums worldwide and won 13 Grammy Awards, amassed a fortune through his numerous and varied business ventures, been interviewed on *60 Minutes* and *Oprah*, worked with the United Nations' Water for Life campaign to combat the global water shortage, lent his fame and made significant financial contributions to relief efforts in New Orleans after Hurricane Katrina and in Haiti after the 2010 earthquake, and, as part-owner of the New Jersey Nets, pledged to move the team back to Brooklyn.

The career of Shawn Corey Carter — a.k.a. Jay-Z — of course also sheds light on the history, current state, and future of hip hop, and Jay-Z's work reveals the many compelling issues on which that music and its creators touch. Jay-Z, as much as any Puritan, emphasizes the importance of hard work, but also knows when to let go. As he has said of the process of achieving success, using himself as an example, "We work hard and apply ourselves in a way that when the job is done, you can look in the mirror and say I've exhausted all possibilities.... I've done all I can do to make this right. After that, let it go for it is out of your control" (*BestLife Online Magazine*). Jay-Z is someone, without debate, who peers into the darkness of the human social condition and works his way through that darkness, in a quest for "Victory" and the ability to sit on his "Beach Chair," images that serve as two of his song titles. But his work is not just about personal success. Oprah Winfrey has crowned him a philosopher king, and his music, like hip hop more broadly, serves as a force, particularly for minorities, of creating a new identity — but also a new rhetoric to augment the identity, a new lingo, new symbols of identity that have become part of a metamorphosis of black and brown youth, who have become part of a crescendo of lifted voices that stretch from the cotton fields to musical stages, from activist rallies to presidential inaugural receptions.

In "Notes on Nature," Ralph Waldo Emerson states,

> Every spirit builds itself a house; and beyond its house a world; and beyond its world, a heaven. Know then, that the world exists for you. For you is the phenomenon perfect. What we are, that only can we see. All that Adam had, all that Caesar could, you have and can do. Adam called his house heaven and earth; Caesar called his house Rome [1981].

Jay-Z calls his house hip hop. It is this younger generation's way of comprehending and dealing with life's changing reality. The birth of hip hop gave rise to a primacy of education, cultural awareness, and consciousness, as well as to insight into inner-city doings and sufferings. The current generation of hiphop artists is dealing with the ideal of achieving importance through fame. As they serve in such cultural roles as gurus, teachers, and worldly philosophers, they provide patterns of inquiry that help us deal with the need to matter, the quest for historical impact. As with so many musicians and writers, their work will stand the test of time, shaping the sounds and beliefs of their audiences.

Jay-Z is one of this generation's leaders. His artistic prowess continues to serve as a proverbial wind for all ages. But, as the essays in this book demonstrate, there are many ways to understand Jay-Z and what he represents. This project represents Jay-Z as much more than a rapper. Its contributors present him as a renaissance man, an entrepreneur, a cultural icon, a socially conscious rapper, even an artistic genius. But not all of them agree with those characterizations, and this collection is meant to help facilitate a discussion about his historic meaning and how to situate him in a tradition; it is meant to allow its readers to draw their own conclusions about his cultural relevance.

These critical essays are birthed from both the love of hip hop and the love of the generations that have been — and are being — influenced by hip hop. As such, the book can be used in hip hop studies, cultural criticism, literary studies, and Africana/African American studies. The essays provide a theoretical framework crafted so as to situate Jay-Z within a historical tradition that sheds light on the cultural phenomena called hip hop. This reader gives students, especially college students, a backdoor lesson on the history of hip hop, as well as its present and future. The body of Jay-Z's work is vast, and these essays explore his commentaries on the themes of life and death, corporate elitism, social consciousness, and community uplift. His work reflects the struggles of hope versus hopelessness, of historical sensibilities and future visions, and it investigates love and loss, the fuel that drives the life and the vocations of so many of us.

Sign, Symbol, and Shawn

Just as Alexander had thoughts of conquering Asia before he died but was optimistic about uniting Egypt and Asia, so Jay-Z is hopeful about the idea of Roc Nation conquering the music industry and merging with other empires to include film, clothing, sports, and more. But unlike Alexander — who downplayed wealth but wanted the most prized possessions in the world, particularly land, and wouldn't stop after one conquest — Jay-Z, as one of the founders of the Roc-A-Fella recording company and the related venture, Roc Nation, has coined himself rap's Gordon Gekko. We are reminded of this Gekko character, played by Michael Douglas in the film *Wall Street*, as Jay-Z frequently coins his own über-capitalist mantra by often stating in his music, that he is not a business man, he is a business. The empire that he has built includes the music world (he has served as the CEO of both Roc-A-Fella and Def Jam Records, and Roc Nation, which he co-founded, is a record label, a talent and management agency, and a music publishing company), clothing (through the Rocawear line), nightclubs (he is co-owner of the 40/40 clubs), and other ventures. Some might even question whether he has fallen prey to the same allures of the American Dream he so often warns his listeners of. In any case, his meteoric rise can be attributed to a keen business acumen, several strokes of luck, partnerships with other successful people, and a marketing brand that has surpassed all others in popular culture.

So can we affirm Jay-Z as the king of pop culture, or is the position a vacuous one? The term seems appropriate, for there has not been another figure who has the amassed cultural marketing capital, through music and other related cultural products, in the two generations of hip hop's history. Or maybe we simply defer to the adage coined by the sixteenth-century Erasmus: "in the land of the blind, the one eyed man is king."[2] Either way, Jay-Z represents the top level of hip hop success and influence. Marvette Britto, a public relations agent for many entertainers, confirmed his "influence as a tastemaker," and she called him "the E. F. Hutton of hip-hop."[3] With such a distinction, he deserves a full-length critical discussion of his historical legacy and artistic acumen. Further, these accolades bestow on him a measure of social responsibility and provide challenges to him, as an iconic figure.

This book includes a towering discussion between two talented academics, Stephany Rose and G. Jahwara Giddings, and a community organizer, Daylan Dufelmeier, who navigate their way through Jay-Z's vast accomplishments but ask, as he often does, what counts as success. In what may prove to be one of the most controversial pieces in this book, Rose brands Jay-Z as a neo-colonialist who should be de-mystified and rationally spanked for his overt pimping of American youth. She writes, "with lyrics emblematic of psychotic materialism, violence against blacks, deliberate objectification, and homophobia, his political thought often parallels the dominant culture's ideologies." When read against Giddings' piece, Rose's argument enters a pugilistic ring of critical proportions. Does Jay-Z commodify whiteness in a manner that threatens the cultural agency often professed by a hip-hop generation? Will we, the readers, be cornered into defending Jay-Z against these critiques? Giddings offers a reading of Jay-Z that seeks to justify his "clear conscientious commitment to cultural-nationalist aesthetic conventions" and identifies whatever has followed — his success, fame, and wealth — as by-products of the same.

> "The whole thing is to learn every day, to get brighter and brighter. That's what this world is about. You look at someone like Gandhi, and he glowed. Martin Luther King glowed. Muhammad Ali glows. I think that's from being bright all the time, and trying to be brighter. That's what you should be doing your whole time on the planet. Then you feel like, 'My life is worth everything.' And yours is too."
>
> — Jay-Z in *Best Life Magazine*, December 2008

In the words of Cornel West, if you are not spiritually, politically, and morally prepared to deal with success, you are headed for what Tennessee

Williams calls "a catastrophe of success." That concept begs the question: In what ways does Jay-Z promote moral prescriptions and flirt with social consciousness, but never become a social critic? If he offers only moments of revolutionary thought and action, but not a life of revolutionary practices, can we surmise that he provides us with an example of someone who wants "the best of both worlds"? Further, what is it that draws people into his narrative? Is his narrative simply the narrative of hip hop itself, or does Jay-Z offer us something different?

My mother said that she likes Jay-Z because he looks respectable. Such a simple yet loaded statement speaks loudly as we deal with a generation of youth whose interest in presentation and arête — or excellence — is overshadowed by a hood mentality and a hood morality of underachievement and "getting by before I lose it." As David Stovall mentions in his essay, "Complicating Shawn Carter: Race, the Code, and the Politics of School," "In K–12 schools, many African American males enact a code, but their lack of constructive outlets for expression and critical analysis often leads to further misinterpretations of their actions, disproportionately impacting their overrepresentations in suspensions, expulsions, and juvenile incarcerations." So can we find in one of Jay-Z's three *Blueprint* albums, or as we peer into his album *Life and Times*, a pedagogy upon which we can reach our youth? This reader's manifest function is to equip the educator, the community or religious leader, and the average hip hop fan with a language and structure for an intellectual debate. The very mention of Jay-Z does evoke certain stalwart positions (as Rose's critique makes clear), but, in many cases, a teacher's ability to link this cultural icon to a tradition can fully engage the attention of students. Clearly the challenge to transcend a visceral emotive response to his work, particularly if it is tinged with a situational memory, can be a monumental task for those whose love for his work — or for hip hop more broadly — is clouded by his Dionysian proclivities. It is an almost impossible task to intellectualize "Big Pimpin'" or "Dirt Off Your Shoulders" when these songs represent not only artistic creativity by the artist, but also social euphoria and even lament, as we shout out: "Man, that song was the shit back in the day!" But, pushed further, Jay-Z's human elasticity allows for non-racial (dare I say post-racial) discussion among his interpreters: A study of his work suggests the virtues and values innate in every person and accessible if they are given the opportunity to hone, enhance, and market their talents. Such discussions are germane to classrooms and water-coolers across the America, as people seek creative ways to engage in issues of race, class, gender, inclusion, democracy, and freedom. This project taps into what all can learn and employ from Jay-Z's life, laments, lucidity, and lyrics. It gives educators a blueprint for providing energetic and substance-laden discussions that free-thinking citizens seek.

But this challenge is made palatable when academics, like Stovall, turn on their academic swag and offer a connectivity and relevance to the spirit of young people. This is also true of A.D. Carson, in his contribution to this book. This rapper-turned-high-school-English-teacher offers a glimpse into his systematic hip-hop classroom. Unlike many hip-hop scholars in higher education, with the academic freedom to easily represent the best of our artistic culture in the classroom, Carson has had to navigate the waters of local school board curriculum control and fight for his right to use a hip-hop pedagogy. In his article, "Oedipus-Not so Complex: A Blueprint for Literary Education through Jay-Z Lyrics," he offers us a guide to using the example of Jay-Z as a storyteller and relates the structure, style, tone, and patterns of his lyrics to classical literature. For the literature professor attempting to infuse the classroom with life and cultural relevance, Carson says, "Why not use the Jigga-Man himself?" Fostering intertextuality and potentially stirring up critical thinking skills, we, as educators, must resurrect what I call academic gangsters (those students and teachers who are cerebrally aggressive and intentionally fearless in drawing fresh pedagogy from wherever we can find it) from the overshadowing of timid "wangsters," who uses the rapper Curtis Jackson — a.k.a. 50 Cent — to define someone who scholastically barks with formidable strength but whose practicing bite is unoriginal, lazy, and bland. To reach today's student the classroom must be a dynamic place of integration, an infusion of the social, cultural, and technical atmosphere, and it must avoid an adherence to pedantic tales of "how education used to be." This is similar to what West calls for in his lectures, namely creating an imprint and avoiding being an echo. This is the classroom's challenge. Locating relevance, facilitating growth, and fostering a spirit of scientific, humanistic, and cultural innovation is what the best of us teachers are challenged to do. This challenge is also situated within the very nature of hip-hop culture itself, in its efforts to be creative and relevant, and (commercially) successful.

As I wrote this introduction, I asked the 58 students in my Philosophy of Hip Hop Culture class at Central State University, "Carest thou not if hip hop perish?" Their fascinations run with the lyrical simplicity of the rapper Gucci Mane (who sounds like an intoxicated uncle at a family picnic trying to gain an audience at the kids' table) and rapper Nicki Minaj (whose bisexual messages of self-invention and reinvention in the form of a Barbie doll promote psychic schizophrenia at best). I want to challenge my students: How can you lie here asleep and allow such unimaginative toxins in your mental system? Are you not the harbingers of hope, the orchestrators of hip hop's present and future? Is not the purpose of education to lead out of such limited visions and to imagine something bigger, brighter, better? If we want to strive toward that goal, it is our responsibility to take ownership in our education and into our collective futures as active, innovative agents of thoughts, visions, and ideas. But if we are forever pushing and peddling someone else's ideas and indulging in the illusion of wealth and wisdom based on the quantity of collection of others' ideas, what will we own? What legacy to hip-hop culture will we leave? This is what Jay-Z provides—specifically, a glimpse into our own mirrors of activity and questions into our meaning, our relevance, our freedom, and our flight from the mundane into the new.

Historically, maybe we can think of the founding fathers of this nation as eager young adults who fled from home in search of a new ideal. If so, we get to the central issue of identity. Now, of course, the founding fathers of this nation had a strong sense of culture they could defer to. Penning a blueprint shaped by the Victorian ideals of England, the humanist ideals of Italy, the architectural prowess and political governance of Rome, they created a vision of America. On their journey of identity, they had ideals of culture, legacy, and upbringing on the one hand, and the need to start anew to create an identity, on the other. This nexus, this fork of the proverbial road, is the one that faces hip hop. And we hope that these essays on Jay-Z provide us with a vision that helps us blaze a new trail, or at least take a less travelled path. Coming from a time when we lost two of hip hop's geniuses, Tupac Shakur and Notorious B.I.G. (one who spoke on socio-political issues and one who spoke more on money than problems that confront those who achieve the American dream), Jay-Z not only inherits ideas on some of the delusions of youths, but also the ambition and wisdom to bring about change. If he is to help a new cultural ideal to emerge, he must articulate the socio-political ideals from Tupac while carrying on the grandiose ideals of American dreaming from Biggie.

This Huckleberry Finn complexity is evident in where we are in hip hop today. The founding fathers of hip hop—like many of us academicians—wrestle with a proclaimed Victorian entitlement of defining what hip hop is. This idea is fleshed out in the essay by T. Hasan Johnson, as he wrestles with the question, "Where do we situate Jay-Z?" By age, he rests on the old-school side of this development see-saw, but his music has been on both sides of hip hop's generational divide. Jay-Z, coming of age in the 1980s, was influenced by the dark rue of New York City, and thus he was born within the foundation of hip hop. Since then, these new folk, what Bakari Kitwana calls the post–hip hop generation, born after 1985, is navigating its way through this sankofa-esque terrain. In other words, people like Jay-Z forcibly look back and draw upon the past, even as they look forward to create a new trail into the future. Fittingly, Nicole Hodges Persley, in her essay, not only places a spotlight on Jay-Z's linguistic prowess, but also situates his prowess within a tradition of oral narrative poetry and improvisational theater. This important discussion not only contributes to the ongoing analysis of foundation and grounding within tradition, but also articulates the complexity of those rappers and hip-hop innovators who use performance (including dance, deejaying, and fashion) to assert their authentic voices. Certainly in its attempt to ground us in signs and symbols, her essay challenges all of us in hip hop to invoke a principle larger than us. These discussions are meant to challenge us—as students, teachers, community activists, and parents—to set standards of excellence. If accomplished, even the subjective nature of the art within hip hop, or in Jay-Z's work as an artist, won't disappear, and it can be discussed within a frame of historic consciousness.

While also paying close attention to Jay-Z's musical contributions, feminist/womanist scholar Melina Abdullah presents Jay-Z's work as "an oppositional gaze," an intellectual battle of critical jabs and conscientious blows. Her aim is to cause the reader to again wonder if this giant, Jay-Z, is tall in stature and success, yet small in his understandings of the terrain women must navigate, as the world is paved with language and ideas from Jay-Z and others.

For the reader who is concerned with critical race theory and nuanced discussions of post-modern analysis, it may be fair to delve into the question of whether critical race theory is a viable tool for analyzing hip hop. In *Parodies of Ownership: Hip Hop Aesthetics and Intellectual Property Law*, Richard L. Schur argues that hip hop and its culture are based on the fight against property law, and thus have spawned an individualist ideal, as opposed to an ideal of social activism for rappers and artists. This fits with the proprietary battles associated with music and sampling, as well as the images, ingredients, and fetishes that riddle hip-hop videos. But when we critique rappers, we critique their words, language, style, flow, meaning, and so on. Hip-hop academicians rarely have intellectual battles over the layering of a James Brown track up against a Stevie Nicks riff. So, in the words of Jay-Z, "What we talking 'bout?" For Richard Delgado and Derrick Bell, the answer was legal analysis and race, and we cannot disassociate Kimberly Crenshaw, Cornel West, David Stovall, and others from this discourse on critical race theory. Clearly, if there are many roles an artist can take, from the mic to the sound boards to the board room, there is plenty room for critical race theory to illuminate those points on the music entertainment spectrum.

But philosophers, post-modern thinkers, and critical race theorists concern themselves with race, message, and meaning. Perhaps intellectuals should be more attentive to what kind of democratic message is sent when Jay-Z or Q Tip utilizes artists of soft and hard rock, while allowing various voices on a track that is as fluid as Duke Ellington's band. Hence the questions of hip hop and cultural authenticity that Elliott Wilson, Adam Mansbach, Bakari Kitwana, Michael Eric Dyson and others debate so eloquently fit within a critical race theory framework. As for rap itself, there is no organic sound except the voice of the rapper, and to be a single voice for a generation requires a lot of maturity patience, love, and hope. While there is individual genius in jazz, it, too, is a collaborative sound, with syncopation and innovation between the various artists. The solo artist has the capacity to articulate the sounds of a people, but so does the band, even while there are no words during the syncopation. Is this not open for analysis through critical race theory? Jay-Z travels with a band for this reason but cites rock and roll as where he got the idea from. While the words may be loaded with numerous meanings and entendres, all you need is a soulful beat to augment your plight.

The extraordinary writer Wallace Thurman, in his novel *Infants of the Spring*, writes about the rise and influence of black art from the perspective of artists from the Harlem Renaissance, who wrestled with the dilemma of carrying on tradition or creating a new reality. In Thurman's book, a number of characters want to be recognized for their merits not as black singers or black authors, but as human beings. Thurman writes, "It will be some years before the more forward will be accepted as human beings and allowed to associate with giants. The pygmies have taken us over now, and I doubt if any of us has the strength to use them for a stepladder to a higher plane" (1992). Given the awesome weight of Jim Crow America, the wanton violence exacted upon people of color, and the powerlessness with which blacks had to subvert such atrocities, we can read the Harlem Renaissance, the period between 1919 and 1939, as a response to the assertion. I can't change the external so I will change the internal, to clear my way to eternality. Governed by an attempt to avoid the deferred dream Langston Hughes writes about[4], Thurman and Jay-Z have learned to take action within their own circumstances.

This is also a message of hope and existential appropriation of meaning and purpose in our ancestors' tales of deferred dreams that fill Sunday sermons or songs like "I got shoes, you got shoes, all of God's chillen got shoes." The Harlem Renaissance held a pulse for the soul era's crescendo, which led to the genius that governed hip hop's vehicle to combat the stereotypes and turn them on their head. However, with today's hip hop, there is a madness that now governs music videos and the lifestyle that rappers try to sell — and even Jay-Z has fallen victim to it. But, common sense philosophy maintains that the idea that creates the problem can't be the same idea that solves the problem. Such life pragmatics are erased as we look at hip-hop's ascendency. From the gutter of urban existences hip-hop uses itself to re-create a vehicle toward self-determination, voice, success, and happiness. Jay-Z purported in his seventh album, *The Gift and The Curse*, also articulated in Jacques Derrida's Pharmakon. A lot of life lessons are based on identifying and imitating. People identify with so many things that we forget to identify with being human. No one suffers from an inferiority complex based on being human; we suffer from inferiority complexes based on the very same things we identify with, like the color of our skin, our height, our weight, or our educational level. Jay-Z shows the trials and tribulations of assimilation into the American Dream by focusing on the invisible man's plight of doing business at the street corners where the sun doesn't shine. By identifying himself with an inferior or common origin, he can later discuss progression, as he does in his 2009 album, *Blueprint 3*, by admitting he went from [illegitimate] drug dealing on the corner to a own [legitimate] corner office. In this writer's opinion, Jay-Z raises the Dostoevsky-like question of how much any individual can influence his surroundings while tearing down universal absolutes of "good-vs.-bad" and self-creating a pathway toward happiness.[5]

This reshaping, or renaming, or reforming, of the self is a particularly important question if, on the innovation scale, the individuals happen to be part of a group of urban laggards. No matter how much prosperity comes from being part of that group, the social status of the group never changes. I am reminded of the hip-hop term "hood-rich," which describes an individual, often using illegal means to secure income, who represents a superfluous lifestyle. In the spirit of Jay-Z's song "Renegade," one must adopt a philosophy of "I rebel, therefore I exist,"[6] or as he says in "Say Hello" on the *American Gangster* album, he is an extraordinary man that daily seeks to rise about ordinary circumstances. Jay-Z echoes Razumikin in Dostoevsky's *Crime and Punishment*: "All men are divided into ordinary and extraordinary. Ordinary men have to live in submission, have no right to transgress the law, because they are ordinary. But extraordinary men have a right to commit crime and to transgress the law in any way, just because they are extraordinary." Developing into an "extraordinary nigga" is why Jay-Z, and those who live lives of relative obscurity, seek to build and sustain a sense of the extraordinary as a subversive response to invisibility. Just as Sojourner Truth asked in her 1851 speech, "Ain't I a Woman," and James Weldon Johnson asked in 1901, in his song "Lift Every Voice and Sing"; just as Booker T. Washington proudly exclaimed in 1901, in *Up From Slavery*, and just as James Brown hollered in "Say It Loud — I'm Black and I'm Proud," Jay-Z forces this generation to change the way they seek to live. This drive is consistent with what the nineteenth-century philosopher Friedrich Nietzsche would call the quest of Übermensch, specifically a radical denial of socially constructed otherness, in favor the self-creation of an Overman. Nietzsche's question is: How does a horizontal moving creature learn to use its vertical nature or rise from the bottom to the top? In other words, why wait for heaven when I can have the sky in my hands if I plant my feet on earth and raise my hands to pull down the sky? Black Panther Party founder Huey P. Newton asked, "Before we die how shall we live?" Jay-Z's answer can be found in a song called "Can I Live" on his inaugural album: where he says that living without action is not his aim as he seeks to die larger than life (*Reasonable Doubts*, 1996).

It does seem that Jay-Z, as Overman, is rooted in a capitalistic ideal, caught in a muddle — like a character in a play by August Wilson. Contributor Daylan Dufelmeier, in the tune of Kenneth Burke, queries whether it is that man uses words or that words use man. In this instance, is it that man uses the industry or does the industry use man? In his essay, "A Forty Million Dollar Slave's

Moment of Clarity," Dufelmeier negates Jay-Z's nature as what some call a transformative figure. The key issue is whether Jay-Z belongs to a group or ideology that has always had to conform to another man's symbols and the limitations they impose.

As Frantz Fanon argues, "The intellectual calls for ways of freeing more and more slaves and ways of organizing a genuine class of the emancipated. The masses, however, have no intention of looking on as the chances of individual success improve. What they demand is not the status of the colonist but his place. In their immense majority the colonized want the colonist's farm." In that respect, the rising tide of black republicanism, echoing a self-indulgent, market-driven ethos, in the form of the "emperor's clothes," has permeated hip-hop culture. Contextually, there is a sense to which this exceptionality model (which holds up those very special few), for African Americans, has made many of us into objects of history with sentiments of black power not in a Huey P. Newton or a Stokely Carmichael vein, but more in an effort toward conquest and domain. As the hip-hop and post–hip hop generation attempts to redefine our identity in this country, the CEO model is what is sought. But since only a talented or lucky tenth (or even a tenth of a tenth) ever get to the level of hip-hop empire that Diddy, Russell Simmons, and Jay-Z have reached, what should we make of their success as entertainers and businessmen? And, as far as progressivism and the ideas that we hold dear, are we watching a replication of a Fanonian construction take shape around us? This point is precisely where contributor Stephany Rose agrees with Dufelmeier and asserts, as does Fanon, that the colonized intellectual has invested his aggression in his barely veiled wish to be assimilated into the colonizers' world. Jay-Z, then, has placed his aggression at the service of his own interests, his interests as an individual. The result is the emergence of a kind of class of individually liberated few that distances itself from the proletariat class. But the irony, as they "keep it real," is that Jay-Z and others claim to represent their proletariat class through individualism and guises of black capitalism.

Nelson Mandela, in his autobiographical depictions of his incarceration at Robben Island, wrote, "You must understand the mind of the opposing commander. ... You can't understand him unless you understand his literature and his language." New York is the mecca of capitalism and to have an "Empire State of Mind," to quote Jay-Z's anthem, is to have an understanding of the literature and language or symbols that are used to drive and motivate human beings. Jay-Z, as a modern-day capitalist, crafts a vision for this hip-hop and post–hip hop generation through his music, his business ventures, and even his concerts. When we attend a Jay-Z concert with digital backdrops depicting the stories through language and symbols, we, like traders on the floor of Wall Street, look up as adoring fans cheering and watching this cultural phenomenon known as Jay-Z.

I remember a discussion section in one of my classes in which we were discussing W.E.B. DuBois and the problems associated with cultural elitism. Whether it was the use of terms like "alienation" and "disconnect," or "paternalism" and "social sympathy," there seemed to be no end as to how the distressed mass of people will react to those who are perceived within this elitist model. When Plato speaks of the philosopher who gains knowledge of the forms (light, goodness, truth, beauty) only after being chained in ignorance and false representation, he describes the backlash against this change in as both swift and pervasive. So one must question whether it is in the interest of the enlightened to return to dark and unenlightened conditions, for, in many instances, such a return will be met with resistance and hate. Where the challenge comes in for someone like Jay-Z, then, is in the representation of elite status. The issue is not how much the elite love us, but that this love must be shown through the perilous balancing act of keeping one foot in the Marcy projects of Brooklyn (where Jay-Z grew up) and the other in Manhattan, home of his worldwide empire. Thus, the question is how the successful create a commonality and avoid elitism, while manifesting and living in their own growth and excellence.

It is here that Gil Cook and Sha'Dawn Battle spit their fire. Cook posits a thesis that focuses on cultural hybridism. In his piece, Cook surmises that, with lyrics demonstrated in "Empire State of Mind," Jay-Z offers one example of his engagement with a discourse on being hood — and being of the hood. In this song Jay-Z presents his hood-ness as containing enough versatility to facilitate his simultaneous existence in disparate worlds, represented by Tribeca (an affluent Lower Manhattan neighborhood) and the hood. Jay-Z represents being hood as an empowering concept he has endowed with value and meaning. In contrast, Battle queries whether Jay-Z even maintains a hood identity, given his use of esoteric language and class analogies. Such a discussion — wrought with the psychological, the sociological, the linguistic, and the philosophical — offers the reader a launching pad for wonderful critique, not just of Cook's analysis but of the substantive claims that undergird his analysis. From code-shifting to underachievement, from the bravado of swag to existential anxiety, as we reach America's youth in the classroom and beyond, Jay-Z — as an artist, a man, and a symbol — offers us a phenomenal pedagogy that can allow us into their lives, hearts, and minds. What we must recognize, especially to the urban youth of America, is that in order to be instructive we must know; but to be effective we must feel.

Performers and hip hop cultural ambassadors Toni Blackman and Davey D both thoroughly understand the importance of cultural hybridity but push the idea further by seeking excellence within a prophetic tradition. In her piece, Blackman, an unashamed lover of Jay-Z, laments over the unrealized greatness she sees in him. She understands him as someone who—as true friends do—loves who you are and challenges you to be the best you can possibly imagine.

She characterizes Jay-Z as an underdeveloped superhero who, if not for a recognition and rededication (even at 40), may leave Earth victim to the kryptonite of unrealized potentiality. On the other hand, Davey D challenges us to recognize Jay-Z's limitations when he claims, "Jay-Z would come to influence us to do a lot of things, but at what cost? Did we lose or gain a more powerful voice on Jay-Z's watch? Did we become cheerleaders or remain agitators?" Regardless of where the reader stands on this debate, it is one that will resonate long after the last word has been read.

Technology, Education, Social Action and Hip Hop

I am forthright with my proclivity toward old-school teaching tactics. While others are power-pointing, Skyping, distance-learning, and the like, I can be found still wiping chalk dust off my shoulders (to play Jay-Z's hit). Those of us who teach at less advanced have to engage in such dated forms of classroom interaction. But I have also had some teaching stints in more state-of-the art classrooms and lecture halls.

Recently I was in a hotel room in rural Ohio and I had no wife, no child, and nobody to call at 5 A.M. So I sat with my Cornel West reader, my Socrates reader, and my compilation of Jay-Z's lyrics, thinking about the life of the mind but also thinking about solitude, memory, and loss. It quickly reminded me of that line in *The Souls of Black Folk* where DuBois says, "I sit with Shakespeare and he winces not." But at the same time I was on Facebook and Twitter letting the world know — or whoever would pay attention at that hour — that I was involved in highbrow intellectual engagement. This interplay or fusing of genres — the book and the computer — speaks volumes to the malaise of attention deficit disorder that many in today's society suffer from. At one level we seek knowledge and information, but it must come quickly and palatably. For example, as I write the word "palatable," I am reminded that there will be a high percentage of students reading this who will hit Google or an online dictionary and look up the word. What happened to the print dictionary? "Hip hop" and "patience" are two words that don't go hand in hand. As we escaped from the sedentary and isolated realities of the 1950s and '60s, and as we took part in a new-found America, post–civil rights, we sought engagement by any cost. The book creates that isolation that hip hop shuns. From the cipher to the dance crew, if there is an intellectual engagement in play, it must be communal and viral. This is sort of Toni Morrison–like, where individual thoughts must give way to community or social interaction.

Every period of technological advancement has had its own social challenges. The print press enabled readership, but also saw the spread of propaganda that raised the question of who was entitled to certain material as a source of information and knowledge. Later, the same thing happened with radio, newspapers, television, and now the internet. With advancement come social challenges. Hip hop, for example, is not opposed to the vocal outcry and public demands that are constitutive to social change. As a freshman at Howard in 1989, I remember April Silver and Ras Baraka, along with rappers Paris and others, being deeply involved in hip hop but at the same time organizing rallies and direct forms of political action. The last few election cycles have seen Diddy's "Vote or Die" campaigns and Russell Simmons' H.H.S.A.N. (Hip Hop Student Action Network) become natural formulations of social engagement in hip hop. These movements were connected to the lyrics of early hip-hop groups such as B.D.P. and KRS-1, and they were naturally associated with the challenges raised by Public Enemy and Poor Righteous Teachers. It is here that T. Hasan Johnson and Davey D launch a serious connection with history and Jay-Z's connection or lack of connection with it. Hip hop, founded on the public outcry, has now been internalized via iPods, download links, smart phones, and receptive nodding heads. Whether they are walking on congested campuses, walking down city streets, working out at the gym, or even entering classrooms, hip hop lovers are reciting rhymes. It seems to me that, if I were a rapper like Jay-Z, I would have to create a rap entitled "D.O.P. (Death of Protests)," as the only social outcry from hip hop lies in a handful of lyrics, or the double entendres that exist on the CDs, music videos, or tracks. Sure, we may call the radio station trying to figure out why they are not playing our favorite song, but this outcry isn't for social change; it's for content change. While it does appear that BET's chairperson, Debra Lee, has responded to the outcry against dumbed down and highly sexualized programming with a radical shift to more serious and emotional content, there is not any ongoing critique of social, personal, or political structures at BET or any of Viacom's channels. We must turn to Cathy Hughes, and her Radio One empire, for a more responsible representation of black life and for a focus on the very newsworthy and political issues that Viacom has omitted.

That raises the question: Is hip hop capable of social change and is Jay-Z able or willing to join the charge? In some cases we are confusing social change with content change, pushed through parental advisory labels, record sales and boycotts, and critiques. Without suggesting a measure of "goodness" or "badness," I contend that, today, content change is the new social change. Like social networking fans who send emails demanding changes done by the webmasters, we are believers in the illusion that by changing our images, our frequent status on Twitter or Facebook, or the music on our iPods, we will have engaged in social change. Many in this post–hip hop generation have become too complacent to text in our *American Idol* votes and simultaneously donate to relief aid.

But do we assuage our psyches by asserting our engagement? Have we learned anything from our past generation? Wouldn't you think Fanon would be rolling over in his grave to see that the social protesting platforms of the oppressed are being tweeted on Twitter? Is this participatory reality or illusion? Hip hop, historically, has sought to engage and challenge, even the dependency on technology with microphones, speakers, and CDs. Technology, then, plays a part in the axiom articulated by the late behavioral psychologist Paul Watzlawick, namely that one cannot not communicate, thereby making it hard to differentiate the artificial intelligence of technology from that of the stories most rappers sell. With this being said, what is hip hop selling? What is Jay-Z selling, or communicating? Is it social consciousness? Social activism? Both? Neither? When Jay-Z argued, relative to creativity and vocal delivery in his song "D.O.A. (Death of Autotune)," that the artist must be mindful of legacy when mimicking according popular trends, was this not being socially conscious? For those who say that it is not enough, what choices do we have, given the highly technological and instantaneous moment we live in? The websites and the blogs—which can be accessed by a mobile phone — are this generation's microphone, with which it will amplify communication of the human struggle. This, then, becomes the new (taken for granted) backdrop of our reality, and it creates a double bind. On one level it creates an escape and a mass comfort level into which hip hop is being forced. But we have erred in our reasoning if we believe that if we change our physical or psychic realities by simply changing our status, then we are engaged!

Falling Prey to the Imagery Trap

This project, as a teaching tool, would be failing in its academic duties if it didn't address the ground-swelling mythologies and rumors surrounding Jay-Z and satanic worship, secret society affiliation, and demagoguery. Within the past year or two, the mere mention of Jay-Z, especially among YouTube aficionados, have pointed to these mythologies while extrapolating language or video images into an otherworldly conversation. Admittedly, I, the editor of this volume, do not know Shawn Carter personally, so I cannot offer a definitive or even speculative affirmation or denial of these assertions. What I will do is use my platform in the spirit of this book as a teaching tool. The image of evil has been bantered about in public space recently about Jay-Z. But I assert that this pattern of conjecture tells us more about the nature of this "evil" than it tells us about Jay-Z. For this attraction involves the beholder's wish to get close to the image. This desire to enter into the image and its world often reveals a desire to retreat from the "real" world. In this case, the image is Shawn Carter and what his personal spiritual affinities are. So we ignore his hundreds of spiritual references and, instead, look microscopically into a world of make-believe and audience-induced creation of the "real." An example of this point can be found in the story of Pygmalion, who retreated from real women, who he saw as sinful, into the world of his creation. Similarly, we run the risk of preferring the world of the image over that of reality, and thus run the risk of being trapped by the image. One should remember the story of Hansel and Gretel, who were attracted to a house, or to an image, because of their hunger. As a result, they fell victim to a witch. One should also remember Oscar Wilde's warning in his preface to *The Picture of Dorian Gray*: "All art is at once surface and symbol. Those who go beneath the surface do so at their peril. Those who read the symbol do so at their peril. It is the spectator, and not life, that art really mirrors" (2007). Wilde thus again draws the connection between the image and the viewer; he points out that there is a basic, and potentially dangerous, desire to go beneath the surface of the image into some dream land of fantasy and illusion. Accordingly we, as consumers of popular culture, look at the images of Shawn Carter in this light (or darkness, if you must).

As you situate yourself in the mix of voices raised in this literary contribution to the universe, please receive this text with what rapper Common calls "Retrospect for Life." For sign, symbol, and man do not rest in the same repository of understanding. The man, who was born Shawn Carter, the artist that we have come to know as Jay-Z, and what we take from his works are all different layers of reality. From the ancient Egyptians to Jay-Z, we, the spectators, are forced to locate ourselves in respect to the art which, by our own naturally tragic flaw, separates us from the truth. It is in this vein that we explore Jay-Z as social critics, not biographers. We recognize that the arguments posed are exercises of creative and rational minds and not a biographical discourse of Jay-Z. Nevertheless, we seek to know; we search to find meaning in both the artist and the art. Let this humble project buttress your search for knowledge and meaning through the life and work of Jay-Z.

A Final Editor's Note

Each chapter concludes with a series of questions for public discussion, classroom exchange, or further research. In keeping with the spirit of this project, I will proffer some guiding questions that are at the underpinnings of what I and Cornel West do as philosophers, theologians, and radical democrats. I hope you enjoy this collection of critical essays but it only becomes "critical," just as any art, if you engage in its meaning.

Consider the following:

1. James Baldwin suggests, "How can one, however dream of power in

any other terms than in the symbols of power?" (1992). Hip-hop stars have found themselves not understanding the social and political context of youth in different countries and criticized in most foreign countries for promoting hedonistic pleasures, and thus creating false hope for youth here, and in most countries, where Bentleys, rims, mansions, G5s are not attainable. The fantasy of "Think and grow rich"[7] or "get rich or die trying"[8] offers a myriad of problems.

2. In the introduction of *Prophesy Deliverance*, Cornel West argues that the pitiful are those who remain objects of history, victims manipulated by evil forces whereas the tragic are those persons who become subjects of history, aggressive antagonists of evil forces. Victims are pitiful because they have no possibility of achieving either penultimate liberation or ultimate salvation; aggressive antagonists are tragic because they fight for penultimate liberation and in virtue of their gallant struggle against the limits of history they become prime candidates for ultimate salvation (2002). We certainly find this motif in the work of Tennessee Williams[9] and Henrik Ibsen.[10] Certainly, in a Christian religious sense, this sensibility of the tragic is found in the Good Friday and Holy Saturday experience. When we think of the liberation struggles of Frantz Fanon, Mandela, Nat Turner, Harriet Tubman, Malcolm X and Martin King and others, they, too, fit this sense of the tragic. Is there any way that we can look at hip hop in this same radical sensibility? So when Jay-Z calls himself a renegade manifested in the track "Renegade" in the *American Gangster* album, can we fit him in that same tradition but as a rapper?

3. Many of the authors are progressive-minded. Some even go so far as to claim we are watching a replication of a Fanonian[11] construction take shape around us where he asserted, "The colonized intellectual has invested his aggression in his barely veiled wish to be assimilated to the colonizers world. He has placed his aggression at the service of his own interests, his interests as an individual. The result is the ready emergence of a kind of class of individually liberated slaves, of freed slaves. and the rise of a black middle class that distances itself from the proletariat class of African Americans that lingering mode staying with today's hip hop models who claim to rep their proletariat class through individualism and guises of black capitalism under the guises of owning their own record labels in the pursuit of creating miniscule amount of autodidactic millionaires making us object of history and not subject of history."

4. Jay-Z and Oprah publicly agreed on their show to disagree on hip hop's counter-argumentation on the N-word. Most of hip hop and post–hip hop Generation view the N-word with a certain apathy or desensitivity. Clearly we recognize the power that language has to shape ideas and change definitions. But this historic power to the term isn't a priori is it? Must we ascribe a Kantian pure and unconditional label to the term due to its universalized malaise? To challenge this generation on the basis of being disconnected to the painful

advent and sustained occupation of the term and its racial praxis is to under-score the very birth of hip hop. As a virtual self-discovery and self-definition in the wake of a post–civil rights era whose newly enacted freedoms certainly dumbed or numbed the following three generations to what James W. Johnson called the "way that with tears have been watered, and treading our path through the blood of the slaughtered."[12] As such, how can we feel the same disdain for a term that is known as a term of endearment to many inside hip hop? I would argue that hip-hop culture has contrived a sort of philosophical, Derridan deconstructionism that speaks to the multiple layers and shifting contexts of language. Further, as a fundamentally social construction, the N-word must be able to undergo a counter-critique of its power and impact. Can we not conclude that hip hop provides this counter-critique by seeking to eradicate the self-evident notions of the term? Why is the term still taboo in America?[13]

Notes

1. As reported by *The Washington Post,* 19 April 2008, "The move (brushing dirt off shoulders) illustrated both a generational and a cultural gap: On MSNBC host Joe Scar-borough's show yesterday, *The Washington Post*'s Richard Cohen said the shoulder shak-ing was "contemptuous and aloof" and "not smart."

2. Quote is attributed to Desiderius Erasmus. "In regione caecorum rex est luscus" (1510).

3. The rapper had gone on the offensive by publicly boycotting and redacting lyrics relative to the Cristal campaign. This included the popular line in his "Fiesta" remix, which he made with the R&B crooner R. Kelly, "After the show it's the after party. Then after the party it's the hotel lobby and after the Belve [the Belvedere Hotel] then it's probably Cris."

4. See Langston Hughes, "A Dream Deferred."

5. Since Plato, philosophy has wrestled with the nature and power of universal cat-egories. Even in a pluralistic society we are governed by rules to not only protect our liberties but also to protect us from other people infringing upon them. In the mean time we accept a social contract of behavior and governance toward the aforementioned end. Daily, decisions are made to secure one's lot in life in spite of society's defined (or imagined) constraints. Dostoevsky *The Brothers Karamazov* and Nietzsche's *Beyond Good and Evil* force us to wrestle with our own existences and make autonomous choices toward embittering our fallen lot.

6. Existentialist Philosopher Albert Camus in his story "The Rebel."

7. This is a popular title of a best-seller, by Napoleon Hill, aimed to seduce the mind into believing that wealth is attainable as a life-force through a series of behavior mod-ifications. It is said that the ideas were derived from American financier Andrew Carnegie.

8. This is the title of rapper 50 Cent's 2003 debut album (turned movie).

9. See specifically *A Streetcar Named Desire* and *Cat on a Hot Tin Roof.*

10. See specifically *A Doll House* and *The Wild Duck.*

11. In the spirit of Frantz Fanon who has had an influence on anti-colonial and

national liberation movements. Steve Biko in South Africa, Malcolm X in the United States and Che Guevara in Cuba were a few of those revolutionaries Fanon impacted.

12. An excerpt from the Negro National Anthem, "Lift Every Voice and Sing," by James Weldon Johnson (1900).

13. Talk show host Dr. Laura Schlessinger was the latest scapegoat in this misguided debate over who can and should use the N-word and under what context.

Works Cited

Dostoevsky, Fyodor. *Crime and Punishment.* New York: Vintage, 1993.
Emerson, Ralph W. *Emerson's Essays.* New York: Harper, 1981.
Fanon, Frantz. *The Wretched of the Earth.* New York: Grove, 2004.
Jay-Z. *American Gangsta.* Roc-A-Fella/Def Jam, 2007.
_____. *The Black Album.* Roc-A-Fella/Def Jam, 2003.
_____. *The Blueprint.* Uptown/Universal, 2001.
_____. *Blueprint 2*: The Gift and the Curse. Def Jam, 2002.
_____. *Blueprint 3.* Roc Nation/Atlantic, 2009.
_____. *The Dynasty.* Roc La Familia, 2000.
_____. *Kingdom Come.* Roc-A-Fella/Def Jam, 2006.
_____. "Oprah Talks to Jay Z." *O Magazine,* October 2009.
_____. *Reasonable Doubt.* Roc-A-Fella Records, 1996.
Nietzsche, Friedrich. *Thus Spoke Zarathustra.* New York: Penguin, 1961.
_____. *Gay Science.* New York: Vintage, 1974.
Thurman, Wallace. *Infants of the Spring.* Boston: Northeastern University, 1992.
West, Cornel, *Prophecy Deliverance.* Louisville, KY: Westminster John Knox, 2002.
Wilde, Oscar. *The Picture of Dorian Gray.* London: Random House, 2007.

PART I

The Groundwork

1

Jigga Speaks
The Tradition of Black Oratorical Genius

Toni Blackman

I am here in Azerbaijan, a country bordered by Russia, Iran, Georgia and the Caspian Sea, to be a part of the "Justice" project, a hip hop initiative sponsored by the Islamic Council of Youth Forums. They've outlined the story and asked if it can be translated into English and into a good hip hop song. El Mir was to drive me from the hotel to the designer's studio to try on the dress for the video shoot. As soon as he put the keys in the ignition I heard the radio with Jay-Z's inescapable presence surrounded us, his voice followed by Nas. El Mir is the least fluent in English out of the group, but the beats blared as we nodded in unison and there were no words needed. It is still morning and two voices are blasting in Baku—Jay-Z and Martin Luther King. They've sampled him for the song we are here working on; both voices appear to be equally important to the guys. People all over the world are mesmerized by Jay-Z's oratorical abilities. Still, even as we delve deeper into examining Jay-Z's position in the trajectory of the black oral tradition it feels strange to equalize the voices as their importance comes from different arenas.

Can Jay-Z be placed within the trajectory of great black orators? Great orators tap into spiritual dimensions. These individuals have the ability to move, touch and inspire, but also know how to use the powers of persuasion. They can influence the masses by uttering a particular phrase in just the right way. Malcolm X, Martin Luther King, Mary McLeod Bethune, Shirley Chisholm, Reverend Jesse Jackson, Nelson Mandela, Sista Souljah, and even Les Brown and Iyanla Vanzant all had or have these abilities. President Barack Obama possesses them. Chuck D of the legendary group Public Enemy, gifted in both rhyme and ordinary speech, held an audience captive for almost three hours during a conference at New Jersey Performing Arts Center the day after Jam Master Jay's death.

Is it fair, though, to compare Jay-Z to these historical figures whose power comes from the political movements they represented? Some say that the change Jay is most interested in is the change in his pocket. Tupac Shakur, who conveyed political messages in his music, can be compared but it may be unfair for Jay. He is part businessman, not part activist. A fairer comparison would be Frank Sinatra, Michael Jordan, or Michael Jackson; each figure acquired charismatic power through the myth of their performance leadership. It is a leadership that results from their charisma and not necessarily because of their socio-political perspectives on life. There are entertainers who speak openly and passionately about political issues then there are those who seem to avoid them at every turn. It could be argued that Michael Jackson's efforts on behalf of children were politically charged, but his outspokenness surfaced when, with Al Sharpton by his side, he called out the music industry. "I know my race, I look in the mirror and I know that I am Black," said Jackson as he boldly detailed examples of racism in the industry.[1] One of the interesting, yet unexplored, facets is the dichotomy between Jay-Z, the artist, and Jay-Z, the orator. He hasn't combined his gifts yet, likely because it is extremely hard to remain authentic in both roles. It would be difficult to maintain a firm hold on the bravado and materialistic proclivities; and at the same time, speak to the tender love he has for his nephews or how the rejection hurt when he came into the music industry and what it took to keep going. Could he speak to an auditorium of young adults in an independent living program, the foster care system's transitional space for youth who are aging out, about gratitude, resilience, and overcoming obstacles with the lyrics to "Ain't No Nigga" on a screen above him? Lyrically, his flow represents the streets, but oratorically, what does he stand for? In this essay, we will explore Jay-Z's oratorical power through his music and examine his potential to become one of the great orators of our time. Those great leaders mentioned above could hold a room with sheer presence, but could they rap? By today's standards, when it comes to flow, delivery, and cadence, an emcee's approach is similar to that of a musician playing an instrument, only with an emcee the voice is his/her instrument. Jay-Z's oratory reveals itself through rhythmic storytelling and set to a hot beat has the ability to inspire on the same levels as any of the greats. Some of my peers argue that Jay-Z is a hustler who simply transferred his skill set from slinging in the streets to now slinging in the music industry, however if any of them were to look below the surface and examine the trajectory of his career they might be surprised to find that Jay-Z's depth is not to be slept on.

One might ask what the art of emceeing (i.e., rap) has to do with oratorical genius. It is just "rap," after all. Those who limit their view of hip hop music to entertainment also have a limited understanding of the black oral tradition. Brooklyn-based sound engineer Fritz Francois asserts that what *they* call entertainment is actually our culture, black culture. On one hand, our mistake is to label it "purely an entertainment product." On the other hand, it *is* an entertainment product created from our culture and that is where the connections between rap music and hip hop become complicated. In the context of the contemporary American value system, money often equals respect. "The schools, the media, capitalism, and colonialism are totally responsible for what hip hop is and what it has become," explains M1 of the group Dead Prez, in an article by Yvonne Bynoe.

The cultural tradition of speaking is parallel to spittin' (i.e., rapping), and even though most of the mainstream offerings currently deliver very little in the way of knowledge, wisdom, and understanding, there are flickers of artistic light shining all over the world. The internet is empowering "emcees" to make a living outside the bounds of commercial and record label filters like artists and repertoire divisions; and in a matter of years, the game will look completely different. Emcees can reach millions of users, reduce the need for middlemen, sell product and merchandise without overhead, and partake in all sorts of independent activity that was difficult, if not impossible, for some artists to do before the internet. The changing landscape of the music industry has affected artists in every genre and is even opening lanes for artists in countries where there is no "music industry." These artists—once slaves to exploitation by management, agents, and record companies—can now at least promote and control their own identity, book their own tours, and sell their own music, if they so desire, and they can do it all in the comfort of their own homes or at a local internet café. As the music industry reshapes and redefines itself, artists are also shifting in ways that will allow more of the oratorical genius of hip hop to reach listeners.

There are numerous articles, including features in both *O Magazine* with Oprah and *Forbes* magazine, about what artists and entrepreneurs can learn from Jay-Z as he continues to swim (without drowning) through the uncharted waters of what success looks like for a grown man in hip hop. The blogosphere—in both the business and entertainment arenas—speaks to Jay-Z's resilience.

Rap is tied to the oratorical tradition's rich history and includes the griots of West Africa. A griot (the word is pronounced with a silent "t") is also know as a Djeli and as an orator preserves the history of the family, his or her community, and culture through praise poem, storytelling, and song. Rap also includes signifying and playing the dozens, where many believe the rap battle tradition has is roots as it also involved the concept of dueling with insults, telling tall tales, and lots of wordplay. Then there is Caribbean toasting and dub poetry, Cab Calloway's call and response, Oscar Brown Jr.'s storytelling, the blues, and the Last Poets ethnomusicologist Kyra Gaunt even ties it to the chanting games little black girls play. Jay-Z's use of call and response is most explained in songs like "Jigga My Nigga," where the audience shouts his (professed) name back at him for listeners to share the chorus with him, His storytelling and multiple drug-dealing tales are tied to what Amiri Baraka writes about in his groundbreaking book about blues and jazz, *Blues People*. Jay-Z works his crowd with the "call and response" as well as any church choir director, carrying on one of the defining characteristics of African music and expression. Then there are the ways that Jay-Z lyrically morphs into Chester Himes or Donald Goines, both black American urban novelists who wrote stories of the streets. They paint vivid pictures of hustlers, pimps, and prostitutes, and they masterfully captured the cynicism of black life in America.[2] Many contemporary rap artists were said to have been influenced by their works. Kool G Rap even called himself the Donald Goines of rap while Tupac and Noreaga referenced Chester Himes.[3]

Surprisingly, there are scholars who argue against the idea that rap is rooted in the West African jali and griot traditions. Thomas Hale, author of *Griots and Griottes*, writes that there is not enough research to solidify the claim, but Chen Lo, a noted MC and hip hop educator, points to a bevy of research that clearly illustrates the links between spoken word artists like the Last Poets and the West African griot. The fact that the branch of hip hop is a part of this family tree becomes obvious. Some critics assert that Jay-Z has ventured into the land of mediocrity while others believe he is inching towards his best work yet. Many critics and fans assert that *Reasonable Doubt* and *The Blueprint* are his best works and that *American Gangster*, one of my personal favorites, misses the mark. However, similar to Br'er Rabbit, the trickster character in many African and African American folktales, Jay-Z admittedly uses his wit to achieve what others have perceived as impossible goals. In songs like "Moment of Clarity" or "Ignorant Shit" he references a conscious effort at tricking audiences into believing in, what he considers to be, language or ideas that a dumbed down audience craves.

Jay-Z, in all of his lyrical glory and business acumen, openly admits to the contradictions of creative direction in his rhymes. This is why deconstructing the genius of Jay-Z and giving him a real space in black oratorical tradition isn't so easy for academics.

Whether an effort to clear his conscience or win over the music intelligentsia, Jay-Z publicly explains his choice to operate within the confines of the formula that built his financial empire. On one hand, this is important to note because it reveals his inner conversations, and creates a small window through which we glimpse his humanity. On the other hand, his admission exposes his motives more than it acts as a confession. This is part of what makes Jay-Z such an interesting figure (2003).

These lines could very well be a confirmation that Jay-Z would rather write Hallmark cards and get paid than write poetry and not get paid. However, one could argue that Jay's brilliance, as noted by music scholar and journalist Mark

Anthony Neal when writing about "IZZO (Hova)," "lies in his astute ability to read musical trends within pop music while re-animating a wealth of semi-autobiographical narratives about his life as street hustler 'Shawn Carter' and hip-hop icon 'Jay-Z.' Jay-Z's lyrical statement says 'Fuck perception,' but reveals that perception does matter so he further explains the strategy he employs."

A great orator is both poetic and prophetic — poetic in the sense that poetic imagery is utilized and through aesthetic or emotional impact one expresses the qualities of poetry. Orators access rhyme and alliteration, metaphor and simile, pay attention to diction, create rhythm, and seem to inherently understand tone. Jay-Z also pays attention to cadence and inflection. One example is his whispering rhymes. He even got sued for stealing this technique from some boxer who gave him a demo. Jay-Z, a student of hip hop, in the tradition of great black preachers like C.L. Franklin and King, is notorious for lifting lines without crediting the source. Sampling is an accepted part of the black oral tradition. Dr. Michael Eric Dyson often references how Martin Luther King did this and the academy tried to call it plagiarism. Jay-Z is walking in the footsteps of those who have come before him more than most people realize. The prophetic orator senses exactly what needs to be said and how something needs to be said in order to move the crowd to make a shift in either thought, behavior or action.

In the prophetic "Mountaintop" speech, Martin Luther King Jr. sensed that he would not "get there with you":

> Well, I don't know what will happen now. We've got some difficult days ahead. But it really doesn't matter with me now, because I've been to the mountaintop. And I don't mind. Like anybody, I would like to live a long life — longevity has its place. But I'm not concerned about that now. I just want to do God's will. And He's allowed me to go up to the mountain. And I've looked over, and I've seen the Promised Land. I may not get there with you. But I want you to know tonight, that we, as a people, will get to the Promised Land. So I'm happy, tonight. I'm not worried about anything, I'm not fearing any man. Mine eyes have seen the glory of the coming of the Lord [1968].

Many people express disgust when rappers and MC's are referenced in the same breath as King and Malcolm X. However, it isn't that far fetched to think that Jay-Z might one day evolve into an effective leader whose oratorical gifts will change the world. For Jay to do this, it would require the same level of remorse for his hustling days that Malcolm X had for his. Famous motion picture actor Ronald Reagan became president. Arnold Schwarzenegger, bodybuilder turned actor, became governor of California, and World Wrestling Federation Champ, Jessie "The Body" Ventura became governor of Minnesota. Bono, leader singer for the band U2, was nominated for a Nobel Peace Prize for his humanitarian efforts, while the highly esteemed actor and director, Danny Glover, sat alongside Harry Belafonte and Dr. Cornel West in a meeting with Venezuela's President Hugo Chavez. Glover's just as known for his leadership as he is for his acting.

Jay-Z is heralded for his business savvy, as was Mike Bloomberg before he became mayor of New York City. Is it possible that Jay-Z might have a transformative experience and find himself in a leadership role of service? Stranger things have happened. Although he has made many philanthropic gestures he's not known for his political leadership or lack thereof. Jay-Z's philanthropy took him on a journey to West Africa in 2006 where he appeared to "get open" after spending a few days with the people in a few countries he visited. He saw children who had no running water at home or at school and were not able to have their basic necessities met. He said, "Where I come from they call it the hood, but that's not hood, this is the hood," referring to the village he had just left. This speaks to his ability to transcend as a potential leader while simultaneously making the case that the process has already begun, and that continued with the influence he had on voter turn out for Barack Obama. He recorded a robocall on behalf of the campaign where an automated machine dialed residents in Ohio encouraging them to vote. He partnered with NBA star LeBron James for special events and Jay-Z did free concerts. According to a *Rolling Stone* article, at a concert in Miami Jay-Z shouted, "I'm not telling you who to vote for, I'm telling you who I'm voting for: Barack Obama!" The article also notes that fans for the Detroit concert had to pick up tickets at the Obama campaign headquarters and were encouraged to register upon doing so.

Bill Stephney says in an oft quoted Jeff Chang article:

> Woe be it unto a community that has to rely on rappers for political leadership. Because that doesn't signify progress, that signifies default. Now that our community leaders cannot take up their responsibility, you're gonna leave it up to an 18-year kid who has mad flow? What is the criteria by which he has risen to his leadership? He can flow? That's the extent of it? If our leadership is to be determined by an 18-year old without a plan, then we're in trouble. We're f—ked.

Jay-Z is no longer a youth, but Stephney's statement still applies to him some ways. Is it fair that rap stars are being asked to lead? On the other hand, once a man becomes a certain age, isn't it acceptable to anticipate his using personal experience and wisdom in ways that uplift those in the world at large? Is the adage "to whom much is given much is required" passé? It is a fair expectation, especially if artists have deliberately engineered their level of influence.

One cannot simply point the finger at Jay-Z. When many of the now 30-something and pushing 40 hip hoppers were ready to take the baton, most of the "Black leadership" was running in the opposite direction from anything associated with hip hop. Hip hop education was rejected even when teaching artists with advanced degrees designed the curriculum. Hip hop theater was excluded by greats like Pulitzer Prize winning playwright August Wilson and actor Al Freeman, widely recognized for his role as Captain Ed Hall in ABC's soap opera *One Life to Live* and the first African American to direct a soap opera, but known to many in the hip hop generation as the guy who played

Nation of Islam leader Elijah Muhammad in Spike Lee's motion picture *Malcolm X*. Similarly, hip hop ministers were being alienated by the clergy (rewind to Reverend Calvin Butts, pastor of the internationally renowned Abyssinian Baptist Church in Harlem, and the bulldozer running over CD's with C. Delores Tucker in Washington, D.C.), while also being dissed by national organizations and prominent public figures. Tucker, who succeed Shirley Chisholm as chair of the National Congress of Black Women and worked in the Civil Rights movement, was recognized by *People* magazine and First Lady Hillary Rodham Clinton, and she received hundreds of honors, but to those in the hip hop activism community and the music industry was known less as a groundbreaking leader and more often described as narrow-minded and irrational. There were organizations on life support that just weren't willing to give any hip hopper a listen. Jazz great Wynton Marsalis's critiques have been as harsh as those by social critic Stanley Crouch have been rude. Although poet and professor Sonia Sanchez and Abiodun Oyewole of the Last Poets have consistently supported the growth and evolution of many hip hop artists, a lot of their peers from the Black Arts Movement, who one would think would "get it," did not. Many were elders, but some were people who simply thought themselves to be "above hip hop." Then in 2001 Reverend Jesse Jackson appeared at the Source Awards chanting "Keep Hope Alive." Enter Benjamin Chavis, who worked with the Southern Christian Leadership Conference with Martin Luther King Jr. and served as CEO of the NAACP, and his leadership of Russell Simmons' Hip Hop Action Network. Some organizations and causes started to attach to hip hop with hopes of reinvigorating their causes and connecting to younger audiences, but they soon found out that it would take more than a photo opportunity to repair the generational ties. Jay comments in "Izzo" that he's raping labels because of what they did to Cold Crush, one of the original hip hop groups, which was there right alongside Afrika Bambataa and Grandmaster Flash and the Furious Five in the early days, so he is aware and acknowledging some level of progress, as well. In "Thirty Something" Jay-Z even took the mantle of elder for a moment when he served a lyrical lashing to some of the younger rappers who were chiding him.

Rejection of the cultural, economic, and social significance of hip hop by the "Black Leadership" in the 1990's to this day has not prevented hip hop heads and organizers from developing their respective areas of interest. As time has passed, times have also changed. It has been a slow process for hip hop to be considered as an art form, a tool for social change and as an educational vehicle. In his book *To the Break of Dawn* Jelani Cobb writes, "When you come to hip hop, 85 percent of the books are about the social politics. At the end of the day, it's not so much a social movement as an artistic movement." Tuma Basa, an MTV executive, raises the question, "How about the economic movement?" He adds that many rappers see rap as a way of feeding their families and elevating them to new income brackets, success that is motivated from a man's basic need to survive and desire to prosper. A lot of the hip hop scholars neglect to add these factors to the discussion.

Perhaps there is value in analyzing the science of Jay-Z's mastery of flow and his ability to choose beats that rock the crowd and fit his voice perfectly. Is it possible that the "science" of Jay-Z could then inform an entirely new crop of emcees who do indeed see their goal as lyricists is to become great orators? Jay-Z, as a rhythmic orator, has mastered every aspect of what it takes to make a song appealing. Imagine a world where artists applied the "principles of Jigga" to their creative process and the "fundamentals of Jay-Z" to their business approach. Emcees of varying content and perspectives would have access to wider audiences and on some levels be able to inject balance into an otherwise one-sided world of rap focused solely on money. True, only a small percentage of artists will ever achieve the string of "number one" accomplishments that Jay-Z has, but even in its decline the influence of hip hop is undeniable. The artist who reaches 5,000 or 50,000 listeners on a regular basis can affect lives as well. Unlike the American market, there are parts of the world where hip hop has maintained its sense of idealism, and Jay-Z, most definitely, has not lost his.

Today, most people consider and define the relationship between the world and themselves as very separate and that becomes a core value of who they are, their personality, and what they do artistically or politically for that matter. Great orators willingly tap into the spiritual dimension. This is not to say that Jay-Z is not deep and it is not to say that he cannot tap into the "spiritual dimension," it just appears that he makes a conscious decision to not go there too often in his lyrics. However, his recent video "On to the Next One" has many Masonic and Illuminati-related visuals that have the blogosphere accusing Jay-Z of devil worshipping. The real question is how far Jay-Z is willing to go to broaden his audience. Is Jay-Z merely playing with these symbols and strategically causing a stir to keep people talking? Jay-Z, the artist, is a businessman who could teach music marketing master classes at Harvard, Howard, and USC. The number of Google searches, hits, and blog posts the day after the video premiered were probably predicted and analyzed as the video was being edited. Jay-Z might not willingly tap into the spiritual, but he is profound in other ways that are endemic to particular people; even those who do not embrace his philosophy can appreciate his flow. People are also inspired by his lifestyle and approach to handling his business. Before considering Jay-Z as a great orator, one might explore Jay-Z as a great businessman. The two are distinct and separate. Some say the same thing about T.D. Jakes, a "man of the cloth." Both men represent what it means to be human. We are complex beings in the world of capitalism. America does that to you. It is a place where we are socialized to believe that the do-gooder, the creative artist, and the money-maker cannot coexist within one human being.

The question is: does Jay-Z have prophetic concepts to share lyrically which might influence his listeners, and if he does *will he share them*? On the hip hop planet that exists in my heart and mind, he does. However, in the real world it is unlikely that he will. It would make him vulnerable to attacks from his many business and rap world enemies. He may also fear the perception of hypocrisy because of the great excesses that he enjoys and boasts about in his songs. One of the challenges of maturing is figuring out how to reconcile one's past while standing audaciously in the shoes that one is becoming. Jay-Z knows how to speak in the language of the people. He is humorous and entertaining, but he has yet to reach a point where he lyrically offers prophetic visions. This statement in no way implies that Jay-Z does not have the capacity to do so. To the contrary, Jay-Z's journey is indicative of one who has not only survived swimming in a sea of sharks, has been both up and down, betrayed by others and admitted to failing several times, but gets back up each time.[4]

As a hip hop icon, Jay-Z has done what most hip hoppers still cannot figure out — how to age gracefully in the rap music industry. People tried to write him off. Many wrote off hip hop entirely, declaring that it just couldn't be done. However, he broke the imposed limitations set upon black artists. Commissioner Gordon, Grammy Award winning engineer and producer, asked while working on a project in Azerbaijan: "The Rolling Stones, Led Zeppelin, The Beatles are all considered to be 'classic.' Critics write that Bruce Springsteen is getting better with age and still on top. Yet, Earth, Wind & Fire and George Clinton is old school?" Adult contemporary radio exists to support these rock acts. For urban music, hip hop is often excluded by urban adult contemporary playlists that favor R&B. One must not underestimate the size and magnitude of the barrier Jay broke. He quietly opposed and confronted an unwritten industry rule that aged out emcees and rappers, a rule that has often prevented black music and black artists from evolving, having longevity, and increasing sustainability. Surely, this one act is worthy of acknowledgement and must be added to why Jay-Z is great. Does it qualify as one of the criteria for making him a great orator? Perhaps, but it definitely adds to the list of Jay-Z's virtues of being a great emcee.

Still, as one of the most powerful voices in rap, across generations and cultures, Jay-Z skips over the subject matter that would secure him a position in the history books. He opts out, settling for the record books (the most sales, the most awards, etc.). He's one of the few personalities with global relevancy, but he consistently chooses to say little on specific issues while the world is in crisis. One could argue, however, that Jay-Z is an artist and entertainer who has freedom of choice to do whatever he wants. He has spoken openly, even going on record to say he could be more like Common and Kweli. One could also say that Jay-Z, a former hustler and kid from the streets, at 40 is just now coming into his own as a man — spiritually and emotionally. In his own way

Jay-Z is engaging the integrity of the art form as a gifted emcee and a master of the craft. His album *The Blueprint 3* is all about leadership in hip hop and maturing as a genre with songs like "On to the Next One" and "We Off That" and even "Death of Autotune." He accepts responsibility by making these statements which will most definitely influence a wide array of listeners.

In his essay in the book *Born to Use Mics*, Marc Lamont Hill notes how the construction of a conscious/commercial divide undermines the cultural landscape of hip hop music.

> Too often commercial figures like Jay-Z and Ice Cube are classified as mere rappers who are only worthy of critical attention in order to expose the troubling dimensions of their music. On the other hand, "conscious" rappers like Talib Kweli and Mos Def are romantically viewed as legitimate cultural workers whose work should be analyzed based on artistic merit. Such distinctions are problematic ... they obscure the complexities and contradictions that operate within every artist's body of work. For example, Jay-Z has written songs that critique the American invasion of Iraq "Beware of the Boys," post–9/11 race relations "Ballad for the Fallen Soldier," and the nation's response to Hurricane Katrina "Minority Report" [2010].

One read the infamous opening lines of "Big Pimpin'," we are challenged by a glaring lyrical disrespect for women: Words do have power. Words have power over our thoughts and our actions. Words influence us both consciously and subconsciously. Angela Davis is one of many who has written about the power and practice of Nommo: "Most West African languages incorporate several of the basic structural elements of music: pitch, timbre, and timing. A word uttered at a certain pitch may have a different meaning from the same word spoken at another pitch." Geneva Smitherman addresses the power of words in her book, *Talkin' That Talk*. She argues that we should let go of the myths about how language affects us. The first to go should be the old adage, "sticks and stones may break my bones, but words can never hurt me." In my art of emceeing workshops with young teens, I present a similar argument when proposing that we use the workshop space to "expand our creativity." I ask, "What happens to a child if his/her mother or father tells the child 'you are stupid' over and over again? What happens if a family member tells a child 'you are ugly'?" Although the questions posed are within a different context, it leads to a much more complex dialogue about language and how it can shape one's identity. The students eventually open their minds to the idea that maybe the words they say can impact and influence others. It also sparks interesting debates about gender, class, race, and current events.

If we were to deduce a theoretical framework for the emcee as orator and what makes one great we would have to examine what it means to be a storytelling orator or a rhythmic orator, and how the dynamics of music impact one's oration. Although the intellectual elite might disagree, the art of emceeing is just as important as sermons and speeches when it comes to documenting the oral tradition from a contemporary perspective. The artist can be mainstream or underground, established or emerging, or even unknown. If he/she has the ability to command an audience with their voice, delivery, and lyrical skill, the audience will usually listen for a period of time. KRS-One, a philosopher and a legendary rap lyricist, is often referenced whenever the topic of command arises. Often quoted and referenced by other artists, his ability to command the stage has earned him the respect of critics, artists, and fans all over the world.

One would have to generate a varied spectrum of theoretical frameworks to accurately and fairly measure the oratorical skills of emcees. Some would argue that the beat is essential to the emcee's delivery while others believe that 16 bars spit a capella is the real test to one's ability to move and inspire the crowd. Then there is the concept of rhythmic orators whose choice of rhythmic patterns are even more important than the content or their choice of words. It is in this space that the emcee becomes another instrument on the track and less of an orator separate from the music. The theoretical framework would need to blend the criteria for what makes one a great emcee with the criteria for what makes one a great orator. Of course, the emceeing basics of flow, delivery, and lyrical content would be included along with the oratorical standards of variable cadence, the use of dynamics, and the ability to generate prose. Brett and Kate McKay write in an article entitled "Recovering the Art of Oratory," "Oratory is not mere speaking, but speech that appeals to our noblest sentiments, animates our souls, stirs passions and emotions, and inspires virtuous actions." A great emcee that is also a great orator can do all of this while rocking the crowd.

The question of whether Jay-Z is a great orator in the grand tradition remains unanswered. He has not yet manifested that aspect of his oratorical gifts. Jay-Z is something new and different — one whose flame was ignited and fanned by these powerful and varied influences of the past. He provokes the idea that a new set of criteria must be generated for the emcee whose oratorical skills are being assessed through music. Jay-Z made his name writing street stories where he plays on being smarter than everyone else. Indeed, he is the only rap superstar over 40 and there is no roadmap for how to sustain popularity, to fulfill expectations for what is the unarticulated norm. Thus, within his brilliance there has to be an idea or strategy for how to not only transition from jerseys and sagging jeans, but also transition from lyrics of the 26 year old leaving drug dealing behind to telling stories of women in a way that lifts them up, writing lyrics that teach some of the strategies that he has used to become so successful and which espouse the wisdom he has acquired over the years. Jay-Z's power to influence oozes that of Shango, a ruler of the arts and entertainment, especially the drum, music, and dance, the god of thunder and lightning, the essence of strategy with the ability to bring swift and balanced justice. As Jay-Z rhymed on "What More Can I Say," he has traded in his jerseys for button up shirts, he single-handedly inspired the shift from what was fashionable — the throwback jerseys — and changed the clothing game across generations. Grown men started to grow up, fashion-wise. A lot of women, even if they do not buy his albums, are fans of Jay-Z for that one reason, and they are buying from another branch of the Shawn Carter tree, his clothing line. That is a simple example of Jay-Z's influential power. Imagine Jay-Z identifying a strategy for taking a young person's natural tendency to rebel and tapping into that through his lyrics. Imagine Jay-Z using his ability to read trends to confront the childhood obesity that is affecting children of all races and economic strata or Jay-Z sharing the details of how he overcame his childhood circumstances. What was his daily routine? What tools did he use to reprogram his thinking? How did he deal with his failures? How did his relationships shift as his success expanded? Consider the magnitude of a social entrepreneurial venture incorporating the business principles Jay-Z applied to building his businesses. Jay-Z embracing the core elements of conscious capitalism philosophy would be a revolutionary act and even though leaders of this movement, like Melissa Bradley-Burns, acknowledge the pressure of balancing big corporate business while staying committed to upholding one's values, one cannot help but imagine the freshness Jay-Z could bring to this concept. Not to mention the number of youth development, social change, and educational programs that could spawn from it.

Call me an idealistic hip hop–head and a dreamer, but as an admirer of Jay-Z and as a student of hip hop, I'm aware that the culture has been written off as dead every five years or so. Somehow, a new seedling of an idea sprouts and takes over the world. When it comes to music and artists, the public delivers harsh judgments couched in impatience and sometimes laced with venom. Constructive criticism is important. It is just as important as compassion. Many of the people still grieving over Michael Jackson's death are grieving because he will be missed and it is sad to lose such a great talent, but some grief stems from regret. There are a host of people who expressed remorse for their judgments of him, who wished they had gossiped less and understood more. In researching Jay-Z's background I spoke to some whose judgments were so harsh they couldn't even have dialogue on the topic of Jay-Z. One can dislike his music, his lyrics, or even his flow, but is it fair to not respect his existence, his journey, and the lessons each of us can learn from them? Regardless of how one feels about him personally, a principal of a charter school might borrow the same branding tactics Jay-Z used to establish himself as an artist and build a foundation for Rocawear as a way to establish a name and consequently funding for his school.

Jay-Z's oratorical greatness will evolve as he evolves. One can imagine that it might be overwhelming for the guy who thought he just wanted to "get paid" to realize that not only does he have to be think about responsibility, he must be responsible. He speaks and the whole world listens. He walks down the street and everyone takes pictures. He stands onstage and the audience sings his songs for him. Most people choose, whether consciously or unconsciously, to live their life at half-measure so they will not have to deal with public scrutiny, so they do not have to be accountable. There are natural born leaders and there are those who grow into their roles. As these individuals reconcile family dysfunction, poverty, being high school drop-outs, being former drug dealers, the early deaths of friends, and forgiving their fathers, and as they learn to be at peace with all of the haters and the doubters, the betrayal of friends and colleagues, oh and let's not forget the effects of post-slavery trauma, it is then that these people have a foundation strong enough to truly express their greatness. Indeed each of these points are specific to Jay-Z's actual history, but in taking a closer look many of the points mirror the collective experience of a lot people from my childhood community and that of many of my peers.

Like Shango, Jay-Z has powers of mystical proportions. This command reverberates all over his person, yet up until now he has only accessed a small portion of this power. Meanwhile, he wields a thunderbolt in his hand. He knows it. Gifted with a supremacy that gives him the ability to influence the masses and amass wealth while doing it. Thus, while Jay-Z articulates his superpowers in his classic "Breathe Easy":

Lyrically, I'm saying:

> Fresh, dressed like a million bucks, infrared hot I'm sayin,'
> this character's relatin'
> to everyone
> hot like the sun
> Jay-Z.
> All the world's aglow,
> lit from his triumphant flow.
> Walkin' city streets, even the pavement begs for mo.'
> Cmon' Jay, you know that you know.
> We are the ones we've been waitin' for.

And psst ... Jay, Malcolm is waiting.

For Further Consideration

BOOKS

Dyson, Michael Eric. *Reflecting Black: African-American Cultural Criticism.* Minneapolis: University of Minnesota Press, 1993.
Perkinson, James. *Shamanism, Racism, and Hip-Hop Culture: Essays on White Supremacy and Black Subversion.* New York : Palgrave Macmillan, 2005.

VIDEO

Freestyle: The Art of Rhyme. New York: Palm Pictures, 2004.

QUESTIONS

1. Paul Robeson was known for his artistry, politics, and business acumen — is there anything about today's *context* that would prevent Jay-Z from assuming a position of social and political influence?

2. Like actors who attempt to perform music, or rappers who try to act, is there anything aspect of Jay-Z's art or persona that could prevent from making the transition into a respected orator?

3. Like his predecessor Notorious B.I.G. and his contemporary Lil' Wayne, Jay-Z is known for not writing lyrics. In light the history of black oral tradition and contemporary political climate, is this an asset or a liability for a possible Jay-Z as black orator?

Notes

1. Michael's speech against racism at Reverend Al Sharpton's National Action Network headquarters in the Harlem neighborhood of New York, July 9, 2002.

2. Dr. Stephen Henderson, a legendary scholar of the Black Arts Movement and author of *Understanding the New Black Poetry*, spoke of prison poetry, storytelling battles, and signifying as precursors of the new contemporary black poetry: rap.

3. Chester Himes was known for more angry fire than his contemporaries Richard Wright and Ralph Ellison, and Himes wrote about black protagonists doomed by white racism and self-hate. An ex-offender turned author,his writings of the '40s and the '50s were rife with urban reality and lore.

4. See the lyrics of "I Made It" of the *Kingdom Come* album for a full explication here.

Works Cited

Bynoe, Yvonne. "Mixed Messages: Race and the Media." In *Race and Resistance: African Americans in the Twenty-First Century*. Ed. Herb Boyd. Cambridge, MA: South End, 2002.

Chang, Jeff. *Can't Stop, Won't Stop: A History of the Hip Hop Generation*. New York: St. Martin's, 2005.

Cobb, Jelani. *To the Break of Dawn*. New York: New York University Press, 2007.

Davis, Angela. "Black Women and Music: A Historical Legacy of Struggle." In *Wild Women in the Whirlwind: Afro-American Culture and the Contemporary Literary Renaissance*. Ed. Joanne Braxton and Andree Nicola McLaughlin. New Brunswick, NJ: Rutgers University Press, 1990.

Dyson, Michael Eric. "Power of Words/Words of Power: Reflections on Martin Luther King, Jr.'s Vision and Legacy." Public Dialogue, Aspen Institute, Washington, DC, 19 November 2008.

DimeWars.com. "News of the World." 1 March 1996. Video.

Hale, Thomas. *Griots and Griottes*. Bloomington: Indiana University Press, 1998.

Hill, Marc Lamont. "Critical Pedagogy Comes at Halftime." In *Born to Use Mics*. Ed. Michael Eric Dyson and Sohail Daulatzai. New York: Basic Civitas, 2010.

King, Martin Luther. "I've Been to the Mountaintop." Memphis, TN. 3 April 1968.

Lo, Chen. "Words, Sounds, Power: The Afrikan Lineage of the Contemporary Hip-Hop Artist." M.A. Thesis, New York University, 2008.

Neal, Mark Anthony. "J-Hova Witness." Popmatters.com. September 2001.

Smitherman, Geneva. *Talkin' That Talk*. New York: Routledge, 2000.

2

The Authentic Cultural Agent

G. Jahwara Giddings

As an often mystifying element of U.S. society, and African-American culture in particular, hip hop has demanded analyses that explicate the genius and dynamics of *Africanisms*. And as the most accomplished and acclaimed hip hop MC, Jay-Z represents and provides the most authentic, and therefore authoritative living, exemplum for understanding the latest manifestation of Africa's indomitable aesthetic impact on our American landscape. Herein Jay-Z is viewed as the most authentic hip hop statesman because of what will be shown of his clear conscientious commitment to culture-nationalist aesthetic conventions and the professional and material successes gleamed from this status. Jay-Z's eleven album opus and platinum status persona and achievement in hip hop illustrate an exemplum of hard working genius in the best tradition of African-American creative icons. Indeed, today Jay-Z stands among such consummate cultural stewards as Toni Morrison, August Wilson Danny Glover, and Colson Whitehead. As an accomplished cultural agent, Jay-Z masterful engages *Africanist* aesthetic conventions. In efforts at advancing established culture-national aesthetic theories (Neal; Baraka; Wilson; Herskovits; Welsh-Asante; Ani; Giddings), achieved herein is a new framework, inspired by Jay-Z's opus, for analyzing the social/socio-cultural significance of African American artists.

An artist of Jay-Z's caliber and accomplishment naturally shapes how we view and understand the generative meaning and significance of an aesthetic effectively sustained through a series of generational innovations. Billie Holiday's commitment to musicianship and cultural authenticity earned her a reputation as the greatest, and thus authentic, female Jazz vocalist. Similarly, Charlie Parker's conscientious genius forged the bee-bop aesthetic and form; Sam Cook, Ray Charles, Aretha Franklin, Marvin Gaye, et al.'s risky break from gospel music, sustained and expanded the rhythm and blues; Bob Marley's revolutionary pan-Africanist aesthetic forged the bridge that hastened the arrival of hip hop, as early as 1973, and earned him cross-cultural immortality. Finally, Kool DJ Herk, Afrika Bambaataa and Grand Master Flash pioneered the hip hop DJ form, prodding two new generations of voice, style, and dance aesthetic, which although transcending *race*, remained inextricably tied, and also true, to African American Culture.

It is this tradition, connected by cultural core impulses that prod Jay-Z and his artist predecessors, to sustain aesthetic principles that future artists, in turn, must negotiate, sometimes embrace, but always innovate. Actually, the hip hop artists' relationship, or response (conscientious or not), to these impulses, frames, motivates or takes shape in such authenticity questions as "is hip hop dead?" "You keepin' it real?" "You an artist or an entertainer?" The negotiations between one's artist identify assertions with the demands from fans, critics, and culture, is central to our exploration of Jay-Z's artistic genius and relevance to the state of an *African American cultural philosophy*.

An often overlooked role in hip hop aesthetics, wherein Jay-Z is a key player, is its provision of meaning to the concept of a cultural African Diaspora. Historian James Sidbury (2007) reminds us that the notion of Africa was indeed *created* by dynamic socio-historic forces within and among earnest communities and personalities of African descendants. The historic process of *Africanizing* the United States continues today in several intellectual and creative fronts, including hip hop, and herein Jay-Z's artistry is an authentic exemplum.

Jay-Z's longevity, achievement and wealth, have enabled him to impact hip hop's ongoing aesthetic contribution to the American cultural mosaic. Conscientiously or not, Jay-Z's 11 album opus illustrates engagement with the themes, concerns and conventions that are at the heart of this important historic cultural process. Jay-Z's pure talent, cultural intelligence, incomparable self-awareness, stellar musicianship, and most importantly, for our purposes here, his fidelity to classical hip hop conventions, are all informed by the following core black cultural principles and characteristics: oral, communal, spiritual and *matrifocal* and which serve as guideposts and *blueprint* for marking his place as a significant African American cultural agent (Giddings).

But first, it is important to note that many Americans' enduring alienation from black life is a genuine obstacle to appreciating Jay-Z's importance, beyond his wealth, to American culture, and in fact has served as fodder for diverse rap critics such as Bill O'Reilly and Delores Tucker. For an illustration of this *African-American* twin world dynamic, let's read novelist Toni Morrison's depiction of a pre–1960s black community, segregated from whites. She imagines a white "valley man" who enters this black hill town for some such business as insurance collection and who:

> might see a dark woman in a flowered dress doing a bit of a cakewalk, a bit of black bottom, a bit of "messing around" to the lively note of a mouth organ. Her bare feet

would raise the saffron dust that floated down on the coveralls of the bunion-split shoes of the man breathing music in and out of his harmonica. The black people watching her would laugh and rub their knees, and it would be easy for the valley man to hear the laughter and not notice the adult pain that rested somewhere under the eyelids, somewhere under their head rags, ... somewhere in the palm of the hand, somewhere behind the frayed lapels, somewhere in the sinew's curve. He'd have to stand in the back of Greater St. Matthews and let the tenor's voice dress him in silk, or touch the hands of the spoon carvers (who had not worked in eight years) and let the fingers that danced on wood kiss his skin. Otherwise, the pain would escape him, even though the laughter was part of the pain. A shucking, knee-slapping, wet-eyed laughter that could even describe and explain how they came to be where they were [4].

Word or Die

Of the four black core values, carried from Africa and preserved and innovated within an insular African-American world, the best known is the oral tradition. In addition to its acknowledged attribution to the literary theory of *Orature*, this tendency to value or privilege verbal over written communication forms, also finds full dynamic expression in hip hop aesthetics. Jay-Z's legendary MC skills, as measured especially by his professed insistence on free-style rap even at recording sessions, illustrate this value. But perhaps more importantly, free-style (rapping) facilitates sincerity, spontaneity, improvisation, realness, truth telling and spiritual exploration. Jay-Z's sincerity shines through unequivocally. His relaxed style and swagger even makes his feat of having Beyonce as the chick who wears chain seem easy and matter-of-fact as opposed to conventional rap braggadocio. Still, beyond the accomplishment, or blessing, of an ego-boosting power marriage to Beyonce, Jay-Z's uncommon swagger stems mainly from an uncanny ability to spit phrases, which in the mouth of any other MC, would seem corny, especially within an art profession where coolness is currency is vigilantly policed by the audience and artists alike. Few other rappers, if any, can get away with expressing excitement over his mother's guest appearance on his black album, especially cooing over the specialness of how at age four, Jay-Z taught himself to ride a two-wheeled bike ("December 4th"). Now this unusual act might be explained in light of a *matrifocal* impulse gone awry; however, Jay-Z's opus is rife with litanies of seeming *corn-ball* phrases, diction and references which speak to his status as a maverick trend-setting emcee.

Jay-Z operates within the hip hop conception of an *MC* as the "Microphone Commando" who welcomes the challenge of "*m*oving the *c*rowd," and also incorporates elements of the more classical *m*aster of *c*eremony diction, resulting in an ingenuity crafted by a unique, purposeful, laser-sharp focus, self-confident, honest voice. The oral traditions of free-style or improvisational rap naturally demands honesty, sincerity and, most importantly, *authenticity*.

To assist our explications of these traditions, Marimba Ani's (1993) expansion of the aesthetics concept to include *kuzusa mtima* (move the heart in Ki-Swahili) as more appropriate for grasping the dynamism of the Africanist creativity and beauty. Fittingly, Jay-Z (2004A) brags that, he grasped the ears of the streets, charts, and hearts of his listeners. ("Hova and Out") Jay-Z's attention to audience, as seen especially in the live concert album, *Unplugged* (2001) is displayed in his periodic measuring, on a 10 point system, of his audience's pulse or energy level throughout the concert. He even plays each side of the audience against each other and at one point revels in his breaking some one of the MTV concert rules, in the name of optimal connection with his fans who all the while constituted a virtual chorus karaoking along with him, his lyrics that they know by heart.

Naturally, live concerts and *ciphers* are ideal hip hop venues for experiencing the oral tradition in full effect. Born of protocols, practices and conventions that facilitate classical, non-literary communication modes, the oral tradition also dynamically facilitates new expressions that still affirm West-Africanist aesthetic values. Such conventions include rhyming, repetition, minimalist phrases including contractions (conceptual and phrasal) all of which aid in memorization and improvisational flow. Also, tonality as an oral convention still has currency as a device for manipulating (and improvising) meaning even within a small framework of concepts. And finally, the creative convention of converting nouns into transitive verbs also serves efficacious wordsmithing and all of the aforementioned oral elements form one of the important bases for the hip hop aesthetics. Jay-Z's masterful poetics, replete with a measured humor and irony, employ, innovate and consequently sustain this aesthetic. A close examination of Jay-Z's lyrics exhibit pure genius in rhyme, reasoning and reflection on life. For instance, in "Already Home," off the Blueprint 3 album, Jay-Z equates himself to Andy Warhol in terms of his impact on popular culture. Still, he does so with impressive finesse and humility, comically begging us to resist bowing in his presence, in-spite of his legendary prowess.

Jay-Z (2009) conscientiously asserts a griot or djeli identity and status by claiming he is the only rapper that continuously re-writes history. He explicates the oral tradition's ephemeral character by alluding, via double entendre, to an untraceable owner or authorship. And he also affirms *communalism* by suggesting ambivalences over ownership of such entities as words, rhymes and beats that are often, and in this case, a collaborative product.

All For One, One For All

It is the *communal* core value that dictates much of these instances of breaking through the proverbial veil that might inhibit optimal artist-audience interaction. It is also this cultural imperative to view and value the self as extended (and dynamic) as opposed to nuclear (and static) that is seen throughout hip hop generally and where Jay-Z's body of work is no exception. Now the inclination would be to limit our search for evidence of communalist concerns/value in Jay-Z's more "conscious" lyrics, if there is any such thing as a conscious Jay-Z lyric! And perhaps because Jay-Z is not being perceived as conscious as his colleagues NAS and Common, he is perhaps the most perfect candidate for this analysis that seeks to uncover the latent commitment to this cultural value. In his *Black Album* self-professed clarifying moment, a self consciously maturing Jay-Z (2003) confesses *dumb-downing* for his audience for optimal profit and rationalizes that conscious lyrics simply don't sell records.

Furthermore, Jay-Z (2003) concludes that he has to dismiss perception and essentially roll with what is sensible as he goes about the business of rap. Clearly he affirms that the greater good of focusing on financial success enables him to be philanthropic. Indeed, this "win-win" pragmatism affirms his commitment to an extended sense of self. As someone from the same social or "street" conditions as Biggie Smalls, Jay-Z is as keenly aware of and compelled to comment and to "keep it real" about the social conditions folks in the neighborhood experience daily. Indeed, there is perhaps no truer rapper-representative of the streets as The Notorious B.I.G. (Biggie Smalls/Big Poppa), and whose "Ten Crack Commandments" track from his *Life After Death* album, is certain testament to this claim. As self-professed heir to Biggie Smalls' legacy, Jay-Z wouldn't be paid without playing/embracing the role of street representative. Jay-Z (2003) is forthright that tried and true, he is Marcy projects of Brooklyn, New York. In the following justification of his supposed thug identify, the Brooklyn Boy cognizant of the limits of many black communities, seems to advocate for his constituency by calling on both the president and governor to pay attention to the squalor of his community ("Justify My Thug").

In this activist-artist role, success requires Bob Marley-like observational keenest of insight. Certainly in the rap game, one's proverbial pen had better be as precise as a surgeon's scalpel in lancing societal abbesses. Amiri Baraka is correct in observing that the Africanist tradition insists that a key function of art is the critique and development of society. In answering this call Jay-Z (2003) rightfully, and inspiringly, reaches beyond the random superficial observational references that the free-style form can generate. In this regard, the philosopher rapper reflects on his own real meteoritic "pauper to president" achievement. He claims, for instance, a status similar to Martha Stewart without the benefits of being Jewish or the status of a Harvard alum, simply by using his own intestinal fortitude ("What More Can I Say").

Recognition and constant reference to and glorification of place of origins is also crucial to one's credibility as a representative of the streets. Just as congress persons are beholden to their constituencies, Jay-Z is compelled to make frequent homage to his hometown, and as a successful native MC is wont to do, he proclaim himself "Brooklyn's Finest" and "New York's Ambassador," even recites odes to his esteemed city as found in "Empire State of Mind"(2009).

In addition to addressing the drugs and poverty plagues, Jay-Z has criticized the problematic educational system with increasing precision, focus and sophistication. On a 1999 pop track with Mariah Carey, Jay-Z casually noted that "school made me sick, teachers said I was too crazy." However, in a new era of President Barack H. Obama's radical and fiscal focus on education, Jay-Z's critique of low school-teacher expectation in "So Ambitious" is now reminiscent of Malcolm X's autobiographical account of the same issue (2009).

Another very key component of (the) communal value is the seeming ubiquitous, almost mandatory collaborations among MCs and R&B artists and here Jay-Z is certainly no exception. Despite Jay-Z's lyrical skills, an album is often a collaboration of not just MC and singers, but also with producers. Jay-Z's extensive and diverse collaborations that have assisted his achievement include:

> Notorious B.I.G, Pharrell (Williams), Kanye West, J. Cole, Kid Cudi, Alicia Keys, Rihanna, Beyonce, Beanie Sigel, Bilal, Ne-Yo, Sterling Simms, Usher, John Legend, Chrisette Michele, Gloria Carter, Memphis Bleek, Timbaland, Young Chris, Scarface, Lenny Kravitz, Paul Anka, Big Boi, Killer Mike, Twista, LaToya Williams, Sean Paul, The Roots, Jaguar Wright, Q-Tip, R. Kelly, DJ Clue, Snoop Dogg, Scarface, Missy Elliott, Amil, Juvenile, Mariah Carey, Jermaine Dupri, Foxy Brown, Big Jaz, Babyface, Lil' Kim, P Diddy, Mary J. Blige.

In addition to Jay-Z's many significant musical partnerships with producer/MC Kanye West, another important collaboration is Jay-Z's "Renegade" duet with the Academy Award winning emcee, Eminem, whose often surprising achievement as one of the most successful emcees is undoubtedly attributed to his internalization of black behavioral core values. In fact, Eminem's skills arguably eclipse Jay-Z's on this East Coast — Mid West 'bi-partisan' MCs effort to represent (for) millions without a microphone. Eminem has spotlighted 8-mile Detroit, Michigan in ways not unlike Jay-Z's representation of his own Marcy Projects, Bud-Stuy., Brooklyn New York. Jay-Z's ultimate testament to community is articulated in the very words of his last album, "Thank You."

Spirit ... Pouring Louie to Dead Thugs

Notions of transcendence, religiosity and ethics pervade the ethos of African descendant peoples from London and Haiti to Carolina Sea Islands and New York, and expectedly the art is a natural conduit for explicating spirituality. Specifically, such communal hip hop conventions as the extended self and the cipher are chief means for manipulating and manifesting the spiritual. Perhaps no single Jay-Z track illustrates spiritualist concerns more than his *Black Album*'s

"Lucifer" continues the profound themes initiated his 1996 "D'Evils" track. Here, Jay-Z (2003) theorizes that we are D'Evils due to the invasion and obsession with money and power." Later in "Lucifer" community concerns are explicated as a holy war and in so doing shifts Ghetto discourse from simple economics to complicated ethics. Whenever the issues of poverty and poor schools are framed only in economic abstractions, i.e., liabilities, property taxes, culpability is anonymous and stasis sets in. However, when these problems are framed in ethical terms, i.e., social-contract, collective responsibility, fairness, solutions are possible because where responsibility is identified, actions are more likely to follow. Explaining that street violence should be contextualized arguing that violence, and economics are inextricably linked, Jay-Z (2003) argues that what is perceived as natural sinfulness often has justifiable social origins/motivation. On the track, "Lucifer," Jay-Z serves as interceder for a friend begging God to forgive him the sins the committed as being caught up in a seemingly inescapable cycle of violence not necessarily originated by him.

Furthermore, Jay-Z's diction on this track mirrors the somewhat old-fashion African Americans practice (beyond Elijah Muhammad's theology) of using "devil" as a metaphor for whites, and as a measure of the evils of the enslavement holocaust, disenfranchisement, banishment, lynching, and the like. Conscious that devilry is so dynamic as to even assume the "form of diamonds and Lexuses," Jay-Z (1994; 2003) employs this familiar metaphor to chase Lucifer "out of Earth." On "D'evil," "Lucifer," and other tracks, spiritual invocations and

Though one hears and reads these explicit spiritual references in recordings, it is the cipher and other live performances where one feels and witnesses spirituality at work. Jay-Z's (2001) recorded performance of his "Song Cry" blues begins with a sort of cipher between himself, Jaguar Wright and the Roots band. Jay-Z's conventional rift: ... uh, uh, uh ... just behind and intertwined with Wright's mostly wordless crooning ... getting him into the grove and right articulating the soulful beauty of the music. With a spiritual invocation achieved, Jay-Z further invokes the music to do his bidding as crying wouldn't be a generally accepted form of the hip hop personae, so the song must cry for him. He tells a confessional tale of love lost to machismo pride, all the while sustained by Wright's blues croons supplying a support base of minor notes that Jay-Z rides all the way to an epiphany climax. In the end, and emerging from a post-coital state where Wright and The Roots had tucked him for the last three minutes, Jay caps his confessional by exclaiming that he was, indeed, lost in ecstasy.

Whether or not Jay-Z actually strayed from, or transcended the stage, he certainly exhibited the sort of sincerity any live hip hop audience expects. It is well known that Billie Holiday (1957) mastered this convention, revealing for instance in a recorded interview, that:

> The blues to me is like being very sad, very sick, going to church, being very happy
> ... there's two kinds of blues, there's happy blues and sad blues ... don't think I ever
> sing the same way twice, don't think I ever sing the same tempo, one night it's a little
> bit slower, the next night it's a little bit brighter, depending on how I feel. I don't
> know, the blues is sort of a mixed up thing, you just have to feel it.

This spontaneity aesthetic, attention and fidelity to audience and context, or even whim, affirms the established tradition of viewing, embracing and engaging the creative spirit as an enterprise that extends beyond the individualist psyche. This aesthetic is no different than that of any given Sunday at high noon (still the most segregated hour of American life), where black preacher, saints, and musicians rely and build on each other's shouts, songs and dances to call, mount, ride, feel and taste the spirits.

Furthermore, an established tradition of personifying such spiritual forces as evil, affirms the Africanist cultural value of appreciating a composite nature of reality as both tangible and ethereal. Lyor Cohen (qtd. in Healy 288) recognized the exhibition of this value in Jay-Z's personality, and in pursuing Jay-Z to join his Warner Bros. record label, celebrates that "Jay-Z doesn't have a [presumption] of what's good and what's bad. He doesn't feel like anything is out-of-bounds for him to witness and experience" and as such Cohen recognizes this worldview as having been "an incredibly valuable thing for hip hop." Still, this is not a Jay-Z singular worldview, but part and parcel of a larger spiritualist orientation, forged by history. James H. Cone (71–77) explicates this culture-based theology, if you will, via the blues tradition, and Toni Morrison paints her Black characters' worldview similarly as follows:

> In their world, aberrations were as much a part of nature as grace ... nature was never
> askew — only inconvenient. ... There was no creature so ungodly as to make them
> destroy it ... a full recognition of the legitimacy of forces other than good ones. ...
> They knew anger well but not despair, and they didn't stone sinners for the same
> reason they didn't commit suicide — it was beneath them. ... The purpose of evil was
> to survive it [90, 118].

Woman

Recognizing the importance of various women in his life, W.E.B. Du Bois (1929) describes the "mother idea" as one of Africa's several legacies and gifts to the world, and as pervasive in the African Diaspora. This notion, conceptualized (Giddings) as the appreciation of women's unique, indispensable and complimentary role in relationships, family, community and society, is very much manifest in hip hop, in spite of hip hop's misogynistic label. The organically evolved hip hop tradition of referring to any woman as "Ma" is a glaring example. Further, one of hip hop's most natural links with its older R&B cousin is the emcee's dependence on vocal hooks, (typically) executed with female voices generating and guiding and supporting melodic tracks for effective emcee flows on recordings or live.

Jay-Z's (2001) "Song Cry" exemplifies this conventional assignment of women to crying and crooning, even on his behalf, as he cannot see tears coming down his own machismo eyes. In this "Song Cry" confessional Jay-Z offers his male perspective and understanding of complementary gender characteristics. Although, to the conventional sensibility this seems a double standard, Jay-Z's sincerity is unequivocal. The process of coming to terms with *dogging* or disrespecting and consequently losing his woman is unequivocal. He attempts to blame her for his own assumption that she would always forgive his wandering ways, but in the process realizes that he was totally at fault, and has to live with that regret forever. Ultimately, one is given the impression that a former "playa," not pensive Jay-Z, has learned from this mistake.

This process of explicating male-female romantic relationship issues is also attempted in Jay-Z's (2001) seemingly misogynistic "Girls, Girls, Girls" which further complicates this Roc-A-Fella artists' relationship to the *matrifocal* ideal. Collaborating with three other male companion emcees, Biz Markie, Slick Rick and Q-Tip, this track is a curious affirmation of Alice Walker's (1983) *womanism* concept. Here, Jay-Z brags, or fantasizes, about romantic conquests of the following ethnic and otherwise diverse group of women: Spanish, black, French, Indian, young, project, model, paranoid-hypochondriac, Peruvian, Chinese, African, and narcoleptic. Beyond its chauvinistic banter and jabs at these personal and cultural stereotypes, this rap effectively affirms the *matrifocal* imperative by satirizing behaviors antithetical to the unique *womanist* values that are the foundations of this cultural principle. Indeed, Jay-Z's jovial policing of these suboptimal behaviors fits quite within the same practice engaged in Brand Nubian's "Slow Down" and Chaka Demas' "Murder She Wrote." Indeed, one gets a sense of Jay's artistry as effective satire, if one is able to get beyond the surface chauvinism. After all, Jay-Z (2003) has since rapped with some measure of gender egalitarianism, that women can occupy that fictive male space of pimp too.

What perhaps, more effectively saves "Girls, Girls, Girls" from the accusations of misogyny is Jay-Z's attempt to address what culture nationalist scholar, Maulana Karenga (2002:335) conceived as the "cash connection" dynamics of black gender relations in the United States (335). In response to Jay-Z's rap of asking the "Indian Chick" which tribe she's from, she retorts the irrelevance of such line of questioning and directs him to affirm his financial status before getting with her. This provides some fodder for the debates on video vixens and other pornographies as economic traps some women find themselves forced to elect. This is expected however in a society where the *matrifocal* value is suppressed, and where the female and the black body has been historically objectified and commoditized. In such an environment all bodies, particularly female and non-white, are on the proverbial auction block.

Among Jay-Z's litany of professed conquests, the "Black Chick" and "Project Chick" are of particular interest to Jay-Z's dynamic relationship to the *matrifocal* principle. Jay-Z's (2001) proclamation that the black Chick "don't know how to act/Always talking out her neck, makin' her finders snap" is met by her retort that "listen Jigga man, I don't care if you rap/You better R-E-S-P-E-C-T me!" Jay-Z's use of this distinctive black woman's anthem suggests some conscious engagement of the *matrifocal* value. This popular and successful Aretha Franklin cover of an Otis Redding original song illustrates the gender relations discord within a society estranged from *matrifocal* principles. Ultimately, as the product or son of a Brooklyn housing Project, Jay-Z (2001) is *communally* compelled to reserve the highest regards, respect, and love for the "Project Chick, that plays her part" and about whom he concludes that "...if it goes down y'all that's my heart." Devotion to the *matrifocal* principle is certainly affirmed even more explicitly in Jay-Z's (2006) "Hello Brooklyn, 2.0" where his home-borough of Brooklyn is personified as a loving, nurturing woman, whom Jay-Z would honor by naming his future daughter "Brooklyn Carter." This 2006 collaboration with the very young and popular emcee, Lil' Wayne, suggests a mentorship that might ensure passage of these discourse traditions and aesthetics *on to the next* generation. For sure, this alone should warrant looking beyond Jay-Z's surface misogyny (hapless or not) if one's to see and engage the thoughtful artist who employs pop and deep-cultural resources for profit as well as cultural meaning and influence.

Conclusions: Living Through Bars

Beyond an expose of Jay-Z's hip hop authenticity and mastery, this is a framework for a theory of hip hop as one of the most effective contemporary keepers of Africanist aesthetic traditions. As illustrated, Jay-Z's eleven album opus offers excellent exemplums of this tradition, when explicated through and Afrocentric paradigmatic lens. In fact, Jay-Z's self-confidence in comfortably engaging non-conventional Rap references and concepts, illustrates the authority and authenticity of a genuine cultural agents. The authority Jay-Z asserts on his craft, colleagues and competitors is professed and exhibited.

An important element of cultural leadership or mastery is consciousness of one's existential relationship to cultural forces. Apparently recognizing his connection to legacy, Jay-Z admits that he did not "invent the game" and as a metaphor for both the hustle (legitimate or illegitimate) and leadership, Jay-Z (2003) thoughtfully explains that what he does is a continuity of pathways his predecessors have laid.

Furthermore, Jay-Z seems aware of the complexities of cultural leadership as littered with paradoxes and issues of relevancy. Seeming to sense his eldership as the industry, plus air and video waves swell with youths, Jay-Z (2006) asserts that 30s is the new 20s, perhaps recalling the fact that he was 24 years old when his first album dropped in 1996. This concern with relevancy might have prodded Jay-Z's cleverly constructed and publicity-hyped retirement with the *Black Album* in 2003, a development unprecedented in the rap industry, where MCs, DJs, B-boys and Graffiti artists typically just fade to black, and often very quickly. This facilitates the issue of passing the torch from the hip hop generation, who was born between 1965 and 1984 (Kitwana), to the post–hip hop generation, who might have no appreciation for Break dancing, for instance, but whose reach beyond conventional commitment to blackness might have facilitated the election of a self identified black man, Barack Hussein Obama, to the United States Presidency. Still, Jay-Z seems to take fullest advantage of his maturity, which might be apparent also in his sensible management of his relationship with R&B superstar Beyonce away from media abuse. For sure, maturity makes his many braggadocios claims as the following, appear as a status he has earned ("On to the Next One")

These bragging rights are affirmed by Mark Healy, who acknowledges that "[t]he world knows that if he's doing it, wearing it, backing it, it's probably worth a second look" (288) and also by acclaimed actor Gwyneth Paltrow, who admits that "there's a generosity and self-assurance that makes him super, super cool. Something just went right along the way for him, because he just has it all" (qtd. in Healy 288) Now, in spite of his earned bragging rights, maturity and self-consciousness as an accomplished artist, Jay-Z and a black man make Jay-Z is also aware of his paradoxical societal status as a black man. So, among Jay-Z's (2003) proclaimed "99 problems" is his need, despite professional status, to navigate a discourse on a racist justice system that imposes high bail because of his African roots. Indeed, Jay-Z's opus inspires further investigations into dynamics of black culture and the potential and imperative, of black artist to forge a *functional cultural philosophy* or a system of norms, standards and practices that create sustainable institutions that ensure cultural development and attendant social progress for African Americans. In more conscientiously engaging in such a project, hip hop can avoid the pitfalls suffered by Jazz, which had experienced a short-sighted reception by many African Americans during its nascent years. As such, promising artists and industry executives such as Jay-Z, Russell Simmons, Curtis "50-Cent" Jackson, And it takes such undisputed agents Lil Wayne, Lauren Hill, Naz, Common, Most Deff, Talib Quali, Dead Prez, Eminem, et al. to commit to this *cultural agent* imperative.

As an important American music genre, on par with Jazz, hip hop must avert its popularly exclaimed and prophesized "death" of this important American music genre. Jay-Z, and the best of hip hop illustrate that hip hop is indeed strong. Still even Jay-Z (2004: 75) understandably participates in this alarm by attributing his 2003 announced retirement to being "honestly ... bored with hip hop" and admits having spent "a lot of time feeling uninspired." His return suggests, perhaps, a misreading of hip hop's climate, a response to a messianic calling to salvage hip hop, or something else. Whatever the motivation, it has been illustrated herein that Jay-Z's opus is at least of the extant black musical vessels poised to pass on core aesthetic values and traditions to subsequent generations of artists.

Jay-Z's status as a hip hop leader, and thus a black cultural agent, is determined, in part, by his engagement of, at least, two generations of fans, while honing wealth and influence the like of which predecessors Billie Holiday, Duke Ellington, Sam Cook, Miles Davis, Aretha Franklin, Shirley Caesar, et al., did not fathom. This suggests the great and serious potential of hip hop in the hands of Jay-Z and the need for further analysis by way of a comprehensive cultural biography of the artist, and the man, and his work's meaning for the approaching third generation of hip hop and Africanist culture in the United States.

For Further Consideration

BOOKS AND JOURNALS

Boyd, Todd. *Am I Black Enough for You? Popular Culture from the 'Hood and Beyond.* Bloomington: Indiana University Press, 1997.
Chang, Jeff. *Can't Stop Won't Stop: A History of the Hip-Hop Generation.* New York: Picador, 2006.
Herskovits, Melville J. *The Myth of the Negro Past.* Boston: Beacon, 1958.
Ntloedibe, France. "A Question of Origins: The Social and Cultural Roots of African American Cultures." *Journal of African American History* (Fall 2006).

DOCUMENTARY

Person-Lynn, Kwaku. *Rap Music: Afrika to Hip Hop.* Spirit Flight Productions, 2003.

QUESTIONS

1. What are some of the historic precursors that gave rise to hip hop culture? Who and what were the forerunners of this musical genre?

2. The author makes the argument that use of women in the music by Jay-Z, and hip hop in general, represents a *matrifocal cultural value*. Paying attention to a song like "Girls, Girls, Girls," can you see this as satirical critique, as the writer suggests, or do you affirm the track to be womanizing in nature?

3. In essence, it is argued that hip hop is organically rooted in blackness and Africanisms. Discuss your view of this argument. How is hip hop black? Do you agree with the author's Africanist claims?

4. What are the four Africanist cultural values as discussed in this chapter? How do they apply with other artists that you can think of?

Works Cited

Ani, M. "The African Aesthetic and National Consciousness." In *The African Aesthetic: Keepers of the traditions*, ed. K. Welsh-Asante. Westport, CT: Praeger, 1993. 63–82.

Baraka, I. A. "Blues People." In *The LeRoi Jones/Amiri Baraka Reader*, ed. W. J. Harris. New York: Thunder's Mouth, 1991. 21–33.

Brand Nubian. *All For One*. Elektra Records, 1990.

Chaka Demas & Pliers. *Ultimate Collection: Chaka Demas & Pliers*. Hip-O, 2002.

Cone, J. H. *The Spirituals and the Blues*. New York: Orbis, 1992.

Du Bois, W.E.B. "The Damnation of Women." 1920. In *Darkwater: Voices from Within the Veil*. Mineola, NY: Dover, 1999. 109–13.

Giddings, G. J. *Contemporary Afrocentric Scholarship: Toward a Functional Cultural Philosophy*. Lewiston, NY: Mellen, 2003.

Healy, M. "Jay-Z: Renaissance Mogul." *Gentlemen's Quarterly*, December 2006. 286–289, 357–358.

Holiday, B. "The Sound of Jazz." *Seven Lively Arts Series*. New York: CBS Television. 1957. *http://www.npr.org/templates/story/story.php?storyId=1072753*.

Karenga, M. *Introduction to Black Studies*. 3rd ed. Los Angeles: University of Sankore Press, 2002.

Jay-Z. *American Gangsta*. Roc-A-Fella/Def Jam, 2007.

_____. *The Black Album*. Roc-A-Fella/Def Jam, 2003.

_____. *The Blueprint*. Uptown/Universal, 2001.

_____. *Blueprint 3*. Roc Nation/Atlantic, 2009.

_____. *Blueprint 2: The Gift & the Curse*. Def Jam, 2002.

_____. *The Dynasty*. Roc La Familia, 2000.

_____. "Hova and Out." *Vibe*, January 2004, 72–80.

_____. *In My Lifetime*. Roc-A-Fella Records, 1997.

_____. *Kingdom Come*. Roc-A-Fella/Def Jam, 2006.

_____. *MTV, Unplugged*. Def Jam, 2001.

_____. "Never Let Me Down." Kanye West. *College Drop Out*. Roc-A-Fella Records, 2004.

_____. *Reasonable Doubt*. Roc-A-Fella Records, 1996.

_____. *Volume 2: Hard Knock Life*. Def Jam, 1998.

_____. *Volume 3: Life and Times of S. Carter*. Def Jam, 1999.

Kitwana, B. *The Hip Hop Generation: Young Blacks and the Crisis of African-American Culture*. New York: Basic Civitas, 2002.

Morrison, Toni. *Sula*. New York: Alfred A. Knopf, 1993.

Walker, Alice. *In Search of our Mothers' Gardens*. New York: Harcourt Brace Jovanovich, 1983.

Welsh-Asante, Kariamu. *The African Aesthetic: Keeper of the Tradition*. Westport, CT: Praeger, 1993.

West, Kanye. *Late Registration*. Roc-A-Fella Records, 2005.

3

The Meeting with a President and a "King"

DAVEY D

In 2010 when you say the name Jay-Z, depending on whom you talk to, you'll get a variety of descriptions: "He's a street hustler," "a gifted rapper—one of the greatest of all times." "He's the God MC," "Jay Hova," "a trendsetter." "He's a music mogul," "a businessman." "He's a drug dealer," "a hip-hop icon and legend." "He's Mr. Joe cool—Mr. Swagger." "Jigga Man" is many things to many people. For the purposes of this essay, Jay-Z is simply a "point of reference."

For a younger generation whose attention has been grabbed by the likes of Lil Wayne, Gucci Mane, and Drake, to name a few, Jay-Z is an elder statesman. He's not your big brother, but your uncle. He's a relic from a bygone era who gets respect because of his business accomplishments, because he is married to Beyonce and because of his overall vibe. Beyond that, many will arrogantly say he's passed his prime. For today's generation Jay-Z is the proverbial "old man" in hip hop.

For others, Jay-Z is one the greatest emcees to have ever blessed the mic. His flows are unmatched. His subject matter coupled with his story telling is compelling. As an emcee he's managed to reinvent himself over and over and stay current. Jay-Z went from being the guy you saw rapping behind Jaz-O, who was one of the hottest emcees at the time in the song "Hawaiian Sophie," to a street hustler from the notorious Marcy Housing Projects with hot flows to a more sophisticated "corporate thugging"/"crime boss" who headed up the "The Roc" (Roc-A-Fella Records) to the music mogul we know him to be today.

For many, Jay-Z is the one commercialized, mainstream artist that an oftentimes fickle, discerning and, yes, somewhat snobby underground has come to respect or even admire. Jay-Z is the cat whose hustle can't be knocked. He's the man who filled the void left by Notorious B.I.G. after he was tragically murdered in Los Angeles on March 9, 1997. He's the guy who made many, especially those in a grieving New York, eventually be able to cope with such a huge loss.

Jay-Z has long been known as the guy who could influence, a trait he's been quite vocal about. In fact, many have long dubbed him the E.F. Hutton of rap, meaning when he spoke, people listened. He's the man who once noted that he could get the hip hop audience to stop drinking Hennessy and start drinking water. He's the man who got us to move from BMWs to Maybachs.

Jay-Z got us to move from gold to platinum and to stop wearing throwback jerseys and start wearing button ups. He turned many on the East Coast onto Southern rap when he first linked up with Juvenile to do the song "Ha" and later when he teamed up with Texas rap legends UGK to do the song "Big Pimpin'." He's the man who got us thinking about Euros over dollars. He's the guy who had even President Barack Obama referencing his song when as a candidate, President Obama gestured by "dusting off his shoulders" to show that he wasn't really worried about battling Hillary Clinton for the Democratic nomination.

Jay-Z fans listened and followed when he helped further popularized Cristal Champaign with his constant references in songs. Those same fans listened when Jay-Z led the charge to economically tank them. Folks may recall that the company's director, Frederic Rouzad, gave an interview with the *Economist* magazine in 2006 and foolishly noted that he felt the brand was being cheapened by the hip hop audience and the company didn't really need them.[1] Jay-Z thought the remarks were racist and thus went on a mission. He flexed his economic muscles and his ability to influence by killing the brand. First, he pulled the beverage from the shelves of his popular 40/40 club and then he made it a point to glaringly omit the name from any of his rhymes. Within two years, Cristal was not only played out, but a forgotten part of what was once an important staple item within the commercial realm of hip hop.[2]

Jay-Z is the one man who in many ways made a generation forget its history and musical legacy because his overall charisma and influence are so strong. For example, what I find most interesting is that many have forgotten that it was Jay-Z's predecessor, Notorious B.I.G., who really name-checked Cristal into people's consciousness after being influenced by the character Frank White in the 1990 movie *King of New York*.

Another example is Jay-Z wearing button ups and being hailed as the trendsetter, eclipsing the fact that hip hop had gone through a couple of eras before this button ups trend set in. People have seemingly forgotten about the Paid In Full era of the mid- to late–80s when people were dressing up and wearing fancy suits from places like Dapper Dans in Harlem while artists like Kool G Rap and Eric B and Rakim were doing Mafia-inspired songs or video where they dressed up. We saw this trend during the John Gotti-Gambino era of the mid–90s where everyone was running around rocking fancy Italian suits and John Gotti-inspired Mafioso names.

Jay-Z, on some level, has made folks forget past greats the same way that Michael Jordan made a generation of basketball fans forget there was once a guy named Dr. Jay who dominated the game. I often chuckle when speaking to younger cats because on more than a few occasions when I've heard this "Jay-Z is the greatest of all time" talk, I'd interject and ask, "What about Big Daddy Kane, Kool G Rap, the Juice Crew? You think Jay outshines them? You think he's better than them?"

For the fan who grew up with Jay-Z in the 1990s, [Big Daddy] Kane and [Kool] G Rap are not even distant memories. At this point in time they don't even register. They're not even up for consideration. As far as they are concerned, Jay-Z was and is the best —*hands down*! For many in that generation, what has captured their imagination is not only Jay's immense body of work, but this notion that he writes songs in his head and knocks things out in one or two takes. "Kane was good, but he can't come off the dome with complex rhyme schemes like Jigga." That's a sentiment I've long heard from Jay-Z era fans who've forgotten that Kane not only flowed (coin phrase for an adept delivery of rap) but was an incredible writer for many.

I had this Jay-Z mystique underscored when I had a conversation with his long-time partner Memphis Bleek. The Roc-A-Fella crew had come up to my old radio station KMEL for a "meet and greet." While folks hovered around Jay-Z, I pulled Bleek to the side and asked him, "Fam, be honest, is it true what I heard? Does Jay really go into the studio and spit complete songs off the dome?"

Being a former emcee myself, I was trying hard to understand the process. Was he doing a bunch of retakes and punch-ins? Was he building upon and reworking old rhymes, a trick I used to do back in the days? Did Jay have things on paper that he would look at that would trigger a bunch of rhymes he had secretly memorized the night before? Bleek assured me in no uncertain terms that Jay-Z was coming off the dome [head] and that was his "get down," or way of approaching his craft. He then took it a step further by adding, not only did Jay record songs off the dome, but so did the whole damn Roc-A-Fella click. Bleek explained how they all fed off each other and this helped to keep everyone sharp. He tampered down his assertion just a bit probably knowing I wasn't fully buying that one and admitted that many of the song concepts are constantly being worked out in Jay's head and by the time he gets to the studio, he spits flawlessly. Stories like that have only added to Jay-Z's lure and "King of the Hill" reputation.

Rising from the Ashes

For many, Jay-Z is a welcome throwback to a critical era in hip hop. He's the guy who rose from the ashes in the aftermath of hip hop's most troubled period. This was in the mid–90s when the infamous East Coast vs. West Coast War unfolded. For those unfamiliar, there had long been simmering tensions felt by artists on the West Coast, not so much with each other but with the way the industry and media outlets based in New York operated.

Many West Coast artists felt disrespected and marginalized by East Coast publications, media outlets and personalities that seemed to harbor an extreme bias, especially in the arena of radio play. This tension was further exacerbated when magazine reviews would come out praising East Coast artists and lambasting their West Coast counterparts even though they were popular and had similar subject matter. Many on the West Coast felt it was unfair that East Coast artists could come to Cali and be shown respect and given love, but the sentiments weren't returned when West Coasters touched down in the East.

Adding to this tension was that people were hearing stories about West Coast artists like Too Short being booed at his own listening party or popular deejays like Joe Cooley being overlooked in deejay competitions. Bad feelings began to build up. The West finally started to make some headway with the popularity and eventual acceptance of NWA and, later, Ice Cube. But tensions built up again when East Coast artists like Tim Dog released songs and videos like "Fuck Compton" off his album *Penicillin on Wax,* where he took shots at West Coast stars like Dr Dre and DJ Quik. This song netted responses from everyone ranging from street artists like Tweety Bird Loc to Snoop Dogg, who went in hard on Tim Dogg on the infamous song "Dre Day."

The East vs. West Coast beef really crystallized when 2Pac Shakur, who was actually a crucial bridge builder between the two coasts, got shot five times outside a midtown Manhattan Quad studio while on his way to visit his good friend at the time, the Notorious B.I.G. and Puffy. Pac was convinced that he was set up by Biggie's people, and he was quite vocal in his accusations. This is when all that bi-coastal tensions really exploded. The feud between 2Pac and the Notorious B.I.G. extended to their respective labels, Death Row and Bad Boy, and their respective CEOs, Marion Suge Knight and Sean "Puffy" Combs, and eventually the streets. The end result of this "dispute" was the senseless loss of several lives on both coasts, including that of two of rap's most popular and influential wordsmiths, 2Pac and Biggie. After Biggie was killed, artists from both New York and Cali were paralyzed and scared to venture outside of their regions to the opposite side of the country. Word had circulated that a vicious cycle of revenge was set to break off with artist like Ice Cube and his Westside Connection group, who by than had recorded a number of anti–East songs, were next in the crosshairs.

Things were in turmoil and leadership was needed to calm things down. For better or worse, Pac and Biggie were elevated and being called the Malcolm X and Martin Luther King of their generation, hence whoever was going to step forward had some huge shoes to fill. On April 3, 1997, almost a month after Notorious B.I.G. was gunned down, Minister Farrakhan and the Nation of Islam stepped in and called for a nationwide peace summit. In the weeks after Biggie was shot, the NOI had quietly held a series of meetings around the country, including New York, Los Angels and Atlanta. They were working behind the scenes to calm things down and eventually bring everyone together.

Key artists from both coasts were summoned to Minister Farrakhan's house in Chicago, for what was an unbelievable, very moving, very emotional meeting. In attendance was a who's who in rap: Snoop was there, Chuck D was there, Too Short was there, Willie D was there, Cee-Lo was there, Common was there. The Dogg Pound was there, Bones Thugs and Harmony were there, Fat Joe was there. (He noted that he had driven 15 hours from a bowling alley in New York). He was still in his white T-shirt and bowling shoes. He was eager to confront this problem dead on. I came through with Kam and Shorty of the Lench Mob. Ice Cube was in California on movie set filming the morning of the gathering. He was strongly urged to shut things down charter a private jet and show up with WC and Mack 10, which he did. He was at the center of attention and had a lot of people upset with him.[3]

Also in attendance that day was Stokely Carmichael, aka, Kwame Toure. It was the last time I would see and hear the former SNCC head speak. That day he spoke to us passionately about the importance of us organizing and how to avoid falling victim to divide and conquer tactics. Latter that day as Minister Farrakhan spoke. It wasn't so much a speech but a compelling conversation that moved many to tears. He laid out a game plan for all of us to follow. He talked to us about the "hidden hand" and told us we were all leaders who needed to step up. Every single one of us in that room spoke to the issue at hand and each person made a promise as to what course of action he or she would take to change things.

When all was said and done, the East vs. West Coast beef was dead. I saw all sorts of people who had beef with each other make amends and offer up olive branches. It was very sincere and on many levels spiritual. It was definitely something I will never ever forget. I can also say that while all of us took a pledge not to give out all the details to that meeting because so many people opened up and spoke candidly, I can say, in the aftermath, that almost everyone acted upon those promises. Many have stuck with them to this day. A lot of artists were fundamentally changed.

Both Minister Farrakhan and Toure explained to us that hip hop was at a crossroads and in need of leadership. We were either going to be this newly inspired politicized force that used our collective talents and influence to challenge the system, or we were going to be slaves to the corporations that help foster the divisions between us. The plan was for us to be agitators who challenged the system. We all left inspired with marching orders to serve our communities and to give voice to those not at the table. Ideally, we were to be more Paul Robeson(esque) in our future endeavors.

There were a handful of people not in the room that day. One was Suge Knight, who was in jail. The other was Puffy, who was seen at an airport and told to come, but for some reason he didn't. The other person who wasn't there was Jay-Z who, at the time, was still in the shadows of his late friend, the Notorious B.I.G.. What I found interesting was that within a year of that meeting, Jay-Z would ascend to being one of the most influential forces and biggest leaders within hip hop. Please note, when I say "leader" I'm not talking about it in a way in which we see someone who is popular and start projecting things on them. That's a mistake so many of us make. We start anointing people who really aren't asking to be in that position. With Jay-Z it's different because he has long flaunted his ability to move the masses. He has openly toyed with the idea of being bigger than life — and more than just an artist. We're talking — Jay Hova.

Over the years, Jay-Z has made moves both within the business and as an artist who has been well thought out and quite calculated. Yes, I'm aware that he's always stated that he's a business man's business man, but make no mistake, Jay-Z wanted more. His actions over the years spell that out. He's a man who has always wanted the respect of the people and to be in a position to ultimately command and move them. Jay-Z coming out of retirement[4] and eventually forgoing his executive seat as the head of Def Jam, talking about the rap game needs him, underscores that point. Jay, plain and simple, wants to be a leader. The question on the table was, "What type of leader?"

Would the man who bragged about getting us to go from gold to platinum or for us to "dead" Cristal and drink more water, the man who could cause a shortage on Dom Perignon, use his influence to get us to move in a particular political direction? Would he get us to challenge the system, or be a cheerleader for it? Would Jay be an agitator and give voice to those not at the table? Does he want to be a Kingmaker? Would he demand that we speak truth to power or be cautious and "pretend" to be too cool to fight?

It's interesting to note that in June of 2001 Minister Farrakhan again addressed key hip hop artists in what was billed as the first "Hip-Hop Summit." It was put on by Russell Simmons. The Minister gave an incredible speech that he described as the best one he ever gave in life. Having been to both the Peace Summit and this event, I could tell that Farrakhan was building off of what he told us four years earlier.

In this 2001 address he spoke emphatically about how rap artists have global impact. He said it was extremely important that they harness their power and start speaking to world issues. He gave a run-down of key international issues including war in the Middle East and upcoming economic troubles and social justice. At this summit was a who's who of hip hop with people like

Luther Campbell, Sean "P. Diddy" Combs, LL Cool J, Wyclef Jean, Redman, Dame Dash, Jermaine Dupri, Ja Rule, Afrika Bambaataa, Kool Herc, Grandmaster Flash, Chuck D, Kurtis Blow, Will Smith, Jada Pinkett, Dead Prez, Sista Souljah, Dr. Michael Eric Dyson, Tricia Rose, Kevin Powell, NAACP head Kweisi Mfume, Eric B, Dr. Cornel West and Congresswoman, Cynthia McKinney, to name a few. Absent from this gathering, Jay-Z.

A President and a King Finally Meet

March 4, 2010, Shawn Corey Carter, a.k.a. Jay-Z, made history of sorts by visiting the White House just hours before his concert at the Verizon Center. He and his wife Beyonce, along with singer Trey Songz and former Def Jam executive Kevin Lyles, among others, are all shown sitting in the Situation Room, which is usually reserved for National Security discussions, while awaiting the president.[5] Eventually Jay-Z met with the President Obama, who joked how ironic it was that a former community activist and a former community hell-raiser (referencing Jay-Z's crack selling days) were sitting in the White House. "Only in America," he is quoted as saying.[6]

Maybe it's me, but I found a couple of things ironic about that meeting. First, I found it ironic not so much that President Obama was a former community activist but, by his own admission, was someone who once used cocaine. Who would've thought? A former cocaine user and a former cocaine seller sitting together in the White House. The fact that both are black is even more ironic, especially when you put into context that around the time President Obama used and Jay-Z sold (late–1980s early '90s) was when the war on drugs was in full swing decimating and permanently scarring entire communities throughout black America. Some of our best and brightest fell victim to that plague.

Adding to all I mentioned, is that both men come from broken homes and humble beginnings where their fathers were absent. The fact that these two managed to transcend that reality, to become the leader of the free world and — as he has been proclaimed in recent weeks—"The King of Hip Hop" is a cold hard truth to put on the table for all to digest. Talk about beating the odds! A President and a "King" sitting together in the White House — How powerful is that? Symbolically speaking, it's a lot to take in. It's an image that both Jay-Z and President Obama were well aware of. After all, both men come from professional arenas, politics and the music industry, where symbols are major cornerstones. Over the years both men have mastered the ability to play up and play off images while exuding an "ultra cool can't be phased" exterior/swagger that has been crafted to make them appear in total control even when under fire. And I might add, I think Obama, although a few years older, may have picked up on Jay-Z's coolness and not the other way around.

In any case, when it comes to playing up symbolism, it might be as simple as President Obama not allowing himself to be seen smoking cigarettes or his making magnanimous gestures of bending over backwards to be bipartisan and above any fray. If you really think about it, his historic 2008 presidential campaign was all about symbolism where each move and word was carefully crafted to touch people in a way that would reinforce the notions of "hope" and "change." Many of us were inspired and enthusiastically brought into it. With respect to Jay-Z, his play upon symbolism might be seen in the way it's been reported on how he conducted himself during that March 4 White House visit. It was noted that Jay-Z made it a point to downplay any conversation about his music, his rap career or beef with former friend and rapper Beanie Sigel and, instead, sparked up a conversation where he got to demonstrate his keen insight, knowledge and interest in the fancy paintings by Josef Albers on display at the White House. In doing so he shattered the stereotype of his being "just a rapper." In typical fashion he went left when everyone thought he'd go right.

We've seen Jay play up symbolism when he did the video for the song "On to the Next One." Rumors had been circulating that Jay-Z was part of the secret society the Illuminati, and every lyric he cited and every gesture made was being scrutinized. Hence, by the time everything was said and done with this video, Jay-Z gave people all over the globe some things to seriously speculate about. Whether he's Illuminati or not, all this conversation has made the one-time street hustler from Marcy Projects appear bigger than life. With all that said, one has to wonder if Jay-Z's visit and access to the President Obama was all about playing up symbolism or seizing the time and speaking truth to power? Did these two powerful men from humble beginnings have a powerful conversation about how to change "humble conditions"? As the self-described ambassador and proclaimed "King of Hip Hop," does Jay give voice to the voiceless? Reflectively, in other words, did the two men talk about how to improve the high unemployment rates in and around Jay-Z's childhood home Marcy Projects in Bed-Stuy, Brooklyn, which, last I checked, may have been hovering around 15 percent to 16 percent? Did Jay-Z holler at Obama about two high profile police brutality cases including the Justice Department refusing to prosecute the five officers who saw fit to shoot 50 bullets into a car killing an unarmed Sean Bell and injuring two of his friends the night before Bell's wedding? Did he talk to Obama about 17-year-old unarmed Pittsburgh honor student Jordan Miles[7] who was brutally beaten by three plainclothes cops as he walked from his mother's to his grandmother's house, several houses apart?

The hip hop community in Pittsburgh, which includes X-Clan member Paradise Gray, who was a part of the Brooklyn based blackwatch Organization, has been helping lead rallies and shed light on this case. Many of the artists are coming together to do a song to raise both money and awareness. Did Jay-Z relay this to the president?

The day Jay-Z met with Obama thousands of students from coast to coast were preparing for a day of action to protest rising public college fees. Affordable education is the number one priority by various hip hop organizations over the years including Russell Simmons' Hip Hop Summit Action Network and the National Hip Hop Political Convention. Did Jay-Z speak to this issue and voice those concerns?

Are these fair questions to ask of Jay-Z? Of course they are. It's not like Jay has shrunk away from being a visible spokesperson. He himself said he was back because "rap needs me." In his 2007 interview with PBS talk show host Charlie Rose he said he was an ambassador for hip hop. When you are the head or representative for a body of people and you meet with someone like the president, what do you convey?

I mentioned the 1997 Peace Summit and the 2001 Hip-Hop Summit because in both events Minister Farrakhan spoke to us and asked us to remember the power we have to speak for those who can't be in the room. He was reminding those of us in hip hop to keep alive what we know as the "prophetic tradition" of being on the side of the oppressed. He was reminding us to have a passion for those who are poor.

When Jay-Z visited the White House he did two things: first, he released a widely circulated picture showing him sitting under the presidential seal in the Situation Room. Next during his concert he bragged about coming from the White House, but he didn't offer up an agenda, talking points, marching orders, plans of action. We got nothing. I'm not even sure if he even extended well wishes to his fans on behalf of the President.

This meeting raises lots of questions. It's not as if politics weren't discussed. During this March 4 meeting, President Obama brought up the fact that long-time Harlem Congressman Charles Rangel and Governor David Paterson were in trouble ("taking their lumps"). Noting that these two powerful African American politicians were involved with highly publicized scandals, President Obama said it wasn't a good black History Month. Jay-Z responded that "both men brought it upon themselves." If Jay-Z could speak to that, should he not have hit on some of the issues resonating within our communities amongst the people?

I find it interesting that at the time of this writing there have thus far not been any pictures of Jay-Z and President Obama shown together, shaking hands, embracing or simply standing side by side from that March 4th visit. One hopes that's only because they are waiting to have them featured in a lofty publication where they can get the most bang for the buck. However, if the two aren't pictured together because of concerns of a political backlash or, even worse, President Obama doesn't recognize Jay-Z as worthy, speaks volumes.

It speaks volumes to what leadership can and cannot do when one is black in America. It speaks to the power one really has or doesn't have when all is said and done. Clearly, I understand, with so much attention on President Obama, everything he does is being super-scrutinized; hence, it's understandable that he and Jay-Z would be a bit pragmatic. One might offer and say they're playing chess not checkers in the sense that they were anticipating and avoiding a political windstorm that could emerge if the two were shown together. They were being prudent. They were being cautious. They were being safe. On some level that's understandable, but where do we draw the line? Is being "safe" what's needed during a time when many in our community are in dire need? Have we have so little power we can't even speak to the issues of the communities that helped get President Obama into office?

The last bit of irony to all this was Jay-Z's opening act, Young Jeezy, being absent from all this. Trey Songz and Beyonce were there, so why not the man who along with Nas penned the 2008 anthem, off the *Recession* album that helped capture the imagination of young urban America "My President is Black." Jay-Z did a couple of "Get Out the Vote" concerts for Obama, but Jeezy had the nationwide hit that was heard bumping all summer long (2008).

Since we're talking about two gentlemen who play to a lot of symbolism, I'm going to attach speculative meaning to Young Jeezy's absence. Yes, we know he has a unsavory, controversial reputation of being a "Trap boy" whose logo was a snowman. You can't get any bolder about your affiliation than that. Jeezy was a part of the dope game in a very real and relatively recent way. His partners that were collected to his label were all arrested and carted off to jail. In some people's minds, Young Jeezy would be that criminal element that the media would have a field day with had he stepped foot inside the White House.

However, at the same time Young Jeezy's album was called *The Recession* and he was harping on that before the economic downturn seriously hit. Young Jeezy represents a significant, ever-present part of our community which is made up of those who are most oppressed, most unreachable, most at-risk, those who have become part of the seedy black market and permanent underclass.

Symbolically speaking, the Young Jeezy crowd is the one that populates our prison system. It should not be surprising that to date Obama in the middle of this recession has increased money for prisons.

In an ideal world, it would've been good for Young Jeezy to have been inside the White House if, for anything, just to let the president know the reason why Trap Boys are out there in the first place. It would've been good to hear him talk about why he called his album *The Recession* and have that voice and perspective planted at the table.

So, in Young Jeezy's absence, we have former "trap boy" turned business mogul, Jay-Z, who, one would hope, would do more than pay a cursory visit and then shout out that he went to the White House. At the same time one hopes that Jay-Z moguling is not President Obama's only connection to that black underclass.

Civil Rights and Hip Hop's Missed Opportunity in 1984

With Jay-Z meeting with the president, it's hard not to reflect that this has been a long time coming. To better understand, this let's go back to 1984, the year civil rights leader Jesse Jackson made his historic presidential bid. I remember that year as if it were yesterday. Many like to say Jesse was the first African America to run for president when, in fact, it was Brooklyn Congresswoman Shirley Chisholm who was the first to run for president in 1972. Brooklyn-born Jay-Z was only 3 years old at the time. Hip hop had yet to be born.

When Jesse ran in '84, it was a big deal. Hip hop was alive and well with groups like Grandmaster Flash leading the way. Ronald Reagan was in the White House smashing on inner city folks by cutting back on social programs and, as far as I'm concerned, with his connection to the infamous Iran Contra scandal, was helping create conditions where our communities would be flooded with crack.

I also remember Reagan for being the guy who refused to help in the global efforts to liberate South Africa from the grips of its racist apartheid regime. He was infamous for vetoing every UN call for economic sanctions in lieu of this ineffective, defanged policy called "constructive engagement," which meant folks did a whole lot of talking but weren't really saying anything.

Long story short, 1984 was a dismal year if you were black in America. Jesse's run for office provided "Hope." I recall the excitement and lifted spirits, much the same way people were feeling when Obama made his historic run in 2008. "Run Jesse Run" was on everyone's lips and, as he won a couple of key primaries in places like South Carolina and Louisiana, the enthusiasm was thunderous.

One of the interesting and somewhat ironic aspects of Jesse's 1984 bid was the role hip hop played or didn't play. The top group at that time was Grandmaster Flash and the Furious Five with lead rapper Mele-Mel being the "King of the Hill" when it came to rap. Mel's baritone voice sent chills up our spine when he rapped songs like "The Message," "New York New York," and "Survival." All three songs got lots of radio play which was unusual because many stations avoided playing rap like the plague. It was also unusual because all of Mele's songs had a message. They spoke to the harsh living conditions of inner-city neighborhoods. Back then, Mel's popularity was unrivaled. In many ways he was our Jay-Z for that time.

When Jesse Jackson decided to run for president in 1984, Mele-Mel hit a high note and penned an anthem song called "Jesse" (1984). He starts out by smashing on Ronald Reagan: Mele-Mel continues his verbal assault by rapping about harsh conditions in America and the hypocrisy felt in certain places[lands] that freedom doesn't seem free. In the last verse, Mele raps passionately about Jesse Jackson going to Syria to secure the release of Navy Lieutenant Robert Goodman, who was shot down and being held hostage. Mele ripped into the clown-like attitude of President Reagan who was "smiling like everything was fine and dandy" and had doubted Jackson's ability to succeed in this mission when all other U.S. efforts had failed. Of course we know Jesse not only succeeded but later went to Cuba and freed other hostages. In the meantime, as Mele noted in the song, Reagan was forced to invite Jesse to the White House.

With each verse came the anthem like a refrain that Liberty and Justice are in the past since the majority of Americans refuse to recognize the legitimacy of Jesse's candidacy, So he urged hip hop fans to get out and vote. It was an incredible song that interestingly enough received very little airplay, marking the first time a record from the group was ignored by radio.[8] In the San Francisco Bay Area where Jackson was enormously popular and was host to the 84 convention, the song "Jesse" was the number one charting song in the PROs—predominantly black record pool — which featured many of the area's most popular disc jockeys. It was played in clubs and was known in the hood but was never heard on the urban stations in the area.

What was also interesting was that I got the sense that Jackson himself hadn't heard the song or didn't really glean the significance. I asked Jackson and people in his camp on three occasions about this song. The first time was in 1988 when I met the reverend at a black lawyers' convention in Houston. Jesse said he had heard about the song, but had not heard it. I thought that was crazy. How did the person who best epitomized the civil rights era not connect with a group that epitomized the emerging hip hop generation?

I asked Jesse about the song in the mid–1990s during the big debates around affirmative action and Proposition 209. He told me that he had finally heard the song a couple of years prior. The irony of a "people's champion" being totally unaware of hip hop's attention to his presidency–Talk about being disconnect. I also asked Mele-Mel a couple of years ago when Reagan died about the song. He noted the song was played at rallies, but they were never tapped by Jesse and his people to do the song or anything like that.

I wondered what difference it would've made if Jesse Jackson had tapped into the energy and innovativeness of the hip hop generation and if we had tapped into the wisdom, expertise and institutional structure of the civil rights generation. However, what we do know is that Mele-Mel and Jackson at that time were praised for speaking to the conditions of the people they represented. They were very clear and very vocal and stayed rooted in the prophetic tradition.

Mele's message type songs paved the way and helped usher in the golden era of hip hop, which was very Afrocentric and personified by groups like Public Enemy, KRS and X-Clan, who all started to make noise around 1987. Jesse's landmark run was followed by his run in '88 and helped paved the way for scores of black elected officials to got elected into office around the country.

In 2010, we had the offspring of civil rights era and the offspring of hip hop's pioneering era meeting in the White House, but was the spirit of speaking truth to power and giving voice to voiceless at the table with them? Obama has been severely criticized for never mentioning poor or using the word poor in his speeches. It's led his critics to believe that his policies and actions are not firmly rooted, or that he does not take into account the struggles of the communities who are enduring hardships.

Jay-Z, on the other hand, while praised for helping people out from his old neighborhood in Marcy Projects, has come under fire for being detached from the realities of the poor communities that have long supported him. He's become a business man at the expense of maybe not being fully focused on those trying to come up. The controversy surrounding his involvement with the New Jersey Nets and their building a stadium in historic Atlantic Yards has put Jay-Z in a precarious position. On one hand, people outside that area see it as a power move and Jay-Z being a mogul on the come up. But a few months back an open letter was written to him explaining that a stadium would be displacing poor residents, mostly black people, who live there. Thus far it appears the building plans are moving forward.

One can't be all things to all people; and, as hip hop advances, the reasons that initially gave birth to it may be farther and farther away from its practitioners. In addition, as we look at this question of leadership, we are now seeing ourselves at a crossroads of sorts. President Obama is seen by many as part of a new wave of leadership, smart, highly educated, business minded, and smooth with the swagger. People like to point to politicians like Corey Booker, Deval Patrick, and Harold Ford as examples of this new class of leaders. These are the types of folks who politically are centrists and won't exactly kick up dust like the civil rights leaders before them. Some call them safe. They play the game and they are not trying to agitate the system.

Within hip hop we have a similar class of leaders. They have money, swagger and play it safe. Some call it Michael Jordan-like, referencing his non-political/very safe position on things. Sure artists like Jay-Z may do a song or two but it will never be one that damages or embroils their brand in controversy. In other words, one is not likely to hear a song from Jay-Z about "Taking about Fight the Power" or "By the Time I get to Arizona." One is not likely to even hear a song from Jay-Z like the one Mele did about Jesse. His brand is his business, and he protects it at all costs.

How does the one of the most influential artists who can make us strive to buy Maybachs over BMWs or platinum over gold, not speak to power in a way that empowers the community? Maybe it's all artificial or backed by corporate interests who would strip away everything if one should stray too far.

Or maybe the ultra coolness is there to save face and not let the world know he's too scared to not be safe. Jay-Z said he's been inspired by Malcolm X, so maybe, just maybe, he's all about making the ultimate chess moves and in time the gloves will come off.

Is Jay-Z all about speaking truth to power or is he about impotent symbolism while making money? The proof is beyond the rhymes: it's in the actions.

For Further Consideration

BOOKS

Forman, Murray, and Mark Anthony Neal. *That's the Joint! The Hip-Hop Studies Reader.* New York: Routledge, 2004.

Hess, Mickey. *Is Hip Hop Dead? The Past, Present and Future of America's Most Wanted Music.* Westport, CT: Praeger, 2007.

Keyes, Cheryl. *Rap Music and Street Consciousness.* Urbana: University of Illinois Press, 2004.

Kitwana, Bakari. *The Hip Hop Generation: Young Blacks and the Crisis in African American Culture.* New York: Basic Civitas, 2003.

Ogg, Alex. *The Men Behind Def Jam: The Radical Rise of Russell Simmons and Rick Rubin.* London: Omnibus, 2002.

Reeves, Marcus. *Somebody Scream: Rap Music's Rise to Prominence in the Aftershock of Black Power.* New York: Faber and Faber, 2008.

Scott, Cathy. *The Murder of Biggie Smalls.* New York: St. Martin's, 2000.

QUESTIONS

1. What is the significance of Jay-Z's absence from the summits hosted to quell the "East/West Coast beef"?

2. Is Jay-Z avoiding to "speak truth to power," or is he using an alternative strategy to change the conditions of the working class? If so, what evidence exists of this strategy?

3. Can we call Jay-Z a "leader"? In what ways are we called to reconsider the role of leadership, especially among our artists and musicians? Do they, can they, really speak for you?

4. Social consciousness and social critics can be said to be two distinctions. How would you define the difference? Which one is Jay-Z? Is one to be valued as better or more effective?

Notes

1. The business magazine reported that an executive from Cristal's maker regarded its hip hop cache as unwelcome attention. Jay-Z accused the company of racism, at which point the company issued a statement saying the official had never made such a comment and that the company has the utmost regard for all forms of art and culture — including hip hop. http://www.npr.org/templates/story/story.php?storyId=5497540.

2. Jay-Z songs like "Fiesta," "Give it to Me," and "in My Lifetime" speak to Jay-Z's particular affinity toward the brand before this soured relationship with the Cristal brand.

3. Ice Cube, during this period, had been in public "beefs" with Mack 10 from West-side Connection, rapper Common even Dr. Dre. It was for these reasons, and his tele-vision/cultural celebrity, that his appearance and "sit-down" was crucial for these reconciliation meetings.

4. With the *Black Album* in 2003, he proclaimed that he was going to retire at that point. But as we know, 2006 he "resurrected with *Kingdom Come.*

5. This photo can be found in many places on the web. http://www.huffingtonpost.com/2010/03/04/jay-z-white-house-visit-r_n_485631.html.

6. In an interview with Elvis Mitchell, Jay-Z was asked again about the feeling he had when he met Obama on that day. "For me, being with Obama or having dinner with Bill Clinton ... it's crazy. It's mind-blowing, because where I come from is just another world. We were just ignored by politicians—by America in general." Found in "JayZ," www.interviewmagazine.com/music/jay-z/.

7. Jordan, an accomplished violinist, had a few months prior to the incident played for First Lady Michele Obama. The officers in question accused Miles of trespassing but the woman whose property he was on knew him and said she had no problem with him cutting through her place as a shortcut. Miles was beaten so badly that he had his dread-locks ripped out his head. A judge dismissed the case against Miles only to have the Pittsburgh police union promise to refile in spite of the community outrage.

8. Mel became known as Grandmaster Melle Mel and the leader of the Furious Five. The group went on to produce the anti-drug song "White Lines (Don't Don't Do It)." Mel then gained higher success, appearing in the movie *Beat Street* with a song based on the title. He became the first rap artist ever to win a Grammy award for Record of the Year after performing a memorable rap on Chaka Khan's smash hit song "I Feel for You."

4

An Urban Singer of Tales

The Freestyle Remixing of an Afro-Homeric Oral Tradition

NICOLE HODGES PERSLEY

Jay-Z is considered one of the most prolific rappers in hip hop history. His ability to freestyle — to improvise lyrics over a background beat or a cappella — has allowed him to present complex stories that sample from a wide range of his experiences, including but not limited to selling drugs, his relationships with women, the marginalization of black youth, and the commercialization of hip hop.

Jay-Z's repertoire of improvised practices are informed by wide-reaching sources of intellectual, creative, and social influence that can be linked to European, African, and African American oral traditions. Jay-Z's oral narratives reveal the complexity of hip hop music and its often-contradictory relationship to representations of blackness in America.

Rapping continues within a larger historical continuum of oral storytelling by African Americans that can also be linked to more ancient African and Homeric storytelling practices (Banks). Imani Perry suggests such hybridity in her assertion, "Rap music is a mixed medium. As an art form, it combines poetry, prose, song, music, and theater" (38). For centuries, as forced migrants to the United States, Africans Americans have improvised their oral storytelling practices. Following Perry's observation of the intertextuality of rap, one can see, hear, and observe a remix from African and European oral traditions that persist in hip hop music and culture. Jay-Z continues in the tradition of many African American artists, from slavery to the present, who sample from a wide range of oratorical, theatrical, and literary devices in order to articulate their experiences as displaced Africans in the Americas. Citing inspirations such as Homer's *The Odyssey,* the late African singer/activist Fela Kuti, and the late African American rapper Biggie Smalls,[1] Jay-Z's raps can be read as an archive of urban tales, both factual and fictional. What we can read in Jay-Z's works is the intersection of African and Greek oral traditions that inform many African American oral practices, including rapping. Jay-Z creates opportunities to use his raps as social critiques that engage important polemic topics of race, ethnicity, gender, and sexuality in performance. To riff on a recurring title of Jay-Z narratives, the artist uses his life as a "blueprint" from which he draws real and imagined stories. The purpose of this essay is to explore the influences of Homeric, West African and African American oral storytelling techniques on Jay-Z's freestyle storytelling practices. In lieu of reading individual songs and analyzing particular lines out of context, I choose to read Jay-Z's oeuvre as one epic story, from the first album *Reasonable Doubt* (1996) to the eleventh album, *Blueprint 3* (2009). Reading Jay-Z's work within this framework allows us to see different influences that shape the artist's freestyle rapping skills as well the important social role he inhabits in the hip hop community as an urban griot. Examining Jay-Z's oeuvre as an epic story also elucidates the ways that European and African oral narrative traditions intersect in African American artistic practices as articulated in many of the elements of hip hop culture.

My analysis is presented in three parts that correspond with distinct phases of artistic development in Jay-Z's career. Using textual analysis, I explore one rap from each phase of Jay-Z's oeuvre, highlighting how influences from each oral mode of performance work together to suggest what I call a remixed Afro-Homeric oral tradition.

In Phase 1, "The Message: Jay-Z as an Urban Singer of Tales," I focus on Jay-Z's career, examining his introduction to rap, his presentation of main themes and characters, and the construction of his message as an artist. Analyzing his hit song "Hard Knock Life: Ghetto Anthem," from his third album, *Vol. 2: Hard Knock Life* (1998), I pay specific attention to three phases of Jay-Z's artistic development which find synergy with the practices of oral epic singers as outlined by Albert Lord in *A Singer of Tales*. Jay-Z's development as a rapper parallels that of oral epic singers as many facets of Greek oral narrative composition are recast in his hip hop freestyle practices.

In Phase 2, "The Bridge: The Making of a hip hop Griot," I explore the influences of African griot storytelling in Jay-Z's narratives and mark the second phase of his career. I discuss Jay-Z's development of a repertoire of tales and his development of a recognizable style that affords him the attributes of an urban hero that is similar to those found in Greek and African oral cultures. Using the freestyle "I.Z.Z.O.," the second song released off of *The Blueprint* (2001), I argue that Jay-Z remixes essential elements of the West African griot tradition outlined by Isidore Okpewho. Jay-Z preserves the generational oral tradition of hip hop freestylers, identifies the needs of his audience, and splits the difference between past and present oral narrative styles in hip hop.

In Phase 3, "H.O.V.A: Remixing an Afro-Homeric Tradition," I explore

African American oral tradition in hip hop as a hybrid set of oral narrative practices that incorporate Homeric and African oral narrative practices. Focusing on Jay-Z's song "A Star Is Born," a single from the artist's last album, *Blueprint 3* (2009), I discuss Jay-Z's use of call and response and remixing of African American folklore, which together, according to Gayl Jones, influences oral and literary African American narrative forms. Examining Jay-Z's work as an oral narrative performer offers new opportunities to consider the oral performance practices of rappers as important facets of identifying how hip hop shapes American identities.

Freestyling Urban American Tales

Michel Eric Dyson asked Jay-Z to write the introduction to his classic hip hop studies text *Know What I Mean?* (2007), acknowledging the rapper's insightful analysis of hip hop's impact on American culture. Jay-Z speaks to the contradictions of American life complicated by race and class and the social realities that hip hop addresses:

> Hip Hop is American. Blackness is American. I am American. ... Yes, our rhymes can contain violence and hatred. Yes, our songs can detail the drug business and our choruses can bounce with lustful intent. However, those things did not spring from inferior imaginations or deficient morals; these things came from our lives. They came from America [Jay-Z in Dyson x].

Jay-Z's analysis of American identity suggests that blackness is one of several articulations of American identity. Jay-Z's freestyle raps critique the contentious and often contradictory relationships that produce American identities. The process of freestyling in hip hop is the act of telling an improvised story to any music that the DJ, producer, or artist chooses on the spot. The MC performs without a script or previous memorization, yet must draw from his or her memory to create a rap that fits the music and the topic presented. Paul Zumthor, in *Oral Poetry*, brings some insight to the improvisational process of oral narrative composition that finds kinship with freestyling. Zumthor writes "the improviser has the talent to round up and immediately organize raw materials—thematic, stylistic, musical ones—that he blends with memories of other performances, and often, memorize fragments of writing" (181). Zumthor highlights that the act of improvising often conveys an appearance of spontaneity that is achieved as a result of having acquired great skill. Jay-Z improvises his artistic practice through the act of freestyling by sampling from a wide range of European and African impulses to articulate Americanness.

Not every rapper has the skill to freestyle. The performer must rely on his or her capacity to recall real or imagined experiences on the spot and hone the ability to organize the information in a narrative form. During an appearance on the *Oprah* show on September 11, 2009, Jay-Z discussed how he uses memory as a device to catalog his experiences. Jay-Z explained that he "works on" stories in his head by documenting his ideas and does not necessarily "write" them down on paper. He explained:

> It's almost like an exercise — you know I used to write so much you know ... get these blows of creativity. You know and if you're accustomed to doing something ... even when if you're not in the house anymore ... I was away ... I was out in the streets ... I was still getting all of these ideas so I had to memorize them ... the more I memorized them every single day ... it built up my memory. It's like push-ups, one, two, ten — you get these ideas and you have to memorize them. You build ... I built a muscle.

Jay-Z's description of his freestyling practices is reminiscent of characteristics of primary oral cultures as discussed in Walter Ong's *Orality and Literacy.* Ong argues that an oral culture does not have a text but there are mnemonic patterns and formulas that are used to help performers in oral cultures to recall stories. Ong calls these patterns and techniques "memorable thought" that can be recalled through:

> heavily rhythmic, balanced patterns, in repetition or antitheses, in alliterations and assonances, in epithetic and other formulary expressions in standard thematic settings ... in proverbs which are constantly heard by everyone so that they come to mind readily and which themselves are patterned for retention and ready recall, or in other mnemonic form. Serious thought is intertwined with memory systems [34].

For Ong, processes of mnemonic recall are part of Homeric Greek tradition and West African oral tradition. In the case of hip hop freestyling, rappers such as Jay-Z use similar formulas and memory techniques that mirror more ancient oral cultures such as the Homeric Greek tradition or West African Ibo oral traditions (Ong 37). Jay-Z mobilizes many of the devices outlined by Ong in his narratives. Through the repetition of themes, sounds, characters and content, he provides his audience with familiar scenarios that contribute to his creation of an identifiable "flow" that is easily recognized by his fans and peers. Jay-Z's freestyles present improvisations of American identity that highlight the intersections of race, class, and gender.

Phase 1: The Message: Jay-Z as an Urban Singer of Tales

"The Message" (1982) is a rap written and performed by Grandmaster Flash and the Furious Five. The epic tale chronicles the day-to-day experiences of many young black and Latino youth living in impoverished communities in New York. The main hook of the song provides an insight into the first phase of Jay-Z's career in which he develops his message as a rapper and defines his audience. "The Message" is frequently referred to as one of the greatest records in hip hop history because of its vivid descriptions of life in urban space and its engagement with the physical and psychological threats of violence, poverty, and lack of resources that impoverished American communities. The first phase of Jay-Z's career, from 1996 to 1999, which spans the albums *Reasonable Doubt* (1996) through *Hard Knock Life, Vol. 2* (1998), documents Jay-Z's early development as an artist. Like many black youth who grew up in poor environments described in "The Message," Jay-Z turned to selling drugs to make money and to take financial burdens off his single-parent mother. In a two-year time span, we see the artist establish his lyrical style, develop the key themes that shape his life, and define his audience. He openly grapples with his relationship to poverty, his friends, women, and rivals. Translating the life lessons he learned on the streets to the rap industry, the artist expands upon the trials and tribulations described in the hip hop classic "The Message."

Jay-Z's heroic journey from the Marcy Projects in Brooklyn to rap superstar parallel many of the learning patterns of Homeric oral narrative poets. Albert Lord describes the fundamentals of oral epic composition in *A Singer of Tales*, building on the scholarship of Milman Parry who discovered a formula within the Homeric poems *The Iliad* and *The Odyssey*. Lord writes that an epic singer is "a composer of tales ... singer, composer, and poet are one under different aspects but at the same time. Singing, performing, and composing are facets of the same act" (14).

If we apply the processes of oral composition that many European epic singers have used over time to train as artists, we can see pronounced similarities between their journeys and those of West African griots. West African oral narrative practices date back thousands of years. From the Malian griots to the Ibo, the griot tradition is one that often operates in contradiction. Many griots are regarded as mouthpieces for the Divine who bring prophecy and important messages to the community. Others are viewed as oral epic singers, community storytellers that document the histories of families and tribes for centuries without writing a single word. Whether seemingly divine or generationally appointed and/ or professionally employed because of oratorical skill, all griots that are successful must have the capacity to improvise and tell a story that is compelling. Like many African American rappers of today, griots are also lauded for their performance styles and musical abilities. This means that the roles of the oral epic singer and the griot are not simply those of musicians and storytellers, but also as performers who weave their personal stories within the tales they tell of the community's past to comment on the present. Kevin Wetmore contends that many connections that we see between Greek and African epic oral tradition are not coincidental. He contends "the introduction of original Greek tragedies to sub–Saharan Africa took place during the colonial era" (47). African epic scholars such as Thomas Hale and Stephen Belcher, cited in

Wetmore, state the griot, known by a variety of local names "gewel, gawlo, jail, jeli, mabo, gesere, jesere, etc." as being the indigenous equivalent to Homer (xvii): (Hale and Belcher in Wetmore 29).

Much of hip hop storytelling incorporates both European and West African griot[2] traditions. An African American rapper such as Jay-Z, who came of age in New York City United States in the twentieth century, builds on an African American oral tradition that incorporates such European and African retentions. Oral narrative performance techniques outlined by Lord offer us a basic working vocabulary of oral narrative practices discovered by Milman Parry that find commonalities with West African griot traditions discussed later.

Lord elaborates on the process of oral composition identified by Parry that incorporates improvisatory and performative techniques that move through several stages of learning for the artist. The first stage of learning oral epic formulas is to find a mentor or experienced singer to follow. The stages identified by Parry are explained by Albert Lord who argues "in the first stage it generally happens that the neophyte has chosen one singer, perhaps his father, or a favorite uncle, or some well-known singer of his neighborhood, to listen to most closely, but he hears other singers too" (23). The second stage of oral epic narrative composition is "the process of imitation both in regard to playing the instrument and to learning the formulas and themes of the tradition" (24). The third stage involves the artist establishing his repertoire and competency as an oral narrative singer as well as his audience. The artist develops the skills that allow him to "learn the rudiments of ornamentation and expansion" (25). This three-part learning process for oral epic singers ends when "the singer's repertoire is large enough to entertain an audience for several nights" (26). Within the first phase of Jay-Z epic oeuvre, we can see links to this process of learning the skills of oral composition as they are manifest in rappers learning to freestyle.

There is no "rap school" where MCs can go to learn their craft. They must learn oral narrative strategies from established MCs through listening to existing storytellers and observing their environment. The singers of oral narratives who follow the Homeric tradition start in an apprenticeship style learning process near the age of 14 or 15. Jay-Z began to follow rappers in his community and began to rap in his early teens. Growing up as hip hop emerged in New York in the late 1970s and early 1980s; Jay-Z was drawn to rapping to express himself. Following in the footsteps of Brooklyn rappers such as his early mentors Jaz-O and Biggie Smalls, he learned to tell stories and began to draw parallels between drug-dealing and rap. We can see a direct link between the oral practices passed down by oral epic singers and rappers. Oral epic singers learn by listening to experienced singers and paying attention to rhythm and melody to work through their process of imitation. Both Jaz-O and Biggie Smalls became mentors for Jay-Z, who learned to rap by watching and listening to these and other experienced artists.

Following in the tradition of Biggie Smalls, Jay-Z learned to freestyle his raps, versus writing them down. His early raps weave tales about the drug game, its relationship to the underground crime world, and the ways his life changed with money. His first major hit from *Vol. 2: Hard Knock Life* (1998), "Hard Knock Life: Ghetto Anthem," narrates his rags-to-riches story by sampling the chorus of his rap from the Broadway musical *Annie* (1977). Here, I demonstrate how all three parts of oral narrative composition come together fusing orality, improvisation and performativity in the act of freestyling. "Hard Knock Life: Ghetto Anthem" was one of the first crossover commercial successes for Jay-Z reaching audiences across racial, ethnic, and class lines. Jay-Z riffs on the storyline of the original song sampled from the musical, drawing our attention to the similarities between the trials and tribulations narrated by white orphans with those of young African American boys and girls living in similar situations. Jay-Z takes center stage as the chorus from the original song plays against a thumping bass beat that serves as a new background for the young female voices who talk about their hard life. The familiar refrain references a life of hard times, children playfully recounting being "kicked" instead of "kissed" which serves as both literal and figurative references to their impoverished home lives, ones that lack both physical and emotional well being.

After this introduction, Jay-Z establishes a familiar scene from the musical and film versions of *Annie,* shifting his audience's attention to his own journey. He makes links to his rise from the social conditions that oppressed him to his new status as a successful artist. In the video for the song, Jay-Z is seen walking through the streets of Brooklyn, greeted by African American children on the street. The black youth pantomime the chorus from *Annie* mouthing the words over the original white voices, linking their experiences of abandonment and despair to those of the white children in *Annie* who sing of their struggles. Jay-Z begins the first verse that begins with his own rags to riches story. Taking his listener on an aural and visual tour of his early times as street corner hustler his present role as wealthy hip hop MC.

Jay-Z engages the second component of oral narrative production by imitating the themes of previous artists such as his mentor Biggie Smalls, who often chronicled his journey from selling drugs to becoming a successful rap artist. Jay-Z, like Biggie, uses his story to present himself as the resilient hero who has overcome social obstacles despite terrible odds. He reminds his audience that he has experienced social desperation and turned to sell drugs, yet has found another way to escape the harsh realities of the street to emerge as one of the finest rappers in hip hop. He encourages his audience to embrace their hardships and to turn them into fuel for success. Urging his audience them to see his life as an example, he reveals his fears and vulnerabilities. Later in the verse, he pays tribute to one of his mentors, Biggie Smalls, establishing for his audience that his flow and skills are indebted to his late teacher and moves forward in his footsteps.

Jay-Z challenges his listeners to embrace the "school of hard knocks," here represented as the streets, and to make the most of their lives. He tells youth to protect themselves from outsiders who want to prey on them and to reach for the stars by making a plan for their lives that will bring them prosperity. Later in the fourth verse, Jay-Z makes a narrative shift and alerts his audience that he has proven himself and is ready to move outside the shadow of his mentors. He has proven to his audience that he can freestyle and has built on the repertoire of his mentors and is able to provide innovative takes on familiar themes to entertain his audience. Jay-Z reminds us of his struggles to the top where competitors doubted him, his battle with his enemies, and of his past as a drug dealer (1999). Overcoming these odds, he rises to the top, finding a new family in hip hop. Jay-Z's freestyle skills captivate his audience with his confident swagger, his boy next door presentation, and his ability to speak to audiences of all races despite the fact that he addresses the African American community in most of his rhymes.

By remixing his social commentary with the *Annie* sample, Jay-Z speaks to the abandonment of black youth in urban spaces and the limited life chances they often have. By connecting the stories of young white orphans, who also critique undesirable living conditions, to his rag to riches story, Jay-Z links American stories of abandonment and survival that are often separated by race and gender, yet connected through class. Jay-Z's narrative performatively reproduces images of race and class that engage both black and white audiences, yet speak to any interlocutor who has a dream of obtaining fame and fortune and is met with naysayers. "Hard Knock Life: Ghetto Anthem" marks Jay-Z's realization that his audience is larger than the African American community and that he can complicate the black-white binary by focusing on issues of class. The three stages of oral narrative composition outlined by Lord are apparent within this narrative context.

Phase 2: The Bridge: The Making of a Hip Hop Griot

In "The Bridge" (1985), the rapper MC Shan calls to his audience asking them to remember, "how it all started" showing the relevance of the past of hip hop history in the present. This rap is cited as a classic in hip hop, yet often sparks debate about whose narratives represent the "authentic" history of hip hop culture in the United States. The song is also important because it incited one of the first major rap battles in hip hop history. Rapper KRS-One, representing the Bronx, contested MC Shan's declaration of Queens as the birthplace of hip hop. Both rappers operate as hip hop griots who document the past and present of hip hop as they contest claims of authenticity in one another's storytelling. Griots take on several, and often contradictory roles, in West African societies. One does not just "become" a griot or storyteller just because one aspires to do so. Just as in European oral epic traditions, West African griots must apprentice and learn their craft over time.

African American rappers have made literal and figurative links to the African continent since the beginning of hip hop. What is important here is recognizing the conscious and subconscious retentions of West African oral narrative practices that persist in African American culture that are manifest in hip hop. West African griots are often regarded as the oral historians of their communities. Kevin Wetmore defines the role of the griot as "a storyteller whose function in an oral society is not only to tell stories, but to serve as that society's historian, lawgiver, teacher, entertainer, and repository for the community's knowledge" (24). Similarly, many rappers often act as entertainers as well as "historians, lawgivers, teachers" because they are successful in their communities and often document what escapes the mainstream archive of American history. Rappers such as Jay-Z orally document the past and the multiple ways it shapes the "news" of the present moment by informing his audience of what they need to know about current events, life dealing with the law, education and social dilemmas. Lilyan Kesteloot contends that we must reconcile the role of the griot as storyteller with the role that he/she takes as a profession that is usually past down generation to generation. She notes that many West African griots inherit the skills of the profession by participating in a rigorous apprenticeship program, some that last ten years (138). During this time, Kesterloot argues griots learn several oral narrative strategies that mirror patterns found in European oral narrative practices outlined by Milman Parry and Albert Lord:

> The young griot memorizes lists of names, codified songs and the diagrams of adventures, a kind of abstract manual. A same time, he learns the art of developing them, embellishing them, of filling them out with proverbs, rumination, digression, depending on the audience and his imagination ... [138].

As a griot of hip hop, Jay-Z establishes his legacy in the hip hop game and the trials and tribulations that have contributed to his flow as a rapper. If we recall Jay-Z's theorization of his process as a freestyler, we can see similar practices of his creating such a "manual" as outlined above by Kesterloot. Shifting the focus and content of his stories to appeal to his audience overtime, as he builds on stories previously told never forgetting what he has said before in his epic tale. As an artist, he demonstrates a self-reflexive capacity to critique his work and to admit that his expanded worldview has enabled him to make new choices that allow him to bridge the past of his audience with the present. This oratorical strategy of creating a "bridge" between past and present is most noticeable in Phase 2 of Jay-Z's artistic practice and oeuvre spanning the time from *Life and Times of S. Carter, Vol. 3* (1999) to *Blueprint 2: The Gift and The*

Curse (2002), and represents the artist's connections between past and present as they demonstrate considerable growth as an oral composer.

Isidore Okpewho contends African griots inherit a responsibility to mimetic principles of realism (14), ecology of art (19) and tradition and originality (22). *Blueprint* (2001), one of Jay-Z's most critically acclaimed albums, documents his navigation of each of these principles as the artist finds a balance between his personal and public life. At this phase of his career, Jay-Z is awaiting a criminal trial for gun possession, is at the center of a now historic rap battle with his contemporary *Nas,* and begins to elevate his "hero of the streets persona" to a rap "god" status. Naming himself "H.O.V.A.,"[3] a word play on the word Jehovah, the artist endows himself with supernatural powers that allow him to escape the challenges presented in his environment. Jay-Z creates what Okpewho calls "ecology of art." In West African griot culture, to be a convincing djeli, (another term for griot), artists had to be aware of their audiences and their relationships to the environment. They could not use obscure language that the people could not relate to but had to "speak in the language of your [their] savanna" (19). The griot/griottes job was to create connections between his/her life experiences and the natural environment while simultaneously crafting stories in a language that his audience could understand and recognize. Jay-Z uses hip hop vernacular to create a relationship to the environment always keeping in mind the fluidity of popular culture, the relationship of past to present and the changing social and political climates of hip hop over time. Like West African griots, Jay-Z uses specific language that describes urban landscapes in ways that are appealing to his audience. He also names himself as a master storyteller by telling his audience that he is better than most MCs that they will encounter. He juxtaposes the familiar with the new remixing ideas and terms that provoke his audiences to think in new ways about their lives and the capacity they possess to imagine themselves as more than their surroundings. Jay-Z reinforces this triumph over tragedy ideology throughout the oeuvre [body of work], but speaks directly to this idea later in Phase 3 of his career on the fourteenth track of *Blueprint 3,* "So Ambitious," where he tells his audience that they have the capacity to create and realize their own visions for their lives. Jay-Z creates what he wants to happen in his world using his narrative strategies speaking his vision into existence. By replacing traditional images of landscapes and animal metaphors used in West African ecology with his own lush imagery of the landscape of urban America, Jay-Z juxtaposes images of depressed urban spaces and of life on the streets with references to luxury goods and elite locales. Using hip hop vernacular, Jay-Z makes connections across class lines that work to expand the worldview of his audience. Eugene Redmond's attempt to relate African griot traditions to African American storytelling in *Drumvoices: The Mission of Afro-American Poetry* (1976) provides an insightful connection that underscores my analysis:

The *griot* began at a very early age to master his technique and information. Like the master drummer, he understudied an elder statesman of the trade. His training demanded a certain psychological adjustment to the significance of his job — which was to contain (and give advice on) the cultural "heirlooms" of the community.... To the black American *griot*-singer-poet the job of unraveling the complex network of his past and present-future worlds is a painful but rewarding labor of love [1976, 18].

We can see connections between the diverse influences of which Redmond speaks in Jay-Z's "I.Z.Z.O. (H.O.V.A.)." Jay-Z's use of mimetic principles and attention to his environment underscore his ability to balance tradition and originality. The song opens with the rappers focus on the ecology of his environment. He thanks his audience and proceeds to name himself as "the 8th wonder of the world." By using the term "wonder of the world," a term used to describe things in comparison to the natural and modern wonders of the world that are designated as sites of awe in the environment, Jay-Z lauds his skills as a rapper and tells his audience how to view him. He welcomes his fans and notifies them that they will witness the "flow of the century" underscoring a connection between his auto-didactic skills being divinely appointed in the same way that natural wonders such as the Grand Canyon and Niagara Falls are products of nature that attract people around the world to admire them. For Jay-Z, his "flow," or freestyle ability, classifies him as a site to be seen. Thanking his audience in the rap for witnessing his greatness, he establishes his place in history, representing himself as a keeper of tradition and one of great originality.

At the end of the first verse, Jay-Z positions himself as a resilient hero, a self-professed rap god he calls H.O.V.A. who is needed by the people. His claim that other rappers want him dead and that the police want to stop him describe the social conditions of many inspiring and established rappers who live the "street" life and compete for fame in a music industry that has few success stories. Addressing his own criminal charges faced in his career, he narrates his escape from death and rise to the top acknowledging himself as an urban "singer of tales" who "tells life stories through rap." A resurrected hero who beat the odds, Jay-Z announces his triumphant return. He warns his audience that his individual sacrifices offer life lessons for his audience. In the second to last verse, Jay-Z establishes further links between tradition and originality. Citing his debt to African American culture and hip hop, he argues that his storytelling is for his people. Highlighting the social stereotypes superimposed on African Americans in hip hop, Jay-Z states that despite his success in corporate America, and both artist and executive, that he is a "nigga." Using this term of endearment used between many African American men and women in African American culture as well as hip hop, Jay-Z aligns himself with the continued struggles of many black subjects who follow him aspiring to rise above their social conditions and to obtain the wealth and success that he models in his career. Jay-

Z positions himself as a master storyteller who has the capacity to right some of the wrongs of history such as the injustices many rappers have suffered. In Phase 3 of his career, he does just that embracing his position as a conqueror that has beat the odds personified in his character "H.O.V.A.."

Phase 3: H.O.V.A.: Remixing an Afro-Homeric Tradition

One of the most important aspects of African American culture is the oral tradition. However, like battles in hip hop over territory, African American writers have debated the value afforded to oral and literary traditions of African American people. Much analysis of African American oral tradition during the Harlem Renaissance structured this disconnect between the oral and the literary in a binary between African American "folklore" and the formal adherence to Western literary forms (Jones 2). Gayl Jones argues many African American writers "draw upon their oral heritage for the power and diversity of its narrative forms and storytelling techniques" (1). Daniel Banks makes insightful links to the hip hop MC and his or her capacity to bridge Homeric and African griot traditions:

> The MC in Hip Hop culture functions in much the same way as the djeli ... or griot (a more commonly known term in the west). The MC, as opposed to many—but not all—commercial rappers, also tells of the community's issues, its values, its ancestors, its heroes and heroines, its triumphs, and its struggles [1–2].

Banks observes the connections between ancient Greek and West African oral tradition that are manifest in the orality of the role of the MC as a storyteller. Relating Jay-Z's freestyle practices to the African griot underscores the importance of the remnants of that oral tradition in the African American community, specifically in the oral practice of freestyling. Phase 3 of Jay-Z's career, which I delineate as the production period between *The Black Album* (2003) and *The Blueprint 3* (2009), documents the artist's play with tensions and connections between European, African, and African American oral modes. By privileging freestyling as a distinctly American vernacular style of storytelling, Jay-Z underlines the ways that race, ethnicity, gender, and class determine and undermine notions of American identity. This period marks the expansion of Jay-Z's worldview, and thus his storylines, as well as his rearticulation of his public persona as not only a rapper, but also as an entrepreneur and social activist.

Jay-Z's oral narratives, during this phase of his career, attempt to rearticulate similar assertions made by African American writers during the Harlem Renaissance who sought to abandon what Jones call a "literary double consciousness and ... an applauding of African American modification of American language" (9). Jay-Z articulates the "folklore" of hip hop, stories of the ghetto, the language of the streets, and the recurring characters of pimps, gangsters, and video vixens through complex characters who live in contradiction to and in collaboration with hip hop culture. He also introduces new themes that attempt to re-signify notions of urban space and characters. Addressing seemingly bourgeois topics such as cosmopolitan vacation locales, luxury goods, and elite friendships, Jay-Z remixes notions of the folk, or common, with the bourgeois. He uses his ability to live between both spaces to mark the fluidity of the borders between groups. By exposing serious intra-racial conflicts in his epic oeuvre that are based on class and gender, Jay-Z honors historic traditions of resilience, survival, and creativity in African American culture.

As "H.O.V.A.," the artist finds the audacity and the ingenuity to chart new territory in hip hop that claims both "folk" and bourgeois elements of African American life. During the Harlem Renaissance, this claiming of folklore, or oral tradition, provided, according to Jones, "the base for contemporary African American writers, who make use of folklore, cognizant of its multiple and complex linguistic, social, historical intellectual and political functions" (9). Similarly, Jay-Z's sampling and remixing of European, African, and African American oral modes charts new territory to understand the intersections and overlap of American experiences and the ways in which hip hop can engage the multiple "functions" of folklore as it also discusses the luxuries of the bourgeoisie.

The Bronx, considered by most hip hop artists and scholars to be the birthplace of hip hop, shaped the contours of the oral narrative form of rapping by depositing oral techniques from Caribbean, West Africa, South America, and Europe. What Houston Baker called a "blues matrix" of African American culture is relevant here. For Baker, the matrix is a point of ceaseless input and output, a web of intersecting impulses in productive transit that incorporates both the "folk" and the "art" of African American cultural production (3). Jay-Z zeroes in on this "web of intersecting impulses" at the end of his epic story. Creating seamless links between past and present, ancient and modern, European and African, folk and bourgeois, he develops an what I call an Afro-Homeric tradition that acknowledges multiple contrasting influences deposited within African American oral tradition. Jay-Z also suggests a global matrix of cross-racial and ethnic exchanges enabled through hip hop music.

By privileging an African American vernacular, hip hop folklore, and call and response traditions of the African American church, Jay-Z rearticulates tensions between notions of the "folk" and the "bourgeois," highlighting their intersections. Jay-Z's remixing, African, and African-American oral modes can be heard in the song "A Star Is Born," from the album *Blueprint 3* (2009). The song can be read as an ode to his rise from urban apprentice to a cosmopolitan oral narrative composer. The title of the song is sampled from the 1937 film *A Star Is Born*, a film that chronicles the story of a young white woman who has a dream of becoming a famous Hollywood actress. Similar to Jay-Z, she is told she has a one in a million chance of success. Through hard work, talent, and determination, she receives a break and becomes an overnight success. Jay-Z riffs on the original storyline of the film in his narrative and also uses the title of the film as the chorus of the song. In the first verse, Jay-Z applauds the creative efforts of his peers lauding their performances as rappers. He references important storytellers who have come and gone in the American hip hop game, alluding to the fact that only a select few have had the success he has obtained. Naming the rappers, MA$E, Kanye West (who Jay-Z mentored), Sean P. "Diddy" Combs, Lil' Wayne, 50 cent, his one-time rival Nas, and Eminem, he lauds his competition focusing on their skills as MCs. Using call and response strategies often employed in African American oral and literary genres, he guides his audience to acknowledge these artists as important contributors to the history of hip hop. In the third verse, Jay-Z employs African griot techniques of establishing tradition and legacy to comment on the breadth of his success. He spins his story back to the beginning of his career arguing he always knew he was going be a star and that no matter how many impasses that attempted to detour his plan, he maintains that it is his skill as an artist that has allowed him to stay on top. Paying homage to his past, he shows the connection between past and present articulations of his own story linking early days as a drug dealer to his success as an entrepreneur. As the chorus resumes, Jay-Z receives the applause of his fans and allows a new rapper to end the song to suggest that he is ushering in a future star and embracing the power of his omnipresent alter ego H.O.V.A. One could also read this mentoring of a new urban storyteller as a call to his audience to reflect upon their capacity to make changes in their communities by reaching out to those in need to help young people find a path to success. Jay-Z's selection of rapper J.Cole to complete the verse can be read symbolically as a new rapper/storyteller embarking on the same cycle of apprenticeship that Jay-Z began with his early mentors Jaz-O and Biggie Smalls. In the final verse, J. Cole pays tribute to his mentor Jay-Z while demonstrating the braggadocio that all MCs must master as lyricists. He argues that he is grateful for the opportunity to rap with a legend, and that his flow and skills reflect his potential as an artist that one day might be compared to Jay-Z.

Jay-Z comes full circle in his career in "A Star Is Born" by giving an emerging rapper the same break he received. Using his life experiences as his "blueprint" to show young African-American youth specifically, and all racial and ethnic groups more generally, that they can succeed despite socially constructed obstacles. He establishes his message and creates a bridge between the have and the have nots to end his epic tale by passing the torch to a new generation of storytellers. In 1937, Richard Wright's "Blueprint for Negro Writing," suggests that African-American writers and artists find value in their lives and their experiences to transform their own lives and society. He writes:

> in the lives of Negro writers must be found those materials and experiences which will create a meaningful picture of the world today. ... And, in turn, this changed world will dialectically change the writer [Wright in Lewis 200].

What Jay-Z's epic tale elucidates is that African American expressive culture contains samples from a range of influences that are manifest in hip hop arts. Using his oral stories to write every day expressions and experiences of black people, Jay-Z reveals himself as epic hero and urban everyman who makes a call to us to ask ourselves "what is 'American'?" As Jay-Z tells it and hip hop shows us, there's nothing more American than hip hop.

For Further Consideration

QUESTIONS

1. Provide a comprehensive definition of griot. How does Jay-Z fulfill the many and/or multifaceted roles of an African griot? Is it even important for African American artists to maintain a linkage and connection to Africa? Why or why not?

2. The author makes note that there is also the concept of the hero in the African world, which is similar and yet different to the Homeric concept of hero. And in particular, there is the role of the hero in the epic tale. Can we not argue that Jay-Z's musical corpus constitutes an epic? Aren't his trials and tribulations, and life experiences similar to that of *The Iliad* and *The Odyssey*, thus making him an epic hero?

3. The author suggests that "Jay-Z's analysis of American identity suggests that blackness is one of several articulations of American identity" and that "Jay-Z's freestyle raps critique the contentious and often contradictory relationships that produce American identities." What role does race and culture play in the production of American identity? Keep in mind that suburban whites are the largest consumers of hip hop music and also that Jay-Z "complicate[s] the black-white binary by focusing on issues of class."

4. The author notes, "Rappers are also oral historians. They preserve the history of the hip-hop community, preserve African American music genres through sampling, and document social issues within the African American community." Does a rapper's lack of objectivity compromise the history he seeks to preserve? In 50 (or so) years can the next generation's view of America be aptly told through Jay-Z?

Notes

1. Jay-Z references Homer's *The Odyssey* in the September 2009 issue of *O Magazine* in the article "Books that Made a Difference to Jay-Z." He contends, "This epic poem was kind of difficult for me to get through, but it has a beautiful rhythm. I got lost in reading about Odysseus' struggle to get home and his longing for someone so strong, as his wife was, waiting for him. That's like a dream — that kind of strength, love, loyalty." Jay-Z is listed as a producer for the 2009 Broadway musical *Fela!* In a November

2009 interview with MTV with S. Roberts, Jay-Z discusses the music of the slain Nigerian musician, stating, "It's an inspiration about the power of music." He mentions Biggie Smalls as an inspiration in several songs.

2. It should be noted that West African griot traditions are expansive and vary from tribe to tribe and place to place throughout West Africa. Though I focus on Isidore Okpewho's analysis of the role of the African griot, I acknowledge that there are many roles and interpretations of what the griot's function was and is based on cultural practice and historic context. My use of the term griot broadly encompasses the role of social and cultural historian as well as accomplished storyteller and performer of cultural traditions.

3. Many fans and critic argue this use of the moniker H.O.V.A. is a blasphemous reference to God. However, few acknowledge the ways in which this metaphor also operates on multiple levels that reinforce the epic qualities of rap storytelling. When Jay-Z uses this reference to himself, he is most often referencing his seemingly "supernatural" qualities as lyricist, a "rap god" of sorts. He capitalizes on his reining status in the hip hop community as one of the most successful MCs of all time and, like any champion, continues to remind his lyrical opponents of his skill sets. Like many griots, he acknowledges his role as a "mouthpiece" for the community (in this case the hip hop community) who has the capacity to deliver inspired messages.

Works Cited

Banks, D. "Hip Hop Theatre: The Voice of Now." *Page and Stage,* 8 December 2008. Retrieved from http://pageandstage.org/themes/homer-to-hip-hop.

"Books that Made a Difference to Jay-Z." *O Magazine,* 2 September 2009. Retrieved from http://www.oprah.com/omagazine/Books-That-Made-a-Difference-to-Jay-Z.

Dyson, M.E. (2007). *Know What I Mean: Reflections on Hip Hop.* New York: Basic Civitas, 2007.

Gregory, J. "Jay-Z Praises 'Fascinating' *Fela!* as Musical Opens on Broadway." 24 November 2009. Retrieved from http://www.gigwise.com/news/53599/Jay-Z-Praises-Fascinating-Fela-As-Musical-Opens-On-Broadway.

Homer. *The Iliad.* New York: Penguin, 2003.

_____. *The Odyssey.* New York: Digireads, 2005.

Jones, G. *Liberating Voices: Oral Tradition in African American Literature.* Cambridge, MA: Harvard University Press, 1991.

Kesterloot, Lilyan. "Myth, Epic and African History" in Mudimbe, V.Y. *The Surreptitious Speech: Présence Africaine and the Politics of Otherness 1947–1987.* Chicago: University of Chicago Press, 1992. 136–147.

Lewis, D.L., ed. *The Portable Harlem Renaissance Reader.* New York: Penguin, 1995.

Lord. A. *A Singer of Tales.* Cambridge, MA: Harvard University Press, 2000.

MC Melle Mel. "The Message." Recorded by Grandmaster Flash. *The Message.* New York: Sugarhill Records, 1982. CD.

MC Shan. "The Bridge." 1985. *Rap's Greatest Hits, Volume 2.* Priority: Los Angeles, 1987. Record.

Okpewho, I. *The Epic in Africa: Towards a Poetics of the Oral Performance.* New York: Columbia University Press, 1979.

Ong, W. *Orality and Literacy: The Technologizing of the Word.* New York: Routledge, 1982.

Parry, I. *Prophets of the Hood: Politics and Poetics of Hip Hop.* Durham, NC: Duke University Press, 2004.

Redmond, E. *Drumvoices: The Mission of Afro-American Poetry.* Garden City, NY: Doubleday, 1976.

Roberts, S. "Jay-Z Becomes a Broadway Producer for *Fela!*" MTV, 24 November 2009. Retrieved from http://www.mtv.com/news/articles/1626972/20091124/jay_z.jhtml.

Saddick, A. "Rap's Unruly Body: The Postmodern Performance of Black Male Identity on the American Stage." *TDR* 47:49 (2003): 110–27.

Wetmore, Kevin J. *The Athenian Sun in the African Sky: Modern African Adaptations of Greek Tragedy.* Jefferson, NC: McFarland, 2001.

Wright, R. "Blueprint for Negro Writing." 1937. *The Portable Harlem Renaissance Reader,* ed. David Levering Lewis. New York: Viking, 1994.

Zumthor, P. *Oral Poetry: An Introduction.* Minneapolis: University of Minnesota Press, 1990.

5

The Prodigal God and the Legacy of Socially Responsible Hip Hop

T. Hasan Johnson

Jay-Z, also known as Shawn Carter, became an internationally renowned hip hop icon in the wake of the deaths of The Notorious B.I.G. (a.k.a. Christopher Wallace) and Tupac Shakur in the mid–1990s. His legacy has already been secured as the wealthiest product of hip hop, an avid freestyler, and a shrewd businessman. In fact, Jay-Z will go down in hip hop history as an icon whose legacy traverses several generations of hip hop, and he has reached a status that will hopefully represent the beginning of an era of artistic prestige for hip hop artists. After all, we must remember that since hip hop is still relatively young (it dates from circa the mid–1970s), forty plus year old East Coast artists like Carter were present at some of the early block parties in New York that framed the foundations of what would later be called hip hop culture. KRS-One, for example, talks about growing up across the street from where Kool Herc's early parties were held (both in apartment buildings and the block parties helmed, later, by Afrika Bambaata). They were fans of the early radio shows by DJs like John "Mr. Magic" Rivas (who died of a heart attack in 2009), Marley Marl, and Kool DJ Red Alert in the early 1980s on WBLS radio. From there, many grew up freestyling in parks, forming their own rap groups and eventually, as it pertains to Carter, joining more established artists like the Jaz-O.

This places Carter in a unique position as an early participant and eventual leader in hip hop who can boast being instrumental in (or at least a witness to) every phase of hip hop's development. From its inception to its current state, questionable as it may be in its direction, Carter was there. However, his long-standing participation lies at the heart of this analysis. As others might, Jay-Z cannot claim ignorance to the potential of hip hop as a force for social justice. He knows what it has done and what it still can do (beyond merely motivating people to purchase certain merchandise), and yet he has not referenced such history. He has not thoroughly re-invoked it in this era, an era where a new generation is ignorant of the social movements and organizations that yielded possibilities for focusing hip hop's energies toward social change — and possibly still could (e.g., the Stop the Violence Movement, H.E.A.L., Blackwatch, etc.).

Worse yet, the most widely known representations of Jay-Z are tied to a hyper-masculine image that advocates that one ignore political issues, subjugate women, and flaunt a gross form of materialism — despite that many of his fans are suffering more economically than ever in this current recession. This is especially problematic when you factor in that Jay-Z comes out of an era in the late 1980s and early 1990s when socially uplifting lyrics were expected from artists. Whether politically-focused (such as Public Enemy), spiritually-focused (such as X-Clan), ideologically focused (such as Arrested Development), and/or generally positive (such as the Native Tongues or Gangstarr), artists across genres challenged the industry in their quest to stay relevant and socially responsible in the wake of the global marketization of gross stereotypes of urban black and brown peoples. Sadly, Jay-Z has moved from this era to becoming the poster child for wanton materialism. Lastly, this is especially problematic considering that even Carter himself has rapped about his family being financially strapped as a kid, describing himself in the context of many during the Reagan presidential regime.

Consciousness in Hip Hop: A Conceptual Map

In what is referred to as the Golden Era of hip hop, roughly from the mid–1980s to the around the early rise of corporate-sanctioned gangster rap, hip hop went through a phase that was unexpected to many avid listeners of the genre — conscious music. Whether dealing with spirituality or non-electoral political mobilization, this era saw many groups of young rappers advocating reading books, meditation, prayer, proper dieting, and even (albeit occasional) sexual abstinence! They participated in rallies against racism, unjust civil treatment, biased judicial practices, and institutional sexism. Although hip hop's advocacy for gay and lesbian interests is still found wanting, this era was nonetheless quite inspiring. More to the point, this mostly East Coast movement sparked interest and reflection from those in other parts of the country, and later around the globe. Not far from the days when hip hop was mostly spread through word of mouth and bootlegged cassette tapes, the motivation to go the record store and buy a new album was still mostly driven by a friend's recommendation.

During this period, it has been rumored that Jay-Z was a member of the

Ansar Allah community, a sect of Islamic practitioners led by then named Imaam Issa Al Haadi Al Mahdi (Dwight York, who would later call himself "Malachi Z. York"), an East Coast figure known for writing profusely on Islamic history and its supposed connections to other esoteric, at times arcane, religious traditions. They were mostly seen, as far as hip hop is concerned, in the video for the song "Peach Fuzz," starring Zev Luv X (who would later be known as MF Doom after a self-reinvention following the death of his brother). Wearing long white robes and selling incense and books on local street corners, their apparent advocacy for orthodox Islam both contrasted and reminded many of the Nation of Islam. In hip hop circles, this would precede the rise of the Nation of Gods and Earths (a small splinter group that spun-off from the Nation of Islam after the death of Malcolm X and led by Clarence "13X" Smith), a group to which many hip hop artists belonged, such as Rakim of Eric B. & Rakim, Big Daddy Kane, Sadat X Allah, Grand Puba, Lord Jamar of the group Brand Nubian, Wise Intelligent of the group Poor Righteous Teachers, the Wu Tang Clan, MF Doom, and J Live to name a few.

These non-traditional rap artists constituted a sort of new constellation of East Coast-based, non-traditional, Islamic influenced spiritual traditions that permeated hip hop until the late 1990s. Meanwhile, on the West Coast, Ice Cube's re-envisioned gangsterism broke from Niggaz Wit Attitudes and made ties with the Nation of Islam. Along with other West Coast artists like Kam, Ice Cube (Oshea Jackson) introduced the Nation of Islam to the West Coast hip hop audience. This led to a bi-coastal declaration of conscious hip hop. On the East Coast, it took form in the Stop the Violence movement (led by KRS-One and Doug E. Fresh), spearheaded by the 1989 song "Self Destruction," while on the West Coast the song and corresponding movement took form with the West Coast Rap All-Stars' 1990 song "We're All in the Same Gang" anti-gang song/movement.[1] This was the climate of the late 1980s and early 1990s in hip hop, a climate that Jay-Z was initiated into as an artist.

Yet one must ask, in the current era of unprecedented corporate radio/ record industry control, could there ever be such a time for hip hop again? Could consumers and artists ever actually make the subject matter of the music relevant to local communities ever again? Can younger generations appreciate the role of social justice-oriented hip hop, though many were not witness to a time in music where there were few institutional limitations? Lastly, as the record industry struggles to regain its footing after the massive shrinking of sales, online downloading, and pirate MP3 technology, how could such a movement in hip hop occur? My solution? Jay-Z. He and other artists of his caliber can help turn the tide if they spearhead a movement with artists, activists, and organizations at every level to accomplish the goal of organizing around issues and content rather than profit.

Jay-Z's Revolution of the Individual

In many respects, Carter's brand of hip hop is not completely unique — at least in terms of subject-matter. Money, power, street respect, cars, houses, expensive beverages, clubs, freestyling, and houses have been common areas of interest in hip hop for quite a while. What makes Jay-Z a phenomenon is his creative talent for setting trends and popularizing the obscure. However, the cost of this talent seems to be is his emphasis on a sort of a narcissistic individualism (though it's not something he embodies alone, particularly in hip hop). Representations of Jay-Z are consistently dogged with an overemphasis on himself, whether the stories he tells in his songs are fictional or biographical, which compellingly suggests to the casual listener that this should be the case for everyone. But sacrificing for others, standing against exploitation and oppression, or even some form of altruism are never engaged or made "cool." Jay-Z symbolizes the hedonistic, self-preoccupied aspect of hip hop's aesthetic taken to its extreme. Unlike other artists, his fame and wealth is unparalleled in hip hop, thus allowing him to engage issues that primarily wealthy white men may entertain — especially in terms of purchasing Maybachs. Such standing would seem liberating in the sense that he should be able to talk about a wide variety of subjects, but it seems that his creative subject matter is limited, something that even he has complained about in the past.

Making songs with artists that have made conscientious stands in hip hop, such as Common, Talib Kweli, and Mos Def, according to Jay-Z, does not even seem relevant, as he has informed us that market demands hamper his ability to produce relevant forms of music. This is also tied to his feeling that he has to dumb down his music for a fan base that seems to not want to hear anything from him. The counterargument could simply be that it is not that his fan base does not want to hear such music, but rather a different fan base may want to hear it, although they may not have the market standing to produce a large number of Nielsen SoundScan ratings — but they would be interested in it nonetheless. A shift in how the market is understood, especially as it relates to different types of listeners should not be taken lightly, as grassroots campaigning for particularly artists has been key in their claiming of new market space. Simply put, as artists who do not produce platinum albums their first time out have had to overwhelmingly opt to produce their work and sell it on the underground market, and more conscious MC's have begun to gain underground appeal, can/should Jay-Z be instrumental in returning the genre to the forefront of hip hop? With his "pull," could he not revitalize the genre by doing different kinds of music, particularly more of the conscious variety, and tap some of the markets that would welcome him if they had a bit more reason to do so?

What is sorely needed in hip hop from those with clout is a radical diversification of thought, word, and action. Much of the music is hampered and curtailed by market concerns and radio sensibilities, but older generations are often disgusted with the limited, sometimes vapid, and repetitive number of topics found in much of Jay-Z's music. Conversely, younger generations have become polarized by such a limited array of issues, dichotomously choosing from an underground current of hip hop that engages a wide variety of topics or the corporate radio stream that is most popularly consumed my masses of listeners. Because Jay-Z sits at the crossroads of both popular and grassroots streams of hip hop creativity, will he address the more esoteric references in his music, much of which still has connections to this early 1990s era of hip hop (often without his audience's knowledge), or will he avoid such connections and continue to reinforce hyper-corporate, radio-influenced hip hop?

Jay-Z and Hedonistic Individualism

In the wake of the history of activism in hip hop, the rise of hedonistic entertainers is best symbolized by MC's like Notorious B.I.G. and Jay-Z. Although neither started the genre, they were both instrumental in sensation-alizing the acquisition of trendy materials and drug-dealing based social power. Jay-Z, having outlived B.I.G., continued to represent the approach and became its most highly esteemed hip hop symbol.

To be fair, he has not always enjoyed his own representation. For example, he has complained about having to dumb down his lyrics for mainstream con-sumption (*The Black Album's* "Moment of Clarity"), pointing out that it's only when he does such things that he goes triple or quintuple platinum. There are several factors that should be considered about Jay's success, and simultaneously reflect the state of hip hop. For instance, Jay-Z's flow has developed and changed over the years. Starting with fast-paced flows and intense lyrical performances, he could rhyme the material performed in the studio on-stage without losing a beat. But he also is rumored to have never written a song down; rather, it is said that he has memorized his lyrics from freestyle performances in the studio. People talk about how Jay-Z has gone into studios, listened to tracks, and then driven around in his car for a while until he freestyled a new hit song. Ironically, this would be something that would prove difficult for some of his producers (namely, Kanye West who, on his 2004 debut album *The College Dropout,* on the song "Last Call," mentioned how he made a beat for Jay-Z and hoped he would not get the "introspective," "meditative" Jay-Z, but more the "light-hearted" Jay-Z). Nevertheless, which Jay-Z a producer might get was hard to anticipate as he would not "write" anything until he meditated on a beat — or at least so it is rumored.

Unfortunately, by the mid–1990s, such talent was becoming more and more infrequent. Fewer and fewer artists mastered the balance between lyrical complexity, metaphorical delivery, and storytelling (as many could only do one — or maybe two — at one time). For Jay-Z, after *Reasonable Doubt*, most notably on tracks like "Izzo (Hova)" and "Hard Knock Life," Jay-Z demonstrated skill with his use of metaphor and storytelling as opposed to just quick, off-the-head flows. More importantly, Jay-Z learned to package his gritty life story into a crisp narrative that made him a sort of bootstrap success-story. In other words, he learned that creating a rise-from-the-ghetto narrative made him more palatable to mainstream audiences (most were used to hard luck stories in hip hop, but were new to MCs that could create a persona they could not only understand, but one they could identify with — even if they did not listen to hip hop!). Essentially, he learned a hidden golden rule in entertainment: help the audience remember your story.

Along with creating a persona in the entertainment industry, the use of a marketable narrative can help with album sales. As KRS-One suggested on his 1995 self-titled album, *KRS-One*, in the song "Health, Wealth, Self," artists should strive to sell their image, not a particular record or project. He goes on to say that the marketed persona supercedes the relevance of the albums that collect dust in an old bin years later. Understanding this principle helped Jay-Z achieve another goal — increased marketability. Jay-Z now sold albums, represented himself on the radio, and marketed himself more easily because people outside of New York, the underground scene, and most notably, outside of hip hop could relate to what he was saying. This meant that suburbanites, rock-listeners, and alternative music fans alike could not only understand Jay-Z, but could understand *how* to understand him. Additionally, at this point, they could also become more acclimated to hip hop music in general — especially artists affiliated with Jay-Z's Roc-A-Fella label. Clearly, production played a strong role in his marketability, and Jay-Z had a reputation for working with the likes of DJ Premier, Puff Daddy, the Neptunes (Pharell in particular), Timbaland, Just Blaze, and most notably, the up-and-coming Kanye West.

The second reason for Jay-Z's success was his rhyme style. For the most part, his choice of subject matter was more easily accessible to those yet uninitiated into the hip hop aesthetic. This may have been part of what he complained about regarding "dumbing-down his lyrics" (especially on *The Black Album* and in his film *Fade to Black*), but it nonetheless helped make his music more popular on MTV and other more mainstream media outlets. Possibly due to his rhyme-writing style, Jay-Z was criticized for years for not addressing more complicated subjects, engaging political issues, or explicating how MCs could be more responsible for the impact of their work on the youth community. Seldom acknowledging these critiques openly, he eventually argued that the fact that he spoke out about the ghetto was a form of political activism in itself. Despite a clichéd remark by MCs by the mid–1990s, Jay-Z seemed adamant about his stance and argued that as long as he rhymed about such things, he was helping to address social ills by bringing the harsh conditions of the ghetto to national and international scrutiny.

Despite the desire to speak out on social issues, Jay-Z understood the difficulty that came with being a social critic in hip hop. As a student of the history of hip hop, Jay-Z was quite familiar with the dangers of being pigeon-holed by his audience, a record label, or any other institution invested in his album sales. Artists like Public Enemy, X-Clan, and Paris demonstrated how restrictive both the record industry and audiences could be toward what you may want to produce and what they want to hear. Alternatively, rappers who were labeled as "gangstas" or criminals had difficulty making any other kind of music than what people expected from them. Whether it is due to intelligence, creativity, or just luck, Jay-Z managed to somewhat avoid inhibiting categories (at least compared to other artists), despite his complaints about the limitations in subject matter available to him.

Tangentially, Jay-Z's approach to spirituality also caught a lot of people's attention. He is abstract, vague, and yet inspiring for many hip hoppers navigating the difficult spaces of non-denominational forms of spiritual inquiry. Jay speaks with the boldness of a member of the Nation of Gods and Earths, the casual practicality of a Sunni Muslim (almost lackadaisically so), and the popular appeal of a Catholic pope. His spiritual message, albeit unclear, has used short statements and occasional references to provide his listeners with a non-traditional approach to spirituality that may be more reflective of today's post-religiosity than anything else. Non-religious, non-denominational, and yet open to the possibility of a spiritual force in the universe, many of Jay-Z's fans identify with his approach to spirituality (often articulated through hard and gritty stories about life, death, violence, and survival). Speaking as a sympathetic (and almost apologetic) ex-drug dealer and criminal, Jay has acknowledged the difficulties of following a spiritual path while addressing the practicality of making a daily living. In many ways, this approach resonated with many of his fans, and quite possibly, it may have also taught some of them about why they should be remorseful about what they do.

The third reason for Jay-Z's success was that he understood the notion of symbolic representation. In essence, he knew that to represent himself as the preeminent rags-to-riches paragon, he could attract those that were living in the same conditions he grew up in, while supplying them with the hope that they could also get out of a life of poverty, criminality, and violence. He also understood that he could attract youth from black, white, Latino, and Asian middle-class (and suburban) communities through his descriptive lyrics on style, taste, and material acquisition. Although some of them may not be able to identify with his "hard knock" origins, they could identify with the desire to be able to purchase nice clothes, buy expensive cars, and drink trendy alcoholic beverages (most preferably with your name endorsed on the bottle). In other words, they could identify with the relationship between possessing the means for increasing their material ownership and the idea that material items are signifiers for status in American society. This phenomenon should be understood as more complex and challenging than it may appear. For the generation of youth born after the 1970s, the civil rights movement, black power movement, and COINTELPRO's war against the black activist community, the turbulent decade of the 1960s does not generally resonate as "real." Instead, much of the legacies of these historical movements are somewhat amalgamated; assumed to be part of the milieu of daily reality for today's youth. Hence, class can be constructed and understood in slightly different ways by today's youth, who are hopelessly mixed and blended racially, politically, and socio-economically in ways almost unheard of forty years ago. Therefore, for Jay-Z's audience, instead of what job, academic degree, or type of house you owned, questions of class and status could be attributed to more fluid approaches to material wealth, like how much money you have access to (although not necessarily whether you received it through legal means), how well you could acquire wealth without working a conventional job, and how well you could find new ways to bring the street experience to the boardroom. Although to some these areas may not be any better than the last set of standards for class stratification, they do allow for larger groups of younger people to participate in society on their own terms.

The fourth reason for Jay-Z's success is his approach to black masculinity. Although not entirely original, his casual approach to "pimpin'," money-making, style, material wealth, and business acumen made him a new type of hip hop icon, a sort of laid-back pimp in control. Arguably taking the New York MC crown in the wake of Biggie Smalls' death, Jay-Z claimed (repeatedly) to be the "best rapper alive" (e.g., in "Dirt Off Your Shoulder," *The Black Album*). He also articulated his disapproval of his rivals (Nas, Prodigy of Mobb Deep, Tupac, etc.) by retaliating against them in his music, suggesting that he would attack anyone who challenged him, and more importantly, be more masculine than them. This resonated with many of his fans, mainly young men who want to identify with Jay-Z's pimp-in-control image. Also, his approach to women, mainly framed with him as a player who controls and manipulates them, suggests a form of masculinity that may complicate black male/female relationships. In the song "Girls, Girls, Girls" on his 2001 *The Blueprint* album, he describes how many girls he has and how well he controls each of them, despite the fact that he portrays most of them as characteristically flawed.

On the surface, the problem is that the type of masculinity Jay-Z exemplifies is often destructive, clichéd, and confrontational. Although this has become the norm for many rappers in hip hop, such behavior still raises questions about whether or not there can be a new, more productive form of masculinity that artists could espouse other than stereotypical pimps and gangsters. For example, in the song "Friend or Foe '98" on his *In My Lifetime, Volume 1*

(1997) album, he tells a story about surprising an assassin who has been planning to kill him. He then proceeds to kill the assassin, but only after taking the time to explain to him how much more of a man he is—suggesting that whoever gets to whom first is more the man. Despite such lyrics, more recently, Jay-Z has redefined his machismo persona. In a recent feud with Nas, both artists demonstrated the capacity for maturity in hip hop by publicly reconciling, as I will discuss later. Nevertheless, Jay-Z's popularity is closely related to his approach to black male masculinity, and after the deaths of his predecessors Biggie and Tupac, he has had to re-evaluate the value of the macho approach to manhood.

Another reason for Jay-Z's success is how his music lends itself to "virtual blackness." Virtual blackness refers to the idea that the socially constructed notion of blackness, rooted in a history of racism, negativity, and depravity, can be experienced vicariously through a medium that separates the listener from the experience, leaving them free to experience stereotypical forms of blackness without the societal repercussions that come with criminal behavior (e.g., jail, violent retaliation, or death). In the past, black entertainers and athletes were often used by white (and other) elite audiences in this manner. However, intrinsic to the rise to of entertainment-based technology, people of all class stations, races, colors, genders, and sexual orientations can experience virtual blackness. This might just be partially what draws mainstream audiences to rap music: the desire to experience "blackness." Such blackness, usually perceived as a form of otherness, is also projected on non-black MCs who participate in hip hop culture. Yet, it is not surprising that the types of blackness mainstream audiences are exposed to in hip hop are limited, or as bell hooks said in her 1992 book *Black Looks*, "we are most likely to see images of black people that reinforce and reinscribe white supremacy [not challenge it]."

In Jay-Z's case, virtual blackness relates to the popular idea that the violence in black ghettoes across America is highly adventurous and entertaining. Because Jay-Z's music has always been associated with such violence, and his lyrics are often quite explicit and detailed, people of all backgrounds and orientations can safely experience "blackness," violence, and ghetto life without enduring the repercussions that come with it. However, in a positive sense, people can also imagine what it may be like to be a black multi-millionaire who drives a Bentley, scoffs at the police, marries Beyonce Knowles, and can command a stadium full of people when performing. Essentially, blackness can now be associated with wealth and success as well as violence and chaos. Yet, the overly indulgent imaginings of black success can also be perceived in unrealistic ways, often to be used to belie the harsh economic conditions that many African Americans experience daily. This, in turn, can create problematic ideas about how black people expend wealth. Thus, if one learns about wealth through hip hop, and by extension Jay-Z, one only learns about the most superficial and materialistic aspects of it, not it's less obvious components (investing, real estate acquisition, and saving for life after retirement).

But, what is the definition of success? For Jay-Z, the question has already been answered — wealth and fame. However, even he has admitted that if he had his way, he would like to create music more like those that don't sell half of what he does. MCs like Common, Mos Def, and Talib Kweli represent the next phase of an underground segment of hip hop usually referred to as *conscious*. Although they have made great strides to distance themselves from this term (arguing that it has limited the types of audiences they can attract, the wealth they can accumulate, and the types of music they can make), they are still able to make music that reaches people, addresses a wider range of issues and topics than other hip hop artists, and even addresses issues of spirituality. Jay-Z criticized Common on *The Black Album* by pointing out how many albums he's sold in comparison, but the line seemed to express a degree of sincerity in his wish to create music not limited to materialism and gangster bravado. On another track, Jay bemoans having to "dumb down" his lyrics, but then quickly states that when he does he sells more albums; he is sort of admonishing his audience for forcing him into his musical style. Nevertheless, this conflicted and complicated assessment of his self-styled persona begs the question, What is success? True, to be worth $320 million is clearly a success for most people, but how successful is it when you cannot make the kind of music you want to for fear of losing your audience? Jay-Z himself followed this line of questioning in his film *Fade to Black* (2004) when, in conversation with another MC in a studio, they discussed how rappers have to make music that stays within a static, formulaic framework of violence and misogyny. Although using another artist to make his point, one might easily assume that he was also talking about himself.

It would seem, nonetheless, that Jay-Z did finally answer the riddle of how to be yourself in the entertainment industry: do it behind the scenes, not onstage. Do it by bringing the street hustle to the corporate boardroom.

Conferring with the God: A Meeting with X-Clan

In April 2010, I met with lead rapper Jason "Brother J" Hunter of the conscious hip hop group X-Clan to conduct an interview on the campus of California State University, Fresno, and we discussed the current state of hip hop, mainstream influences, and the importance of having something to argue in his music. When asked about his thoughts on Jay-Z, popular hip hop, and activism he argued that what we generally consider the mainstream needed to be re-evaluated. He suggested that there are many "streams," and that the underground has its own mainstream. In that respect, he urged that people disassociate from the assumption that there need be a dichotomous practice of buying music from either one source or another, but rather tap into a variety of streams of which people have produced work. He further argued that he does not have any personal conflicts with Jay-Z, but stressed the importance of the responsibility one has when in a public position to speak for those who cannot easily speak up for themselves. Lastly, he argued for the importance of creating a school/training center (something he is very close to completing) where artists can learn and develop their skills (ranging from MCing to interviewing, producing, and even marketing their own products). He suggested that such environments should be tied into the communities to which they belong, and that artists should learn how to better relate to the markets of both the large scale music industry and the local industries that they are attempting to navigate simultaneously. In such fashion, Jay-Z could be a vital aspect to the training of the next generation of MCs by taking a center position in their training and helping to link mainstream resources to grassroots-mainstream creative productions, thus allowing for a fervent cross-fertilization of ideas and topics for creative reflection that range outside of the current norms of materialism, consumption of goods, and sex.

In essence, Jay-Z's origins in hip hop from the late 1980s and early 1990s positions him as a unique figure who could "re-inject" a conscious sensibility into mainstream, radio-friendly hip hop. However, his hyper-emphasis on materiality and his hyper-avoidance of political activism have potentiality cost hip hop a great deal. To counter this, he needs to reconnect with the tradition of socially accountable MCing, especially in this era of corporate media control, and help make principled activism an acceptable aspect of the art.

For Further Consideration

BOOKS AND ARTICLES

Banks, William M. *Black Intellectuals: Race and Responsibility in American Life.* New York : W.W. Norton, 1996.

Bynoe, Yvonne. *Stand and Deliver: Political Activism, Leadership, and Hip Hop Culture.* Brooklyn, NY: Soft Skull, 2004.

McWhorter, John H. *Losing the Race: Self-Sabotage in Black America.* New York : Free Press, 2000.

Tyson, Christopher. "Exploring the Generation Gap." Urban Think Tank, http://www.urbanthinktank.org/generationgap.cfm.

QUESTIONS

1. The author makes this point known by stating, "Jay-Z cannot claim ignorance to the potential of hip hop." Is it poignant to assess Jay-Z's with a lack of ownership to his

societal obligation to positively uplift the African Americans and the challenges of inner-city life? Must we challenge Jay-Z to this responsibility as an artist?

2. The author poses a question as to "could there ever be such a time for hip hop again?" What is the golden era of hip hop and how has it affected you and your surroundings today? Should we chalk that era up to a passing fad? Or is it fair to challenge Jay-Z, who knows hip hop's potential, to use his self-promoting hustle to engage in the social and political challenges that surround hip hop's birth?

Note

1. Southern hip hop artists, or rappers from the Dirty South, have been active for quite some time, but the conscious movement in the South could be traced most especially to the Dungeon Family, most notably containing Outkast, Goodie M.O.B., and the production group Organized Noize circa the release of Outkast's first album in 1994. Also, there were also parallel movements elsewhere, such as the Bay Area in California, where artists like MC Hammer led a movement of party music with a conscious, albeit Christian bent.

Work Cited

Chang, Jeff. *Can't Stop, Won't Stop: A History of the Hip-Hop Generation*. New York: St. Martin's, 2005.

Kitwana, Bakari. *Why White Kids Love Hip Hop: Wangstas, Wiggers, Wannabes, and the New Reality of Race in America*. New York: Basic Civitas, 2005.

KMD (featuring Zev Luv X). "Peach Fuzz. <http://www.youtube.com/watch?v=-t4zTrAoucI>.

Kool Mo Dee. *There's God On the Mic: The True 50 Greatest MC's*. New York: Thunder's Mouth, 2003.

Langhorne, Cyrus. "DJ Premier Announces Mr. Magic's Death, 'He Passed Away This Morning.'" October 2, 2009 <http://www.sohh.com/2009/10/breaking_hip-hop_pioneer.html>.

Rose, Tricia. *Black Noise: Rap Music and Black Culture in Contemporary America*. Middletown: Wesleyan University Press, 1994.

PART II

The Challenges

6

Zen and the Art of Transcending the Status Quo

The Reach from the Hood to the Suburbs

Bakari Kitwana

"There's the gift, there's the spirit, and there's the work — all three have to come together."
— Jay-Z, O *Magazine*, September 3, 2009

Despite America's longstanding race problem, the country has shown resilience in its ability to periodically reconsider the ways we define the black-white divide in our national culture. America during the period of Reconstruction. The post war years. The civil rights movement of the '50s and '60s. The period of integration in the 1970s. And now as we enter the contemporary post-racial Obama Era, it seems that we are once again engaged in moment where many are rethinking the race question — particularly blackness and how it will be politicized, debated and defined relative to mainstream American life.[1] If so, what are the key influences that have emerged in our time to give this new direction shape? And if we can agree that hip hop for Americans under the age of forty-five is one of those forces, then Jay-Z — given his influence across race and class, alongside his wealth and political perspective — is a pivotal figure to consider.

Before groaning, "Oh no, not hip hop," let's review the dynamics of our contemporary moment.

By the end of the 1980s, the United States entered an era where individual and corporate wealth unequivocally trumped nearly everything else. Three

99

decades later, the nation is experiencing the greatest divide ever between its super rich and extremely poor. This economic division exists within the black community as well. At the same time that there exists an unprecedented black privileged class,[2] black poverty has become a fixture in American life — whether we look at annual black unemployment rates, which have remained consistently at least twice that of our white counterparts for the last 40 years, or at national poverty statistics that disproportionately represent blacks.[3] Public policy offers no viable solutions. More often, we bear witness to a firmly embedded tendency on both sides of the political aisle to blame poor black people themselves for their own plight.

Of course, this flies in the face of black collective political aspirations, a clear departure from the trend of the '50s and '60s civil rights legislation. Since the 1980s, there has been a slow but steady turning back the clock. With the election of Barack Obama, instead of the progress that many anticipated, the dialogue seems to have slowed, if not regressed. And our national conversation on race has become a perpetual stalemate, a debate in which reason is no longer a viable tool for moving the discussion forward. We seem to have opted instead for a recurring elementary old racial politics that fails to evolve and which ignores the complexities and nuances of race in our time. How do we jumpstart a new discussion in such an unyielding environment?

This era may require that new means be utilized to infuse fresh ideas into national culture. These alternative approaches must take on increasing significance. The mainstream hip hop phenomenon emerges in this climate. Over its nearly 40-year existence, hip hop has proven itself to be a crucial bridge connecting several generations and narrowing racial and cultural divides. Likewise, given the centering of capital accumulation and wealth's influence in our society, the mainstream hip hop phenomenon embraces that tradition, even as it subversive nature offers an opportunity to resist it. Both facts make hip hop an ideal terrain. So despite all of the contemporary black folks of substance, intellect, wealth, and achievement, it is not far-fetched to fathom that a rapper, an entertainer, a multimillionaire could become the ideal messenger for the shift in thinking necessary to advance the national conversation on race.

Jay-Z offers us unprecedented icon/tastemaker status. In much the same way that Hugh Hefner changed the way that Americans think of men and sexuality (from their sexually repressed roots to empowered, confident, and vigorous), Jay-Z is reshaping the idea of black bourgeois culture. In short, Jay-Z is making sexy the notion of elite class blacks who identify more with the black masses — and with what Harvard philosophy professor Tommie Shelby calls, in his 2005 book *We Who Are Dark: The Philosophical Foundations of Black Solidarity*, a "pragmatic Black nationalist political tradition" — than with liberal or conservative American political philosophy, a.k.a. the status quo. To that end, Jay-Z is a bridge between the black poor and black elite in a way that current activists in the tradition of Malcolm X can never realize, in a way that the current crop of black elected officials, the political descendants of Adam Clayton Powell, Jr., can never realize in today's political landscape. The viability of this brand, in an age of celebrity culture, in and of itself, may present an opportunity to re-imagine the race question in our time.

Making sense of this brand identity requires us to unravel what Jay-Z has to say about race and class, as I will discuss later. Understanding this brand identity and its potential impact also requires a sense of clarity about the distinctions between wealth and class status, how ideas about both have evolved in America, and the unique ways each play out in the black community. Sociologist Mary Pattillo-McCoy informs us in her *Black Picket Fences* that primarily sociologists and economists have defined the way we think of class, specifically who is middle class or bourgeoisie. Historically each has defined class differently. Simply put, economists define middle class strictly by income. Sociologists use more of a sliding scale based on other factors, such as college education, homeownership, and employment. A more striking indication of who *is* black middle class is who *isn't*. Henry Louis Gates, Jr., reflecting on W.E.B. Du Bois' idea of "The Talented Tenth" in his essay "Parable of the Talents," reminds us that in 1950 ninety percent of black Americans were too poor to qualify even as middle class. E. Franklin Frazier documents a black bourgeoisie during the same time period whose identity was about pedigree (often mixed race and/or able to trace one's lineage to free blacks before the Civil War). Otis Graham in *Our Kind of People* documents that same class's evolution into the present and instructs us that inclusion is more a function of status than strictly wealth. Likewise, Ellis Cose's *The Rage of a Privileged Class* gives credence to how wealth has evolved in black America such that many newly wealthy blacks have surpassed traditional black elites in terms of wealth — even if they don't share their historic class distinction.

The national debate over how to increase taxes on the rich without punishing the middle class reminds us that wealth in America isn't what it used to be. There is the top three percent of American households who make $250,000 a year or more who are considered rich. And then there is the super rich, the top 0.1 percent — whose combined income in recent years is as much as the bottom 120 million Americans. Hence the wealth that distinguished a middle-class and upper class black elite of yesterday pales in comparison to wealth (multimillions and billions) accrued by folks like Jay-Z today. Whereas Frazier's black bourgeoisie came into existence a result of racial discrimination, the new black bourgeoisie moment that Jay-Z personifies is an end product of the '50s and '60s civil rights movement's legislative successes, the equally important values and outlook of the black Power movement of the late 1960s and early '70s, as well as the subsequent hip hop explosion, an era exemplified by poor young blacks who find themselves perpetually locked out of the mainstream economy and are thus are forced to make their own way. Take all of the above factors in consideration, alongside our national obsession with wealth accumulation, and today's nouveau riche arguably have more leverage in our national culture with and beyond traditional elites—which leads us back to Jay-Z and his influence.

When E. Franklin Frazier in 1955 and Nathan Hare in 1965 penned *Black Bourgeoisie* and *The Black Anglo Saxons*, respectively, neither could have foreseen a world where a young black high school drop-out from one of America's most economically neglected neighborhoods would rise to head a major American record corporation and simultaneously emerge as a businessman, entrepreneur, and pop culture icon whose music and very taste would exert inordinate influence on a generation of young white American across class. Undoubtedly, Frazier and Hare were aware of black cultural influences on American life—from the blues' cross-cultural reach, beginning in the late 1800s, to jazz's impact in the 1920s big band swing era, as well as its bebop movement in the post-war years. Although young upper class whites gravitated to black culture in all these earlier eras, the definitive face of black cultural influence was white. What distinguishes the contemporary moment is that Jay-Z is unequivocally black, both in his physical appearance and in the worldview he advances in his lyrics—an outlook in which everyday black folk culture is central. He represents, in essence, a new brand of black bourgeoisie: the multi-millionaire, pop culture icon, and tastemaker extraordinaire whose identity strikes an unprecedented balance between his class origins and his current economic status.

To be sure, Jay-Z's reach is more influential when one considers the extent to which it penetrates into our very psyche as a nation, across class, gender, race, and generations, the way that Chris Rock's HBO special stand-up performances did during the late 1990s (*Bigger and Blacker* in 1999 and the earlier *Bring the Pain* in 1996, in which he intoned "I love black people, but I hate niggers")—but more so.[4] The cultural influencer status Jay-Z wields allows us to begin to imagine how the best of black political thought, which during successive generations has centered on ensuring the country live up to the philosophical vision of its founding, can once again help reshape the idea of racial equity and social justice.

Political Philosophy in the Lyrics of Jay-Z

It has been widely conceded, especially outside of hip hop circles and in some cases within them, that contemporary mainstream American hip hop is void of a meaningful political critique. By contrast, emerging global hip hop artists, such as British born M.I.A., are said to offer more searing political critiques of the American status quo. Top American hip hop artists like Jay-Z, grouped in with artists like 50 Cent and Lil Wayne, are dismissed as preoccupied with violence, sex, and consumer culture. However, because of the ways that he expands and critiques the status quo at the same time, Jay-Z is equally if not more relevant.

When his music departs from ballad form, his lyrics are often such dense and layered collages of ideas and experiences—along with glitzy packaging and multiple personas—that surface readings, alongside anti-mainstream hip hop analyses from hip hop purists, have led to the widely held and erroneous conclusion that Jay-Z has sold out his roots and has exclusively bought into bourgeois culture. However, a careful examination of his body of work, eleven albums over fourteen years, reveals that Jay-Z is more concerned with transcending the status quo than acquiescence to it.

His critique of the status quo makes brief appearances along the way on songs like "Who You Wit II" in 1997 (*In My Lifetime, Volume 1*), "Hardknock Life (Ghetto Anthem)" in 1998 (*Volume 2 ... Hardknock Life*), and "So Ghetto" in 1999 (*Volume 3 ... Life and Times of S. Carter*). But by 2001 with *The Blueprint*, he begins to round out a more robust political perspective that centers around three important axes: (1) a critical race analysis that recognizes American power as a white supremacist construct, (2) a class analysis of American society that recognizes inherent class stratification where a minority elite exert inordinate influence over a majority poor, and (3) that he along with other blacks of extreme wealth are occupying a unique space, which transcends what has been historically deemed in the black community as "bougie."

"Chartering a private plane ain't bougie," Jay-Z told me several years later when I interviewed him about the materialism and consumer culture that dominates his lyrics. "I call it the browning of America. There has to be a more equal playing field. And we're starting to see some changes. What myself, Puffy, Will Smith, and Denzel are doing, it's all new territory."

Perhaps Jay's political message gets lost on his debut and subsequent two albums as a casualty of the time. In the early stage of his career, New York hip hop artists are trying to reclaim dominance as the national center of the hip hop world, having witnessed New York hip hop's influence wane by comparison to rising stars out of the west. The vibrant solo careers of artists like Ice Cube, Dr. Dre, and Snoop Dogg on the heels of NWA's success and even the popularity (with hip hop audiences) of films like *Boyz 'n the Hood* and *Menace II Society* helped brand a west coast hip hop aesthetic that in many ways began to redefine hip hop far beyond its New York City origins. Jay-Z's first album, *Reasonable Doubt*, emerges in that climate. With albums like Notorious B.I.G.'s 1994 *Ready to Die* and Tupac's 1995 *Me Against the World* coming right before his 1996 debut, Jay is also facing fierce competition.[5]

Jay's lyrics in these early efforts—which often shout out materialism, reinforce capitalism, and glorify street culture—highlight the east coast manifestation of west coast gangsta. The fierce battle for rap supremacy, personally and collectively, is ever-present in the braggadocio that seems to hold greater sway in earlier part of his career. Jay's preoccupation with transcending the status quo is a recurring theme in his music and interviews.[6] Even in his brand of bragging is found the idea of transcendence: he intends to not only be the best, but to rewrite the play book—from "Can't Knock the Hustle" and "Brooklyn's Finest" to "Nigga What, Nigga Who."

With his fourth album, he offers a turning point, in which the title says it all—*The Blueprint*. It's a metaphor. It's more braggadocio. But given the range of his thought, it's not hard to believe that his title is deliberately laden with multiple meaning, and thus it can also be taken literally: this is how you come up. This is a blueprint, a plan, the science for how it's done. It's as if he saying, "Here are the secrets to my success. The key is rooted in my business savvy, yes, but it's also rooted in my political outlook." *The Blueprint*, then, is in part a turning point where his focus is no longer on strictly competing with his contemporaries. Instead as he put it in his own words, he's "chasing history."[7] Lyrics from "Izzo," "Renegade," and even "Can't Knock the Hustle" attest to this.

To further grasp hold of the range of his political perspective, however, requires us to look deeper into his preoccupation with the status quo. Examining multiple songs across his entire career, paying special attention to snippets in various songs and then viewing them as a collective, yields a holistic political vision. One place where this vision is presented in the most concise fashion is on the 2003 *The Black Album*, particularly in the lyrics of the songs "Public Service Announcement" and "What More Can I Say." We turn now to a full examination of both.

"Public Service Announcement" begins with a sample from the popular 2000 film *Gladiator*. *Gladiator* has all the components of the hip hop gangster film.[8] The protagonist (like the hip hop hero, the average black kid caught up in the new economy of post civil rights era) is thrust into a dog-eat-dog world. His status in that world finds him in a place where he must do bad things, especially vanquish his enemies, in order to survive. He is still God fearing and God loving, but with his back pushed to the wall, he does what he has to do to live a life of dignity and honor and, if possible, all the trappings of monetary success, even if it costs him his life. In the case of this film and countless other films celebrated in hip hop circles—*Juice, The Godfather, King of New York, Carlito's Way, Scarface*—it does.

Jay-Z begins in the first verse shouting out expensive jewelry and cars and engaging the typical hip hop braggadocio. In the second verse, he jumps right in with a concise description of his political philosophy, by referencing the South American revolutionary Che Guevara. What seems an odd contrast and, to some, an all-out contradiction ("Che Guevara with bling on") is instead the political philosophy steeped in the reality of the hip hop era; namely, the generation of blacks coming of age after the civil rights and black power movements and in the throes of escalating neoliberalism. Like Maximus, the gladiator hero in the film, Jay-Z, and by extension the larger hip hop generation, makes the best of the era of existence.

Ernesto Che Guevara is widely considered an outlaw among Western political elites and an enemy of the United States because of his opposition to United States imperialism in Argentina, Cuba, and throughout the world. To date, he remains a thorn in the side of United States interest from South America to the Caribbean to Africa. In contemporary American culture where nearly everything is for sale, Che Guevara has also come to symbolize radical chic. His image is on T-shirts, watches, buttons, hats, etc., and as such has become ironically absorbed into consumer culture: the radical, revolution for sale. You can even buy symbols of revolutionary culture and in the process theoretically make it a part of American culture itself.[9]

So Guevera is loved by those who would resist an oppressive system, a kind of Robin Hood taking from the rich to give to the poor. Che identifies more with "the restless many" than the "prosperous few"—despite his class status (a physician born into an aristocratic family). Jay, too, even as he identifies with the majority working poor class, poses a huge contradiction: he embraces core symbols of consumer capitalism (ostentatious jewelry, cars, and the very idea of crass consumer culture that values products and objects over people and culture). He is young, black, famous, conformist, and yet radical. This is the quintessential post–Afro-centric era hip hop hero, a merger of PE radicalism, and NWA's street/gangster sensibility with the conformity and wealth of a Russell Simmons, the merger of bourgeois culture with street consciousness *and* political consciousness.[10]

The historic dispute concerning the future of the race between W.E.B. Du Bois and Booker T. Washington, or its recurrence in the late 1960s split between integrationists and separatists, is resolved in the hip hop moment. "The struggle" as a descriptive expression used by '60s activists to described the political movement is redefined by The Notorious B.I.G. as a reference to the daily life struggle for those locked out of the mainstream economy to provide for one's family ("Everyday Struggle"). Jay-Z updates it further, appropriating it outright. To do so, he bridges three ideas: international class struggle (by referencing Che Guevera), black political consciousness (Malcolm X's oft-quoted and misrepresented line, "by any means necessary"), and street consciousness (speaking directly to the street element with the familiar salutation "Nigga").[11]

This leads us into Jay's choice of words in the same verse, the phrase largely identified with Malcolm X and his political philosophy.[12] What African Americans studies professor Manning Marable calls Malcolm X's "uncompromising slogan" was popularized by Minister Malcolm X in the last year of his life. Jay-Z advocates a new black bourgeois politics that borrows heavily from Malcolm

X's brand of black nationalist political thought, which sees a critique of capitalism as crucial to understanding institutional racism and white world supremacy. It is a black nationalism rooted in the history of black political struggle, extending from Martin Delaney and Marcus Garvey into the 1960s black power movement; it is what Harvard philosophy professor Tommie Shelby calls "one of the oldest and most enduring traditions in American political thought" (Shelby 24).

At the end of a June 28, 1964, speech announcing the formation of the Organization of Afro-American Unity, Malcolm X put it this way: "We declare our rights on this earth, to be a man, to be a human being, to be respected as a human being, to be given the rights of a human being, in this society, on this earth, in this day, which we intend to bring into existence by any means necessary." It is important to remember that Malcolm X's political vision at its zenith connected the black liberation movement to the struggle for human rights of all people around the globe. The June 28, 1964, speech in New York City at the Audubon Ballroom was given after his split with the Nation of Islam.

It is fitting for Jay-Z's purposes that Malcolm X appropriates the phrase from Jean Paul Sartre's 1963 play *Dirty Hands* (Act V, scene 3), which is steeped in a class analysis: "I was not one to invent lies: they were created in a society divided by class and each of us inherited lies when we were born. It is not by refusing to lie that we will abolish lies; it is by eradicating class by any means necessary." While during Malcolm's era the black struggle was more obviously defined by race, in the post–civil rights era, the class struggle within the black community has been pushed center stage.[13]

Of course, critics would argue that Jay-Z choosing to evoke the four-word refrain may be a simple coincidence, a general familiarity of any young person coming of age in black urban America in the 1980s and '90s, especially someone in his early 20s when Spike Lee released his film *X*.[14] However, the numerous comments that reinforce this politics and that litter various songs suggest that his is a more contemplative reflection. It's a shrewd, calculated self-assessment, a coarse description of how he perceives himself, his evolution, and by extension his generation's evolution from the previous generation. Part of this political perspective includes living with our contradictions, which means, in this case, that we are no longer going to apologize for what E. Franklin Frazier and countless hip hop artists call "getting money," or for what James Peterson calls "the come-up."[15]

Not only does Jay-Z not offer an apology, but in "Public Service Announcement," in particular, he indicates how unapologetic he feels, and he adds that if he had to do it all again, he would. In confessing that he would do it again if he had to, and that a change in economic status from being poverty stricken to being in the top two percentile hasn't reformed him, he touches here on a recurring theme in his work that is central to the political philosophy he espouses in his lyrics. It's an important reminder to himself that the money and fame hasn't made him identify more with the new class status than with the black poor communities that produced him. He is committed to class suicide and in some ways redefines it. This is camouflage, guerilla warfare, his ability to win the war "by any means necessary." But as much as he borrows Malcolm's philosophy, he subtly adds to it. In the end the casual listener can't discern which side he is on. It is as if he is on both sides and on neither side all at the same time. In the process, he is redefining the very idea of the black bourgeoisie.

On "What More Can I Say," at the same time that he is charting/branding his new black bourgeois philosophy, he is shouting out a now clichéd sexist philosophy of trophy women, or multiple "divas," and status-driven consumerism with references to newly acquired sneakers, "deuce seaters," caseloads of top-shelf champagne, paid-for Mercedes Benzes, and privately owned jets that typically fly to places like Turks and Caicos. This muddles the terrain largely because it seems to fly in the face of the politics he espouses otherwise. Again this is deceptive. It is in part a nod to the old black bourgeoisie or what Nathan Hare calls "The Black Anglo Saxons," where the black middle class emulates white consumer culture, a.k.a. the status quo. Hip hop's foray into mainstream popular culture begins to some extent in that place.[16] Within the first decade of its existence, however, even though hip hop begins there, it simultaneously flies in the face of the status quo. Instead of Tommy Hilfiger and Polo Ralph Lauren of the early '80s, hip hop gives us Cross Colours, Karl Kani, and Enyce by the late '80s (which is a radically different animal than black business in the age of segregation). And this phenomenon, like so much of Jay-Z's philosophy or Zen, is within hip hop's own tradition. By the late 1990s, Jay-Z is not only building on that tradition, but also significantly enhancing it.

That he believes in this aspect of the hip hop ethos, and has become one of its chief advocates, is evident by the ways he brings it home in the third verse of "What More Can I Say." There he articulates a generation-specific black bourgeoisie that his core black core grassroots audience—*and* elites of other races—identify with at the same time. The emphasis here is that he is more than just another rapper, and that his commentary in this vein is more than just self-aggrandizement. Instead, he brings attention to the role he is actively playing to redefine American bourgeois culture. Part of his evidence, he suggests, is that he has arrived at a level where his influence, reach, and wealth is on par with white elites, a fact that Forbes magazine routinely reiterates.[17] So often the intra-race discussion is so enticing to those outside the culture that any inter-race commentary is readily dismissed as "reverse racism." To do so (even though his use of the racial epithet "cracker" doesn't help) misses the point.

Consider the lyrics of "What More Can I Say" as he continues discuss his place within the Ivy Tower of Harvard, not as a cultural elite but as existential renegade daily creating his reality and not seeking it. This is a radical juxtaposition between those who create and those who observe. Here we must return to what he tells us throughout his music about race and class in America. If we haven't absorbed that analysis by now, we would miss his point here. He's not white but he's there on the elite list. Hence, he must really be having an impact. To paraphrase, he's not bragging here. He's bragging when he talks about his rhyming ability. But here, he's boasting so his cross-racial, cross-class audience absorbs the extent to which he has made it is unprecedented. Yes, he's bragging because it's a part of the hip hop genre that is his medium. But here he's not bragging simply to inform us on how much money he has, but to let white elites know they can't keep blacks down, to let it be known that the foundation of racism — black inferiority — is a myth, and so elites can't pretend to his core audience that he's not on their level. With nothing, boxed in, locked out of the mainstream, he's not only escaped the trap that institutional white supremacist culture encapsulates the black poor within, but he's gotten richer than most in the process. And what could be sweeter than taking the very environment that was meant to enslave him and using that as the means to get there? Better yet, he's just getting started.

Amidst the self-congratulatory narratives, odes to capitalism, and misogynistic shout-outs throughout his 14-year career, Jay is also recounting the black struggle. This means educating his audience on the new black pain, the post–civil rights story of a new generation facing new realities. At the same time, he is encouraging listeners—black, white, and others—almost seducing them to identify their American identity with blackness, as he does in his rhymes, because in the worldview he constructs in his lyrics the two are a seamless whole.

So the black youth perspective on the issues of the day is—via hip hop—gaining a national and international hearing. Instead of letting the mainstream narrative stand that the black poor are ignorant of their rights in their engagement with the police, Jay-Z and others offer another view in "99 Problems" (*The Black Album*, 2004). To counter the mainstream critique that blacks are poor because they can't compete, he offers "What More Can I Say." For the narrative that black folk are disproportionately in prison because they commit more crimes, Jay-Z says it's not that simple and carries that alternative perspective (calling for a different style of policing in urban communities) into the national arena.

Jay-Z's critique is the rhetoric of standard American patriotism when he comments on 9/11 in his song "Minority Report" (*Kingdom Come*, 2006). But he is critical out of a pragmatic black political perspective when he critiques the way the American government failed its black citizens in the aftermath of Hurricane Katrina in the same song. Likewise, complex dualities exist in his career-wide embrace of crass consumerism and his critique of how elite establishment powers that be keep their foot on the neck of the underclass. The complexity of this duality is at the core of his political philosophy. In that, Jay-Z is transcending the status quo. He offers in its place a perspective of blacks in the new millennium that fits into the American story both as they embrace the status quo and reject it. All are present in the way he brands a new black bourgeois culture and carries the message on his sleeve as his public persona from the hood to the suburbs.

One of the unique components of the hip hop medium is its ability to traverse so many borders rapidly and effortlessly. Jay-Z's range creates such a fine line in his messaging that most critics don't discern the differences. Instead there is the tendency to argue that snippets of a revolutionary narrative are compromised by the anti-black, capitalistic, homophobic, and misogynistic ones. What is lost in the cacophony of these critiques is the arrival of a new generation black bourgeoisie, redefined in the hip hop generation's image. And Jay-Z more than any other hip hop artist independent or mainstream personifies this.[18]

Transforming National Culture

Hip hop's ascendance from poor black and brown communities to influence national culture is one of its least examined variables—and it is simultaneously one of its most salient.[19] Examples abound of hip hop permeating the entertainment world and beyond, from television and film, various musical genres, clothing styles, dance styles, marketing trends, the use of language, and more. Conservative critics from former Education Secretary Bill Bennett to Fox News host Bill O'Reilly for years have emphasized this circumstance as a problem for the future of the republic, especially in the ongoing conservative fight to brand "family values" and "American values" as white culture. Such a phenomenon as hip hop's dominance of popular culture, they argue, threatens to undermine middle American values, suggesting that an alleged inferior culture will over take the assumed superior one.

HBO's 1994 documentary film *Gang War: Bangin' in Little Rock*, which centers on a group of working class white youth in Little Rock, Arkansas, in the mid–1980s, largely reinforced this notion. Although this is a film about the spread of gangs across the country, arguably the films more dominant message is white youth fascination with the aesthetics and values of black, street, and hip hop culture. Middle and upper class whites are not immune. Incidents of white college students at elite colleges and universities hosting "pimp and ho" and "gangster" theme parties have been documented across the United States.

Several cases included white students blackening up. The occurrence of these incidents at institutions like the University of Connecticut Law School, Hope College in Michigan, Tarleton State University in Texas, and the University of Chicago during the 2006–2007 school year (and more recently students at the small liberal arts private school, Bethel College, in Minneapolis, in May 2010) suggest that the trend persists in a different form among white elites.[20]

There is certainly a voyeuristic dimension to the tendency of white middle class Americans taking a bird's-eye view of the "authentic" black experience that is historic (seen during the heyday of blues, jazz, and rock and roll, respectively).[21] Jazz critic Stanley Crouch, and later hip hop critic Kevin Powell, each refer to this phenomenon as "a cultural safari." In our interview, Jay-Z put it this way: "First of all music is something you just feel. Period. And with hip hop it's like a movie. You get to put on this pair of headphones, close your eyes and go through this movie without experiencing it for the most part. You get to go through this fantasy world, where the ultra, super hero guy who nobody could harm, has been through a tough situation and he came out great. Take the CD out. Take the headphones off and go shoot hoops. That's a very easy education."

But to what extent do we see Jay-Z's branding of a new black bourgeois culture or his political philosophy — essentially a hip hop politic which takes on additional nuances and reach given Jay's wealth and influence — penetrate mainstream national culture, particularly American elite or bourgeois circles? Let's return to our analogy of Hugh Hefner as cultural influencer. In the case of Hefner, we are able to look backward over a half century and connect the dots to measure his impact. By comparison with Jay-Z, we are at the cusp, looking forward. For now, there are few hard indicators.

One might take note of Thomas Chatterton Williams' observations in his memoir *Losing My Cool*, one of the few books to date that reflects on hip hop's impact on middle class blacks coming of age in the 1990s.[22] On the one hand, he suggests that hip hop was the primary influence during his formative years in Newark suburban middle class community Fanwood, New Jersey. On the other hand, he says no, that hip hop and Jay-Z, who he specifically singles out, have no values of substance to offer. Instead, he takes refuge in traditional black bourgeois approach: absorption into Euro-American culture.

Losing My Cool, even though Williams is in denial of this fact, is a very lucid example of the part of the story that hip hop's critics have always gotten right: that aside from aesthetics of hip hop, primarily it is the values of elite culture that are being transmitted, regurgitated to hip hop listeners. Even if they are fed back in different package — updated, revised, sans class privilege, and a bit more sexy — essentially these are the core values of capitalist culture: profit first, wealth accumulation, fierce individualism, and dog-eat-dog exploitation.

The findings from several recent studies add to what we know about post baby boomers and how hip hop-hop enters into their worldview across race, class, and gender. According to the 2007 survey "The Black Youth Project,"[23] a first of its kind survey of young people (aged 15 to 25; equal parts black, white, and Latino) about their views on hip hop, race, sex, politics, and more, 81 percent of white youth say they listen to rap music, 63 percent of white youth believe police discriminate much more against black youth than white youth, and at least 60 percent agreed with the statement "rap music videos portray Black women in bad and offensive ways." In addition, 43 percent of white youth surveyed agreed with the statement "it is hard for young Black people to get ahead because they face so much discrimination."

Add to these insights the historic presidential election of 2008. Most political observers agree that the outcome suggests that many white youth across class are more accepting of and willing to vote for a black presidential candidate. In the fall of 2008, in the days leading up to the election, a rapsessions.org survey, "Understanding the Hip-Hop Voting Bloc," found that 88 percent of whites from 18 to 44 years old said race didn't matter in their choice for president.[24] Finally, in the days following the election, a CIRCLE report "Young Voters in the 2008 Election" concluded that 68 percent of all young people aged 18 to 29 (and 54 percent of whites aged 18 to 29) who voted in 2008 voted for Barack Obama.

Additional first-hand research by this writer, in interviews and observations drawn from traveling the country (in 48 of the 50 states) over the last sixteen years, in which I engaged young people across race in conversation about hip hop, gender, and politics, points to a significant population of white youth across classes that, while not buying into street culture wholesale, is certainly embracing the aesthetics of hip hop. Many are also more familiar with the history of black political struggle and more enlightened about black culture and black people as a result.

I also increasingly see young black middle class youth who feel that hip hop isn't the end-all or be-all that it was for those born in the late '60s and early '70s who felt "hip hop saved our lives."[25] The unprecedented campaign and election of Barack Obama in 2008, which allowed mainstream media multiple ways to publicly discuss the black experience, has certainly contributed to this.

But are these various cross-racial, cross-class hip hop audiences really informed about the full range of black political thought, especially as a one-dimensional counter-narrative is seeping into national culture via mainstream news media and the internet — one that breeds racial antagonism with divide and conquer as an end goal? What will be the lasting impact on the political outlook of young Americans who are really absorbing the multiple and sometimes conflicting messages in the lyrics of artists like Jay-Z, artists who offer a more complicated analysis of race in contemporary America?

The extent to which this is affecting America and our ideas about race in national culture is impossible to determine in the present.[26] We don't measure Hefner's influence on national culture directly with hard examples—but looking back we know it is there. When we do, we can clearly identify broad cultural shifts and maintain that yes, certainly he has been at the forefront and a significant part of this national identity shift. I expect that Jay-Z will have a similar impact over time. To be sure, fifty years down the line, we will look back at the hip hop era as a major influence on the way we as a nation think about race. And within that, we will point to Jay-Z as a primary influence in ways we couldn't have before imagined.

For Further Consideration

BOOKS

Gates, Henry Louis, Jr. "The Parable of the Talents." In *The Future of the Race* by Henry Louis Gates, Jr., and Cornel West. New York: Knopf, 1996.

Graham, Otis. *Our Kind of People.* New York: HarperCollins, 1999.

Pattillo-McCoy, Mary. *Black Picket Fences: Privilege and Peril Among the Black Middle Class.* Chicago: University of Chicago Press, 1999.

Shelby, Tommie. *We Who Are Dark: The Philosophical Foundations of Black Solidarity.* Cambridge, MA: Harvard University Press, 2005.

Williams, Thomas Chatterton. *Losing My Cool: How My Father and 15,000 Books Beat Hip-Hop Culture.* New York: Penguin, 2010.

QUESTIONS

1. The author suggests that Jay-Z's political philosophy is an extension of the black nationalist tradition of Martin Delaney, Marcus Garvey, and Malcolm X. Do you agree? Given Jay-Z's obsessions with consumer culture, is this a stretch?

2. Given Jay-Z's nouveau riche status, think about what Otis Graham (author of *Our Kind of People*) says about the black elite and the influence Jay-Z has with "old money" white elites, such as Paris Hilton. Is it far-fetched to imagine that Jay-Z can have influence with the traditional black bourgeoisie?

3. If you agree that Jay-Z has the capacity to influence national culture, as the author suggests, is Hugh Hefner the best example of a similar impact? Are there places in your life and in American culture where you already see that impact? Explain.

Notes

1. For a more detailed discussion of "post-racial," see my essay "Between Expediency and Conviction: What We Mean When We Say Post-Racial." Throughout 2009, I led a 10-city discussion tour on the topic, along with M1 of dead prez, Joan Morgan, Jabari Asim, Lisa Fager, Tricia Rose, Timuel Black, MC Serch, and Lisa Fager Bediako. Video clips of this discussion are available at *www.rapsessions.org*. Also, see my essay "Joker's Wild."

2. Regarding the size and growth of the black privileged class, see Mary Pattillo-McCoy's *Black Picket Fences* (13–30) and Henry Louis Gates, Jr.'s, essay "Parable of the Talents" (19). Also see *The Rage of a Privileged Class: Why are Middle Class Blacks Angry? Why Should America Care?* by Ellis Cose. The great recession has further compounded these dynamics.

3. For details on unemployment rates of blacks, see the Bureau of Labor Statistics. Regarding poverty, the U.S. Census Bureau reports that the official U.S. poverty rate in 2008 was 13.2 percent, up from 12.5 percent in 2007, the first significant increase since 2004. In 2008 39.8 million Americans were in poverty, up from 37.3 million in 2007; 2008 was the second consecutive annual increase in poverty. The racial breakdown: 8.6 for whites, up from 8.2; 11.8 percent for Asians, up from 10.2; 23.2 percent for Latinos, up from 21.5; and 24.7 percent for blacks in 2008, the same as 2007. The 2008 rate was the highest since 1997, but 9.2 percentage points lower than in 1959, the first year estimates are available. Also see National Poverty Center at the University of Michigan's Gerald Ford School of Public Policy.

4. Whereas Chris Rock has bought in to middle class norms in a way Jay-Z hasn't, his medium, comedy, allows him distance from cultural ideas he's selling (this is his stage presence). Hip hop doesn't allow Jay-Z that distance and he seems to welcome that. Hip hop's "keep it real" philosophy is predicated upon how similar his reality is to what he writes and a shrewd capacity as an artist to tease out where necessary the differences, taking special care to speak multiple audiences with various messages at the same time.

5. Following the death of Tupac in the fall of 1996 and B.I.G. in the spring of 1997 — they together ushered in a new era of hip hop artists with mainstream popular culture icon status— the question in hip hop circles emerged, "Who is now the best?" — and in New York City, "Who is king of New York?"

6. See lyrics for Jay-Z's "Izzo (H.O.V.A.)," on his 2001 album *The Blueprint* and his preoccupation with being "the best rapper alive" in his lyrics ("Dirt off your Shoulders," *The Black Album*) and in interviews, such as ones with *XXL* magazine and on the *Angie Martinez Show*.

7. "Chasing history" is a phrase Jay-Z has used to describe his approach, such as in an interview with Charlie Rose in which he discussed his album *American Gangster*, on November 9, 2007.

8. I discuss the idea of the hip hop gangster film in detail in my chapter "Black Gangster Films."

9. The photograph of Guevara by Alberto Korda is said to be the world's most recognized image. See *Che's Afterlife: The Legacy of an Image* by Michael Casey. The other layer of Jay's philosophy that is exemplified is his hustle. He suggests that his hustling skills are so thorough (again, generation-specific critiques of capitalism, black middle class, and status quo challenge all at the same time) that he can sell you anything, even Che Guevera. And yes, with Jay-Z as the messenger/salesman, young Americans— those committed to American capitalism and radicals alike — will love Che, despite his politics for the former, and even if he has bling on for the latter.

10. For an extended definition of street consciousness, see Cheryl Keyes' *Rap Music and Street Consciousness* (5–6). One who exhibits street consciousness is one immersed in or acutely awareness of the culture and politics of everyday life rooted in black urban America. I draw a distinction between street consciousness and black political consciousness that Tommie Shelby defines in *We Who Are Dark*— although the two can often overlap. This is especially true as hip hop meets Five Percent culture on the streets in the late 1970s and early 1980s in New York City.

11. He seems to be answering a recurring unspoken question in hip hop lyrics and culture, "What do we as a generation inherit from civil rights and black power movements?" I discuss this in more detail in *The Hip-Hop Generation*, 133–39.

12. Jay evokes Malcolm's "by any means necessary" comment a second time on *The Black Album*, in the song "Allure."

13. Much of the anti-hip hop criticism in the black community has been driven by middle class and upper class blacks looking down their noses at poor blacks. In one of his most important books to date, Michael Eric Dyson thoroughly investigates this dynamic in his *Is Bill Cosby Right? Or Has the Black Middle Class Lost Its Mind?* Thomas Chatterton Williams' *Losing My Cool* restates Cosby's argument critiquing the use of the "N word" and joins it more succinctly with mainstream conservative critiques of the black poor but, given his age, fashions it as a hip hop generation self-critique — instead of a intergenerational dispute.

14. Leading up to the release of the 1992 film, Amiri Baraka questioned Spike Lee's capacity to do justice to the legacy of Malcolm X, criticizing Spike for his "petit-bourgeois nationalism" (see Trescott). So it's ironic that Spike Lee helps introduce Malcolm X to a generation that then connects Malcolm's political vision to a new brand of black bourgeois politics, one that differs from Spike Lee's own political outlook.

15. See James Peterson's "It's Yours: Hip-Hop Worldviews in the Lyrics of Nas."

16. On the first published rap recording, Sugarhill Gang's "Rapper's Delight," Big Bank Hank rapped on the baller status of their day: swimming pools and color television.

17. In January 2010, *Forbes* published its "Hollywood's Top Earning Couples" list, which looked at earnings between June 2008 and June 2009. With $122 million, Jay-Z and Beyonce topped the list (which included actors, athletes, and musicians). They also topped the 2009 list with $162 million. Coming in at number two were Harrison Ford and Calista Flockhart with $69 million. For *Forbes*' highest paid musician list, Jay-Z was number six with $63 million. (Beyonce was number three with $87 million.) U2 was first on the list, followed by AC/DC. Bruce Springsteen and Britney Spears were numbers four and five, respectively. In 2009, *Forbes* released its "Hip-Hop Cash Kings" list. Jay-Z was number one. In 2008, he was number two, behind 50 Cent. He was number thirteen on *Forbes*' 2010 "Top 15 Wealthiest Black Americans" list with $150 million, significantly behind Oprah Winfrey, who was number one with $2.76 billion. For clarity's sake (and the sake of the big picture), Oprah came in at number 141 on *Forbes*' 2009 "Richest Americans" list.

18. The only artists that come close to bridging the gap between black political analysis and status quo are the rap group dead prez with their revolutionary but gangsta mantra. Ironically, Jay-Z appears on their 2004 album *Revolutionary But Gangsta*, on the remix for the song "Hell Yeah (Pimp The System)." However, Jay's position in the marketplace stretches beyond extreme, crosses race, and includes the black bourgeoisie and the black poor. dead prez doesn't enjoy the same reach.

19. A distinction must be drawn between the more substantial white audience that has no investment in hip hop whatsoever beyond its presence as contemporary popular culture. Then there is a core white audience, the innermost circle of the concentric circles, the activist-minded and politicized who I call white hip hop activists, who are processing Jay-Z in a radically different way than the general audience.

20. See "Majoring in Minstrelsy: White Students, Black Face and the Failure of Mainstream Multiculturalism," by Tim Wise. Also see "Blackface Incident Stirs an Uproar on Bethel Campus," by Jenna Ross.

21. I discuss these various audiences in my essay "Coalition Building Across Race" (53–54, 168–77).

22. Other books that consider coming of age in what I consider to be the tail end of the hip hop generation or moving into the post–hip hop generation include *The Beautiful Struggle: A Father, Two Sons and an Unlikely Road to Manhood* by Ta-Nehisi Coates; *Other People's Property, A Shadow History of Hip-Hop* by Jason Tanz; and *It's Bigger Than Hip-Hop: The Rise of the Post-Hip-Hop Generation* by M.K. Asante.

23. The lead researcher on the Black Youth Project is University of Chicago professor Cathy Cohen. The ground-breaking national survey, funded by the Ford Foundation, gives hip hop researchers an unprecedented look at the views of youth themselves. Dr. Cohen gives a more detailed critique on the website www.blackyouthproject.com and in her book *Democracy Remixed: Black Youth and the Future of American Politics.*

24. "Understanding The Hip-Hop Voting Bloc Survey" examines the political views of two age groups: 18- to 31-year-olds and 32- to 45-year-olds. The survey was conducted from August 22 through September 11, 2008, via the internet by Knowledge Networks, Inc. The survey sample included 302 blacks, 344 whites, and 307 Latinos. The participants include young Americans from across the United States and people of diverse socioeconomic backgrounds, from those whose income is under $25,000 a year to those whose income is $75,000 a year plus. The poll carries a margin of era of 3.2 percentage points. This study is concerned with the two generations born after the civil rights movement. It seeks to identify issues that matter to those young Americans who have lived their entire lives in post-segregation America and hopes to identify the ways these younger generations of Americans are processing race, gender, pop culture, and other life experiences in such a manner that distinguishes them from previous generations of Americans. Finally, the study hoped to identify the subtle disparities that persist between those born between 1965 and 1984 and the post–hip hop generation (those born between 1985 and 2004). Additional findings are available at www.rapsession.org.

25. These include black kids who don't identify with hip hop as their primary cultural point of reference. Thomas Chatterton Williams (*Losing My Cool*) suggests otherwise. In 2004, I spoke with students in a classroom visit after a lecture at Clark Atlanta University. They stunned me when they said hip hop wasn't the primary culture they identified with. It was the first time that I'd encountered young people who had come of age in the hip hop era who expressed this sentiment. Four years later, in 2008, in the throes of a highly racialized presidential election, I was teaching a hip hop course, the Politics of the Hip-Hop Generation, to a class of 170 students at the University of Chicago, and my African American students often reiterated this point.

26. However, I imagine it is having an impact as much as hip hop was when the idea of a black president went from an impossible thought to a contemporary reality. I address this in detail in my *Why White Kids Love Hip-Hop*, which projects the possibility of a cross-racial hip hop audience turned hip hop voting bloc electing Barack Obama in the years ahead.

Works Cited

Asante, M.K. *It's Bigger Than Hip-Hop: The Rise of the Post-Hip-Hop Generation.* New York: St. Martin's, 2008.

Casey, Michael. *Che's Afterlife: The Legacy of an Image.* New York: Vintage, 2009.

Chomsky, Noam. *The Prosperous Few and the Restless Many.* The Real Story Series. New York: Odonian, 2002.

Coates, Ta-Nehisi. *The Beautiful Struggle: A Father, Two Sons and an Unlikely Road to Manhood.* New York: Spiegel and Grau, 2008.

Cohen, Cathy. *Democracy Remixed: Black Youth and the Future of American Politics.* New York: Oxford University Press, 2010.

Cose, Ellis. *The Rage of a Privileged Class: Why are Middle Class Blacks Angry? Why Should America Care?* New York: Harper Perennial, 1994.

Dyson, Michael Eric. *Is Bill Cosby Right? Or Has the Black Middle Class Lost Its Mind?* New York: Basic Civitas, 2005.

Gates, Henry Louis, Jr. "The Parable of the Talents." In *The Future of the Race* by Henry Louis Gates, Jr., and Cornel West. New York: Knopf, 1996.

Graham, Otis. *Our Kind of People.* New York: HarperCollins, 1999.

Jay-Z. Interview on the *Angie Martinez Show*, 1 February 2009.

_____. Interview with the author, 17 December 2003.

_____. Interview with *XXL* magazine, October 2009.

Keyes, Cheryl. *Rap Music and Street Consciousness.* Chicago: University of Illinois Press, 2002.

Kitwana, Bakari. "Between Expediency and Conviction: What We Mean When We Say Post-Racial." In *The Speech: Race and Barack Obama's a More Perfect Union*, ed. Tracy Sharpley-Whiting. New York: Bloomsbury U.S.A., 2010.

_____. "Black Gangster Films." In Kitwana, *The Hip-Hop Generation.* New York: Basic Civitas, 2002. 121–41.

_____. "Coalition Building Across Race." In *Why White Kids Love Hip-Hop.* New York: Basic Civitas, 2005.

_____. *The Hip-Hop Generation: Young Blacks and the Crisis in African American Culture.* New York: Basic Civitas, 2002.

_____. "Joker's Wild." *The Crisis,* December 2009.

Pattillo-McCoy, Mary. *Black Picket Fences: Privilege and Peril Among the Black Middle Class.* Chicago: University of Chicago Press, 1999.

Peterson, James. "It's Yours: Hip-Hop Worldviews in the Lyrics of Nas." In *Born to Use Mics: Reading Nas's Illmatic*, ed. Michael Eric Dyson and Sohail Daulatazai. New York: Basic Civitas, 2009.

Ross, Jenna. "Blackface Incident Stirs an Uproar on Bethel Campus." *Minneapolis Star Tribune,* 10 May 2010.

Shelby, Tommie. *We Who Are Dark: The Philosophical Foundations of Black Solidarity.* Cambridge, MA: Harvard University Press, 2005.

Tanz, Jason. *Other People's Property: A Shadow History of Hip-Hop.* New York: Bloomsbury U.S.A., 2007.

Trescott, Jacqueline. "The Battle Over Malcolm X: Spike Lee vs. Amiri Baraka: Who Should Immortalize the Man on Film and Why?" *The Washington Post,* 18 August 1991.

Williams, Thomas Chatterton. *Losing My Cool: How My Father and 15,000 Books Beat Hip-Hop Culture.* New York: Penguin, 2010.

Wise, Tim. "Majoring in Minstrelsy: White Students, Black Face and the Failure of Mainstream Multiculturalism." *Racism Review* 22 June 2007.

7

Black Marketing Whiteness
From Hustler to HNIC

STEPHANY ROSE

"There ain't no causes — there ain't nothing but taking in this world, and he
who takes most is smartest — and it don't make a damn bit of difference how."
— Walter Lee Younger in Lorraine Hansberry,
A Raisin in the Sun

White House, Black Market: The Critical Framework

In recent years, American scholarly shifts in approaches to studying race as institutionalized expressions of power have allowed dialogues to emerge articulating the social, economic, and political benefits whites in the United States have due to the existence of race. Scholar George Lipsitz has advanced such shifts with his compelling iterations on privileges afforded whites based upon constructed understandings of race. His theories regarding "the possessive investment in whiteness" speak to the profit margins — both tangible and intangible — whiteness as a commodity produces for peoples classified as white. Undoubtedly, because of the possessive investment in whiteness — a fabricated identity that allows its adherents unequal access to citizenship and property[1] — "all racialized minority groups have suffered" (Lipsitz 372). Problematically, however, what is left out of the conversation is the roles racialized minorities have played in the flourishing of whiteness, which to be more specific can be understood as a matrix of "imperialist white-supremacist capitalist patriarchy" (hooks xiii).

The exponential success of whiteness has not come by the investment of whites alone. Like with most other commodities in a controlled economy, a "black market" has emerged where non-white communities throughout the globe have developed consciously and sub-consciously, by force and/or fascination, valued notions of whiteness and its perceived supremacy. Due to this phenomenological occurrence, those originally most alienated and ostracized by the production and consumption of whiteness—peoples of African descent—have grown to be, in many instances, the most persistent investors in the black market in whiteness, much to the debilitating development of black communities throughout the globe and the advancement of white power.

The black market in whiteness permeates a variety of aspects amongst black lives and communities. Currently, hip hop culture provides the most popular representations and influences of black American lives throughout the nation and the globe. As a result, it presents an accessible, though non-totalizing, mechanism for studying the black market in whiteness infused throughout black America. The iconic figure Jay-Z—drug dealer turned emcee and then turned executive—is only one of many enigmatic displays of the black market in whiteness. Shawn Carter/Jay-Z reveals a myriad of inconsistencies within counter discursive minority rhetorics and performances as understood within hip hop when concerns of hyper-consumerism, social and economic elitism, gender, and heterosexism arise. Often productions and consumption of hip hop disclose consciousnesses in producers and consumers alike that are coterminous with the dominant culture, despite a proverbial sense of denial. Jay-Z is, however, a complex enigma—much like hip hop itself—and it is because of the varied contradistinctions he represents that he is chosen for this discussion, since any analysis of him warns against oversimplification.

This essay provides a centralized and condensed exposition into black market occurrences and implications in whiteness via black American hip hop culture. In this exploration, the public and professional personas of Shawn Carter/Jay-Z are used as a synecdochical account of hip hop, serving as case study to exemplify the theoretical underpinnings of the black market in whiteness. However, to minimize Jay-Z—and ultimately hip hop culture—as simply a trope of white Americanism would be a gross misrepresentation. Still, for the focus of this discussion aspects mirroring white Americanism within black culture are dissected in order to highlight the grander discourse of a black market in whiteness.

In the Master's Robes, in the Master Role

Historically, the dominant American culture has projected primarily negative images of blacks in America. The popularized image of black Americans created by white America is condescending, dehumanizing, and inferior, which has its origins in the institution of New World slavery (Fredrickson; Morrison).

In Marlon Riggs' classic documentary *Ethnic Notions*, Larry Levine asserts, "When you see hundreds of them [black caricatures and memorabilia], in all parts of the country persisting over a very long period of time, they have to have meaning. They obviously appeal to people. They appeal to the creator, but they appeal also to the consumers, those who ... look at the cartoons, or read the novels, or buy the artifacts." Indeed much is revealed — the racist notions of black people penetrating national consciousness and accepted on some levels by the dominant and subordinate communities alike. And in the same documentary, Barbara Christian further points out, "It is not just that it's in the figurines ... it is that we [blacks] are seen that way, perceived that way, even in terms of public policy. And that our lives are lived under that shadow, and sometimes we then, even become to believe it ourselves."

Since the arrival of the first enslaved blacks to what is now the Americas, (re)constructing and constituting identity has been and remains a constant site of contestation. Due to physical and psychological enslavement, Africans in the Americas learned to see themselves in relation to Europeans in the Americas. In the United States, each generation of blacks, on average, grew more and more "American" and less "African." Today, the psychology of many blacks in the United States is embedded with the adoration of European American ideological precepts in all aspects of existence: community, religion, governance, economics, and beauty. Therefore, centuries beyond chattel liberation, in mass blacks remain nocuously chained to white ideologies, culture, and perceptions of themselves.[2]

In "'The Blackness of Blackness': A Critique of the Sign and the Signifying Monkey," Henry Louis Gates Jr. outlines rhetoric and social dynamics conveyed in representations of signification within African American traditions. Gates explains the act of signifying as a method of codifying and re-codifying those instances known as the black experience in various settings and times. "If Vico and Burke, or Nietzsche, Paul de Man, and Harold Bloom, are correct in identifying 'master tropes,'" writes Gates, "then we might think of these as the 'master's tropes,' and of signifying as the slave's trope, the trope of tropes, [... for] Signifying is a trope that subsumes other rhetorical tropes" (686). In examining Gates' comments, it is imperative to note that when the "master trope" is accepted as whiteness,[3] then in non-white communities often cultural productions metaphorically resemble the putting on of the master's robes and roles by the subjugated in the perceived absence of the master. However, the very existence of the master's articles of clothing and the assumed posturing by the imposture mark the master as ever present and valued. Therefore, in spaces and practices deemed almost exclusively black, ideas engaging whiteness percolate nearly every interaction either consciously or subconsciously through the structured formations of sign and signification. As a result, black Americans who pursue images of American normalcy innately participate in the promotion and perpetuation of hegemonic whiteness, for the standard of normalcy in the United States is founded upon dominating white ideals. Furthermore, for blacks in America the putting on of the master's robes may inevitable lead to more than appropriation, but becoming the masters themselves as with numerous free blacks in antebellum America who were slave and plantation owners (Koger 1985).

Looking for Cheddar: Capitalist Ideals and the Aesthetics of Hip Hop

While many rightfully may view hip hop as a counter-discursive measure and non-hegemonic, more often than not, popular representations of the culture are invested in the black market in whiteness by reifying notions of the perceived supremacy of whiteness due to a valued appreciation of white aesthetics and ideologies by producers, laborers, and consumers of hip hop. Hip hop culture in many ways has become paltry and immersed in the normalized rhetoric of white American society. Contemporarily, American hip hop largely is a manifestation of neo-colonialism in a Fanonian perspective where the oppressed have become the oppressors. Unarguably, there have been moments when a major currency in hip hop was anti-establishment — social and political relevancy built upon vestiges of radical activism of the Civil Rights and Black Power movements— when artists such as Afrika Bambaata, KRS-One, Queen Latifah, Lauryn Hill, Public Enemy, and others advocated counter-hegemonic frameworks with dexterity for newer generations as the focal point of the developing culture. Yet the power and promise of hip hop has been polemic since its inception and commodification. Examining the polemics of hip hop culture that oscillate between accepting and rejecting the structure of white supremacy demonstrates microscopically the black market in whiteness occurring globally.

Reminiscing on the development of hip hop in Nelson George's seminal article, "Hip Hop's Founding Fathers Speak the Truth," Grandmaster Flash and DJ Kool Herc discuss how the making of "Rapper's Delight" was in many ways a usurpation of the *organic authenticity* of hip hop. George's article suggests that hip hop's "founding fathers" conceived their cultural performances as productions separate from the mass/dominant culture and market. Flash and Herc speak to George about how in the origination of hip hop culture the mass market was beyond their conceptualization just as Big Bank Hank and the Sugar Hill Gang's growing mass appeal was not felicitous in their perspective. Flash and Herc discuss their perspectives through the following:

> FLASH: I was approached in '77. A gentleman walked up to me and said, "We can put what you're doing on record." I would have to admit that I was blind. I didn't think that somebody else would want to hear a record re-recorded

onto another record with talking on it. ... So here it is two years later, and I hear "To the hip-hop, to the bang to the boogie," and it's not Bam, Herc, Breakout, AJ. Who is this?

HERC: And when I heard [Big Bank] Hank [of the Sugar Hill Gang], I was like, what? I knew Hank. I didn't really appreciate that Hank knew me personally, had been to my house, was from the neighborhood, and never once said, "Herc, I'm doing something." Never, until this day [52–53].

As a result, the existence and success of "Rapper's Delight" serves as a watershed in the evolution of hip hop into a modern day image of globalization. Greg Dimitriadis remarks, "'Rapper's Delight' ruptured the art form's sense of continuity as a live practice known to all its 'in-group' members ... it came to mark the art's entrance into the public sphere of worldwide cultural discourse.... The decentralized face-to-face dynamic [... gave way to] one mediated by way of commodity forms such as vinyl, video, film, and CD" (27).

Though the commodification and commercial success of "Rapper's Delight" placed hip hop into a wider market, it is sanctimonious romantic revisionism to project that hip hop was not being utilized to participate within a capitalist economy aforetime. Any form of commercial exchange within hip hop regardless of grand or minute financial success is still the commodification of hip hop. George demonstrates this earlier in his conversation with these pillars of hip hop of whom each speak of subtle ways the pioneering generation commercialized what was developing as hip hop from deejaying private and club parties in order to feed and support one's family, to bets placed on battling crews and "pay for play" breakers—breakdancers who began articulating, "Well you gonna have to pay to see me dance," according to Kool Herc (George 47). Informal as the economy may have been, in relationship to the United States' mainstream economy, the progenitors of hip hop culture crafted and exchanged the production of what was developing as hip hop in economic ways shadowing a profit-based capitalist structure. This does not discredit the elements that were counter-normative from the inception of hip hop, but it does acknowledge that the art forms were also financially supporting and promoting members of the "in-group" through socio-cultural capital measures allowing them to better participate in the dominant social structure. There is no denial that counter-hegemonic iterations were being birthed in the 1970s through hip hop; however, hip hop historians, scholars, and stakeholders often articulate a revisionism of the culture that suggests what was being constructed was quintessentially in rejection of the dominant structure, when in actuality it was being produced and used to garner more successful participation within the pre-existing dominant structure.

Acknowledging that much of the youth culture that developed and maintains hip hop in the United States signifies a reflexive relationship with the dominant white American culture, ultimately allows for a redressing of displaced castigation of hip hop because what is vilified in actuality is the mores and ideals of the larger society. The characteristics of hip hop that in recent years are viewed negatively and condemned by those who exist inside and outside of hip hop communities are not unique characteristics to hip hop culture; they are fundamental qualities of American culture. Because they are, it is unjust to merely single out the behavior of some within the hip hop community as anomalies when the concern is complicated by one's interaction and existence inside a matrix shaped by principles of whiteness—capitalism, Protestantism, patriarchy, and heterosexism. However, one cannot be uncritical of such actualities within hip hop if the ultimate objective is the destruction of white supremacy and the development of truly libratory practices. We must address critical questions in order to foreground revolutionary objectives. How can and/or do hip hop artists speak against the structure of white supremacy while representing the structure and still be accountable to both community and institution within their labor system? And, how possible is it to destroy the master's house while living in it and utilizing the master's tools?

Knocking the Hustle for Real

When Shawn Carter emerged as a formidable participant within hip hop, he did so through the self-proclaimed identity of Jay-Z, the hustler. In 1996, after several failed attempts to break considerable ground within the music industry, Jay-Z released his third radio single, "Can't Knock the Hustle," off his debut album, *Reasonable Doubt,* as a partner and primary solo artist of the independent record label, Roc-A-Fella, Inc. The song, engrossed by desires and displays of possessions and rising to the top of one's financial and social enterprises, has since become the central theme to Jay-Z's career. Heralded as a master anecdote, this song, amongst many, paints a narrative of Jay-Z as one of the more prosperous hustlers to ever hustle. Some critics have suggested that Jay Z's scope of a hustler is oversimplified in "Reasonable Doubt." The assertion is that violence and wanton thrill seeking is not the commensurate to the hustler spirit, as it is more akin to gaining access to resources and living a luxurious lifestyle which lacks a larger cultural contextualization and critique. Hustlers, by their particular nature, are confidence persons ("con men") who epitomize the very ideals and components of a hegemonic capitalist structure.

Hustling and a hustler's mentality as a "celebrated" ideal in the black community materialize out of black masculine culture of the late sixties and seventies. bell hooks explains that "Black power militants were ruthless in their critique of capitalism ... announcing for the black man that whether or not he had a legitimate job ... no longer mattered since nothing about the capitalist system was legitimate ... everybody was a thief ... on the take" (16). Though a revolutionary critique of capitalism was and remains quite apropos, the by-product of their militant ruthless critique, coupled with limited job opportunities and an ever-present sense of patriarchal masculinity that required access to money and power, calcified sentiments of nihilism among many black men. It did not settle into an abdication of capitalism, but fortified even greater desires to become major players within the dominant capitalist structure. "[B]y the late sixties and early seventies most black men had made the choice to identify their well-being [sense of self], their manhood with making money by any means necessary" (hooks 17).

Hence, the hustler persona was lauded for his ability to access money despite the means by which it was acquired. More often than not, those means were not of traditional wage earning, due to the systemic alienation of black men. Though two arenas—sports and entertainment—afforded black males considerable success, the average hustler turned to criminal and illicit practices. Alongside a new hedonistic ethos for money in black communities, the mass introduction of drugs invigorated the black criminal stratum to deeper depths. Thus, when Jay-Z speaks of being a hustler, he commemorates the lure of hedonistic materialism built into his schemes as a drug dealer. The extent to which Shawn Carter's drug ventures may have flourished may be overzealously embellished throughout his music, given that Jay-Z has said, "As much as we keep it real and things like that, that's just a great basis for fantasy. We'll take something that really happened and we'll exaggerate it to times ten or twenty" (qtd. in Kitwana para 48). Still, the actuality of him selling drugs and acquiring money through illicit channels remains,[4] making him a participant in the fostering of spiritual, physical, and psychological violence in the black community. The spirit and purpose, as reflected by his "motto, stack rocks like Colorado/bottle off the champagne/Cristal by the bottle," propagates the "materialism [that] replaced spirituality as the definer's of life's worth" after the mass introduction of heroin and crack to black communities from the late 1960s on into the '90s (Nelson 41).

As much as the hustler and hustler's mentality is a newer phenomenon in black communities, it is a much older practice in larger white American society. It particularly reflects a combined ethos of the capitalist economic structure and the mythos of the self-made man.[5] The self-made man, born in the infancy of the independent U.S. republic and "a model of manhood that derives identity entirely from a man's activities in the public sphere, measured by accumulated wealth and status, by geographic and social mobility," is a direct result of volatile masculinities constructed in a racialized and marketplace-driven society (Kimmel 17). Because the history of citizenship in the United States is built upon a history of race, gender, and class—one could not enjoy the fullness of citizenship unless one were white, male, and a property owner—individuals and communities have been working to renegotiate the terms of their citizenship within U.S. society since the birth of the nation. What manifests in contemporary hip hop culture are residuary effects of desires to more fully participate in the larger national schematic after centuries of alienation and exclusion like other disenfranchised groups, a narrative played out by so many chasing the American dream. Yet what is misconstrued by many blacks in guerilla pursuit of full enfranchisement in American nationalism is the impossibility of the task, because race and the master signifier of whiteness demands difference and exclusion.

Shawn Carter/Jay-Z in so many ways parallels F. Scott's Fitzgerald's early twentieth-century literary character James Gatz, who through his pursuit of the American dream utilizes an underground illicit culture to transform himself into The Great Gatsby — a personification of the extravagant American nouveaux riche. A look at the thematic narrative in "Oh My God," Jay-Z accounts, through rhymes, his humble beginnings with an absent father, who experiences the American Dream after a travail from the depths of in inner-city jungle-like conditions. Similarly, Gatsby, who is of lowly North Dakota origins, transfigures himself into a semblance of greatness by accumulating financial excess through bootlegging liquor during prohibition and surrounding himself with opulence. The life characterized by Gatsby, complete with fast and rare cars, mammoth mansions, lavish all-weekend parties, powerful men, and beautiful women at his disposal — all achieved through bootlegging and organized crime — is quite similar to the life lived lyrically by Jay-Z. Both demonstrate the possibility of rising from rags to riches in the United States by any means necessary.

One of the major critical debates to arise over *The Great Gatsby* focuses on the implications of the American dream. Edwin Fussell argues that the American dream is a representation of "romantic wonder," the interplay between quest and seduction. The surrendering to the pursuit of the dream "is a flight: from reality, from normality, from time, fate and conception of *limit*." Thus, for Fussell, Fitzgerald shows in *Great Gatsby* "the corruption of that dream in industrial America [... which] is universally seductive and perpetually unreal" (291). Numerous other scholars[6] build upon interpretations of pursuing the dream as presented by Gatsby, but none raise the question of who is allowed to dream in the dominant national conscience. Gatsby's tragedy rests upon a false sense of inclusion, the illusion that he has become the quintessential American, when in actuality he is merely mirroring the lives of those who are. Those who typify Fitzgerald's fictive representation of American society in the social practices and consciences are those who believe in white superiority and distinction, fear the loss of white supremacy, and fear minority rule.

"[M]oney," as Ronald Berman distinguishes, "is not the [greatest] problem: the social order is [where] a rich man's son understands that when poor boys rise, rich boys have less space to breathe in" (39). What is of greater concern, however, is that the whiteness that permeates this society is rooted in a hierarchy which Gatsby threatens; his threat is symbolized in his economic mobility and momentary passing. Because the system is based in false conceptions of race, Gatsby is able to pass as one of the elite on the basis of his white skin and his newly, yet illicitly acquired, money. The fragile permeability of the positioning that Gatsby encroaches on is what incites fear in his antagonist, Tom. Accordingly, Tom desperately tries to maintain a barrier between the two by pronouncing Gatsby to be "Mr. Nobody from Nowhere," but the utmost attempt becomes a racist assault when Tom insinuates that because Gatsby is not Nordic and is without inherited money, Gatsby is not just beneath everyone; he is in essence not white, but black (Fitzgerald 130).

Correspondingly, Shawn Carter may have gained some levels of access into the dominant American society via the creation of Jay-Z; however, many instances have revealed the limitations of his tertiary existence and the necessity of maintaining social order due to the primacy of racial structures in white American and global societies. In 2006, in a rude awakening to the hip hop community, Frederic Rouzaud, managing director of Louis Roederer, the maker of Cristal Champagne, told *The Economist* magazine of his displeasure in having many within hip hop freely advertising, purchasing, and consuming the champagne. He stated disapprovingly, "[W]hat can we do? We can't forbid people from buying it. I'm sure Dom Perignon or Krug would be delighted to have their business" ("Jay-Z launches bubbly" para 6). Even though Jay-Z and numerous others of the hip hop community have tremendously increased the mainstream and economic presence of the wine, their business reached a point of undesirability by its manufacturers. In the end when the question seems to be whether a company's main objective is to sell as many units of its merchandise, the answer by corporations like Louis Roederer, Tommy Hilfiger, and Timberland appears to be "No." A nuance of white supremacy dictates that access and availability diminishes elitism and one would prefer to perceptibly loose business than exclusivity becoming commonplace.

Though Jay-Z went on record regarding the racist offense and disavowed himself as a client of Louis Roederer, removing Cristal from his 40/40 clubs, he failed to comprehend that the one act is part of a larger systemic network: if it is not Louis Roederer, then it is another corporate representative of the white infrastructure. Hence, Jay-Z's lyrical critique of white corporate power controlling America is underdeveloped and evanescent at best, because it echoes the sentimentality of protest art warned against by Richard Wright and James Baldwin. It begs of inclusion and appeals to a false sense of morality within whiteness. Rhetorically speaking, Jay-Z and hip hop are successful in demanding and claiming public space as well as quite vocal in the calling out of white America. Regardless, after many of the performances are done, what remains "is safely ensconced in the social arena, where indeed, it has nothing to do with anyone, so that finally ... this report from the pit reassures us of its reality and its darkness and of our own salvation; and 'As long as such [art is being produced] ... everything will be all right'" (Baldwin "Everybody's Protest Novel" 1703). And everything is all right: business as usual remains as racism, sexism, and elitism continues to keep the nation oppressed despite four decades of hip hop.

If whiteness by definition is the loss of oneself and cultural identity for an embraced materialism as a source of power, domination and hierarchy (Baldwin, "The Price of the Ticket"), Jay-Z repeatedly provides his audiences with his sense of self-loss in order to maintain consumer relativity. With lyrics emblematic of psychotic materialism, violence against other blacks, deliberate objectification, misogyny against women, and homophobia, his artistic thought privileges a black market value in whiteness despite laden contentions of regret and confliction. For example, in the lyrics to "Moment of Clarity," Jay-Z narrates his conscious abdication of a more critical and counter-hegemonic discourse through his music for a rhetoric of capitalist appeal. In this song, Jay-Z admits to honoring a paradigm of capitalism over a consciousness more steeped in black liberationism that he's contemplated and alludes throughout his career, but he recognizes it as more appropriate for a Talib Kweli or Common. Though hip hop womanist scholar Dawn-Elissa Fischer appropriately argues against placing "conscious" rappers, like Kweli, Common, or Mos Def, on political pedestals, the immediate issue is what Jay-Z acknowledges for himself. His accounts in manufacturing and selling goods and products— not elevated, counter-hegemonic discourses of racial accountability and liberation — are more "im-por-tant" to him. He suggests that maximizing financial capital is the means for him to provide cultural assistance. What fails to be considered perilously is the contradiction being financially rich and egalitarian creates. Being "rich" in a capitalist economy dictates the binary positioning of the poor; thus, his agenda to "help the poor" should not be confused with eradicating poverty, for it is structurally impossible to live in excessive material luxury without someone being impoverished. Furthermore, his theory of philanthropy is a false sense of philanthropy because one cannot piously provide an offering to a community that he has already pilfered. Jay-Z's transparent philanthropic aim is a conscious admission to becoming a major participator in the black market in whiteness. Lastly, Jay-Z would have the audience to gloss over his reference to sharing in the same consciousness of "them"— translated as wealthy, white men dominating the executive positions throughout the music industry — who "hate" him because they did not "make" him a "rich black man." His discursive explanation reveals a consciousness coterminous with the dominant culture despite his articulated sense of denial.

In "Fear of a Black Planet," Tricia Rose warns against limiting the cultural politics of those within hip hop to representations in lyrical content, for "the politics of rap music involves the contestation over public space, expressive meaning, interpretation, and cultural capital" (276). Jay-Z's political agenda then is not only made evident by what he says, but contextually within his well-established public career. His justification for not speaking differently and focusing on sales within the industry come at a time when he has already achieved pinnacle status in the profession and the threat of not selling at all is unfathomable. Also, as an established entrepreneur and executive, the threat of poverty was/is no longer pressing upon him at the time of the album's release. Thus, considering the level of control over the production of his own cultural capital, he is in a better position than Kweli or Common to articulate a more vocal radicalism and as Adam Mansbach suggests, "he doesn't wanna do it, he hasn't developed a critique — but he feels the need to excuse himself" (Pride). If any ideology is significantly pressing upon Jay-Z, it is a capitalist one of wanting more and having the most. Does that exclude him from completely having a conflicting agenda with the black market in whiteness? No, because whiteness perpetuates the paradigm of minorities, especially blacks, in poverty, which Jay-Z has defied. Yet, in his defiance is the desire to reproduce, not dismantle the same structure and refusing to repudiate a lack of critique perpetuates a syndrome of "black skin, white mask."

In summation, Jay-Z projects an image of hip hop that serves as a means of situational escapism and not structural dismantling. Though he vacillates between condemnations of white-induced poverty on black America demanding that white America by consistently asserting that blacks are owed for debts unpaid, and personal repudiations of his past drug dealings, his willingness to engage hip hop, as just another hustle, keeps him entrenched in the black market in whiteness ("Izzo [H.O.V.A]").

Conclusion: Hate the Game, for It Remains the Same

It goes without saying that dismantling oppression is a complex, generationally consuming affair in which many are lost in the process. In the beginning phases one thinks the desired outcome is to gain situational power (maneuverability) similar to the childhood game "King of the Hill," where multiple competitors attempt to knock the dominant individual from the precipice on which he/she stands. It is a game predicated upon violence and individualism, for even if the competitors work collectively to remove the current "king," the rules mandate a singular winner. So, collectivity gives way to individuality and the cycle of competition begins again as the players fail to realize it is the game itself that is destructive.

What hip hop has yet to accomplish is a defacing/destruction of the dominant ideology. What has merely taken place is a shift in positioning, a maneuvering of pieces within the same infrastructure, but, to reference hip hop vernacular, *the game remains the same.* Shawn Carter has proven that it is possible to move from the bottom rungs of the social ladder to become a critical participant in mainstream corporate America. Unfortunately, for many purveyors of hip hop "too much reliance [is] on short-term institutional struggle for power and too little emphasis on the long-term ideological work of constructing counter-hegemonic ideas and institutions" (Morrison, "The Struggle for Hegemony" 148). Hip hop can claim the victory of being America's culture of popular choice, birthed out of the voices and lives of the subverted and excluded. Jay-Z is just an example of how hip hop has become part of the racist capitalist system. Therefore, the focus of this research is not to blame Jay-Z as much as it is to demonstrate an example of the system that hip hop has become engrossed within. To date — a culture without exploitation, hierarchy, and violence — hip hop is not.

Writing about the aesthetics of black art during the Black Arts movement, a movement that many scholars credit as the parent of hip hop, Larry Neal argues that as an artist, "your ethics and your aesthetics are one" (31). If this is evidence of the ideas that later give birth to hip hop, then one must question the ethical and non-ethical representations postured throughout the aesthetic/artistic representations that is hip hop. Furthermore, Neal states, "The motive behind the Black aesthetic is the destruction of the white thing, the destruction of white ideas, and white ways of looking at the world. The new aesthetic is mostly predicated on an Ethics which asks the question: whose vision of the world is finally more meaningful, ours or the white oppressors'?" (30).

What is presented as most valued throughout the trajectory of Jay-Z's career is a culture of capitalism, copious consumerism, and oppressive power by artist and audience alike. It's not surprising blacks and whites alike yearn for Jay-Z's narratives of "coming up/rising up" in the game, because one of the prevailing meta-narratives framing American society as bootstrap living. Pulling one's self up by one's bootstraps hits the core of American identity. The dominant and subordinate cultures alike have bought into the notion of not attacking poverty and classism because it is one's responsibility to figure out how to *make it.*

Even as Jay-Z begins to develop a more socially conscious perspective, he acknowledges how entangled he is within the dominant socio-economic oppression of American culture. After the wake of Hurricane Katrina and the prime time disenfranchisement of black citizens throughout the gulf region of the United States, Jay-Z spoke of the poverty-stricken predisposition of hurricane survivors who were marginalized even more by the government and media. Of himself he stated that he gave a million dollars to the relief effort but didn't give any of his time so as to ensure its impact. He later concludes that maybe his effort was, indeed, futile as he simply continues to support the oppressive and unsympathetic forces that alienated the very people the hurricane stranded ("Minority Report").

For Further Consideration

BOOKS

Freire, Paulo. *Pedagogy of the Oppressed.* New York: Continuum, 2000.
Jones, LeRoi . *Blues People.* New York: W. Morrow, 1963.
Tate, Greg. *Everything but the Burden: What White People are Taking from Black Culture.* New York: Broadway, 2003.

QUESTIONS

1. If being a "product" of the hustle means that, by default, one can't "knock the hustle," then does revolutionary art truly exist?

2. Critiques of celebrities who make donations (of time or money) to nonprofit or community-based causes often suggest that such generosity is false or insufficient. In what ways can (or should) celebrities demonstrate their desire to have a positive affect on the lives of people who consume and/or experience their art?

3. Based on one of the author's key points in this article (and that of many other scholars), the black experience in America is inherently and eternally tied to a relationship to white people-historically, politically, economically, and psychologically. Agree or disagree: Such a filter is indeed the hustle itself and will always support the victor.

Notes

1. See James Baldwin, "On Being White and Other Lies"; Richard Dyer; and George Lipsitz.

2. W.E.B. Du Bois' articulation of this phenomenon is that of a veiled existence for blacks in America. This veil or second sight "yields no true self-consciousness, but only lets him [the African American] see himself through the revelation of the other world" (618). In short, "this sense of always looking at one's self through the eyes of the others, of measuring one's soul by the tape of a world that looks on in amused contempt and pity" prohibits the creation of totally autonomous and holistically positive representations of one's self and community (618).

3. Kalpana Seshadri-Crooks theorizes "the inaugural signifier of race, [is] Whiteness, [it] implicates us all in the logic of difference ... [and is] a master signifier (without a signified) that establishes a structure of relations, a signifying chain that through a process of inclusions and exclusions constitutes a pattern for organizing human difference."

4. Sean Cane, co-producer on "Can't Knock the Hustle," recounts being paid to produce and mix the song "with a shoe box of money. ... It was ones. We had to count it.

Jay and Dame [Damon Dash], they came with the shoe box of money. ... It wasn't a lot. It was less than 10 Gs, put it like that" (qtd. in Monroe).

5. For an extensive exploration of the self-made man, see Michael Kimmel's *Manhood in America: A Cultural History.*

6. See, for example, Marius Bewley; John W. Bicknell; Robert Ornstein; and Brian Way.

Works Cited

Baldwin, James. "Everybody's Protest Novel." Indianapolis: College Division, Bobbs-Merrill, 1949.

_____. "On Being White and Other Lies." *Essence,* 1984. *http://www.cwsworkshop.org/pdfs/CARC/Family_Herstories/2_On_Being_White.PDF.*

_____. "The Price of the Ticket." In *The Price of the Ticket: Collected Nonfiction 1948–1985.* New York: St. Martin's, 1985.

Berman, Ronald. "America in Fitzgerald." *Journal of Aesthetic Education* 36.2 (2002): 38–51.

Bewley, Marius. "Scott Fitzgerald's Criticism of America." *Sewanee Review* 62 (1954): 223-46.

Bicknell, John W. "The Waste Land of F. Scott Fitzgerald." *Virginia Quarterly Review* 30 (1954).

Dimitriadis, Greg. *Performing Identity/Performing Culture: Hip Hop as Text, Pedagogy, and Lived Practice.* Intersections in Communications and Culture, Vol. 1. New York: Peter Lang, 2001.

Du Bois, W. E. B. *The Souls of Black Folk.* In *Three African-American Classics.* Mineola, NY: Dover, 2007.

Dyer, Richard. *White: Essays on Race and Culture.* New York: Routledge, 1997.

Eble, Kenneth E., ed. *F. Scott Fitzgerald: A Collection of Criticism.* New York: McGraw Hill, 1973.

Ethnic Notions. Dir. Marlon Riggs. San Francisco: California Newsreel, 1987. DVD.

Fitzgerald, F. Scott. *The Great Gatsby.* New York: Scribner, 2004.

Fredrickson, George M. The *Black Image in the White Mind: The Debate on Afro-American Character and Destiny, 1817–1914.* New York: Harper and Row, 1971.

Fussell, Edwin. "Fitzgerald's Brave New World." *ELH* 19 (1952): 291–306.

Gates, Henry Louis, Jr., "'The Blackness of Blackness': A Critique of Sign and the Signifying Monkey." *Critical Inquiry* 9.4 (1983): 686.

George, Nelson. *Hip Hop America.* New York: Penguin, 1999.

_____. "Hip Hop's Founding Fathers Speak the Truth." In *That's the Joint.* Ed. Murray Foreman and Mark Anthony Neal. New York: Routledge, 2004.

hooks, bell. *We Real Cool: Black Men and Masculinity.* New York: Routledge, 2004.

Huey, Steve. Rev. of *Reasonable Doubt,* by Jay-Z. *Allmusic.com.* Rovi Corporation. 4 Jan. 2010 *http://allmusic.com/cg/amg.dll?p=amg&sql=10:hzfpxqthldje.*

Jay-Z. "Can't Knock the Hustle." *Reasonable Doubt.* Roc-A-Fella Records, 1996. CD.

_____. "Izzo (H.O.V.A.)" *Blueprint.* Roc-A-Fella Records, 2001. CD.

_____. "Minority Report." *Kingdom Come.* Roc-A-Fella Records, 2006. CD.

_____. "Moment of Clarity." *The Black Album.* Roc-A-Fella Records, 2003. CD.

"Jay-Z Launches Bubbly Boycott of Cristal." *USAToday.com,*15 June 2006. 5 January 2010 *http://www.usatoday.com/life/people/2006–06–15-Jay-Z-cristal_x.htm.*

Kimmel, Michael. *Manhood in America: A Cultural History.* New York: Free, 1996.

Kitwana, Bakari. "Jay-Z, Hip-Hop, and High Society." *Black Book* (Spring 2004). 3 Jan. 2010 *www.bakarikitwana.com.*

Koger, Larry. *Black Slaveowners: Free Black Slave Masters in South Carolina, 1790–1860.* Columbia: University of South Carolina Press, 1985.

Lipsitz, George. "The Possessive Investment in Whiteness: Racialized Social Democracy and the 'White' Problem in American Studies." *American Quarterly* 47.3 (1995): 369–87.

Monroe, Justine. *http://allmusic.com/cg/amg.dll?p=amg&sql=10:hzfpxqthldje.*

Morrison, Toni. *Playing in the Dark.* Cambridge, MA: Harvard University Press, 1992.

_____. "The Struggle for Hegemony." *The Journal of American History* 75.1 (1988): 146–50.

Neal, Larry. "The Black Arts Movement." *TDR* 12.4 (1968): 29–39.

Ornstein, Robert. "Scott Fitzgerald's Fable of East and West." Rpt. in Eble, 60–66.

Pride, Felicia. "Angry Black White Boy: An Interview with Adam Mansbach." *Backlist* Issue 11 (2005). 1 Jun 2007 *www.thebacklist.net.*

Rose, Tricia. "Fear of a Black Planet': Rap Music and Black Cultural Politics in the 1990s." *The Journal of Negro Education: Socialization Forces Affecting the Education of African American Youth in the 1990s* 60.3 (1991): 276.

Seshadri-Crooks, Kalpana. *Desiring Whiteness: A Lacanian Analysis of Race.* New York: Routledge, 2000.

Way, Brian. *F. Scott Fitzgerald and the Art of Social Fiction.* New York: St. Martin's, 1980. ix.

8

A Forty Million Slave's Moment of Clarity

DAYLAN DUFELMEIER

The Black Album was supposed to be Jay-Z's final album, his capstone to a long and illustrious career. However since *The Black Album* Jay-Z has released three more successful albums, solidifying his place among the entertainment greats and emphasizing why his manifesto, *The Black Album* is worthy of examination. On this album lives his powerful song "Moment of Clarity," in which he takes a jab at the music industry, explains his career choices, and also lays out a life/industry road map. The poetic depth of Jay-Z's lyrics is eminently suited for intellectual criticism — not that they are intensely personal, but that his concerns are a kind that the African American society at large shares with him. In "Moment of Clarity," he sums up much of his career in the first verse; a humble beginning to the black album (which was supposed to be his last album) listen to me and I'll tell you the truth.[1]

Jay-Z's "Moment of Clarity" provides listeners a look at the inner thoughts, motivations, and criticisms of one of the most successful rappers of all times. Despite his numerous accolades, acclaims, and skills, Jay-Z still has to answer to and navigate the power relationships in the music industry. William C. Rhoden discusses a similar relationship in *Forty Million Dollar Slave,* putting forward the idea that black athletes, starting in slavery, served as a source of income for the typically white owner. Rhoden also argues that present-day black professional athletes have almost no decision-making power, yet remain the sole attraction, while generating massive wealth for the typically white owners. This discrepancy creates a paradox allowing the typically white owners to buy and sell black talent without regard for the individual athlete. Rhoden's theoretical analysis of the professional sports industry is easily transferable to the entertainment industry, a lens from which to examine Jay-Z in the music industry both as an industry veteran and former CEO of a major record label. Because of Jay-Z's rags-to-riches story, he on one hand is someone with whom the average listener can identify, but his experience is also uncommon, since he is one of the few, if not the only, rapper/artists who became CEO of a major record company (he stepped down at the end of his three-year contract). There was a long-held belief in the black community that black ownership of sport franchises, or record companies, was the solution to power inequalities, yet Rhoden's *Forty Million Dollar Slave* demonstrates the fundamental relationship between owner and artist does not change regardless of race. Jay-Z, like Robert Johnson, owner of the Charlotte Bobcats and former owner of BET, remains a participant and upholder of the "system" despite his decision-making role.

In *Forty Million Dollar Slave,* Rhoden demonstrates that in the early days of horseracing black jockeys were dominant and common until it was perceived as a threat to white supremacy; then the rules were changed. This would become known as the "jockey syndrome" which "is distinguished by a changing of the rules of the game when competition begins to gain ground" (Rhoden 68). Throughout history and up to the present day one can see this same phenomenon happening continuously from Major Taylor, who dominated cycling in the late nineteenth century, to present-day NFL players, fined for celebrating after scoring a touchdown (Rhoden 88). Rhoden maintains,

> In virtually every decade since the 1950s, black athletes have been at the core of some stylistic or structural innovation in sports. From the alley-oop pass and the spin move in basketball to the spike and ritual of the end-zone shimmy in football ... Jackie Robinson's daring on the base paths, Muhammad Ali's mocking brilliance and fire in the ring, Wilma Rudolph's willowy grace and speed or Michael Jordan's aerial exploits.... The dilemma for the black community is that in the post-integration world, the community has no right, no claim, indeed no way, to profit from this" [152, 153].

The music industry runs parallel:

> Most of the musicians who succeeded in making big money in jazz, like Paul Whiteman, Benny Goodman, and Artie Shaw, were white, even though the origins of the music and most of the really innovative players have always been black. Until the late 1930s there was no integration in jazz groups, except for a handful of recordings on which the musicians sometimes used pseudonyms [Weissman 248].

The critical point here is that African Americans laid the foundation for the multi-billion dollar music industry yet reap no financial compensation, very similar to the way slaves received no compensation for their work in the foundation of the southern textile industry during slavery (Kelley 2). Incidentally, Jay-Z and rappers in general are the contemporary installment of the continued exploitation of African-American talent for white profit. In "Moment of Clarity" Jay-Z gives his listeners insight into his thoughts on this: the music industry dislikes me because they are not who I am, everyday people love me because I can speak their language and my music makes them jam.[2]

In this first part of the second verse, Jay-Z provides us with a wealth of information, a self-reflection on his position in the music industry and with his fans. On one hand, he is aware that the music industry does not like him because he never needed the industry to make him wealthy (although that is seriously complicated because of the amount of money he has made in the industry as a rapper, but we'll let him have it). On the other hand he is well aware that as a former "hustler and booster"[3] people who find themselves in those occupations really like him because he "made it"—he is a contemporary Horatio Alger story. The next part of the verse speaks to a much larger issue, that of "formula" music: "I dumb down for my audience/and double my dollars." "It is a lie, a myth, to say that the record labels and the radio stations and the magazines and the television outlets are giving the people what they want. On the contrary, the power brokers determine what the people should request, then make the people think that they are asking for it of their own accord. It is called marketing" (Powell 147). The formula music is typically gangsta rap. This sub-genre has often provided a "window into, and critique of, the criminalization of black youth" and as a result it has achieved a level of authenticity the music industry sought to exploit" (Green 115). According to Russell Simmons, "75 percent of hip-hop albums are purchased by white consumers, and the global market is constantly expanding" (qtd. in Green 80). Jason Tanz explains why the industry does what it does: "I think back to the Hush Tour I took of the South Bronx, and hearing LL Cool J rap about his desire to leave the ghetto even as we white tourists paid seventy-five dollars to file into it for a few minutes" (192). There is a lot of money in the exploitation of the authentic black experience, which is complexly intertwined with being poor and unintelligent. So when Jay-Z says, he's not as lyrically complex as he would like to be because he makes more money, he is referring to participating in formula music because he "doubled his dollars." Rhoden calls this phenomenon in professional sports "the conveyor belt, where the athlete learns to accept the power structure as is because it is the smoothest, most profitable ride" (194). Both Chuck D in *Fight the Power* and Rhoden point to an excellent example in the NBA when Mahmoud Abdul-Rauf (previously Chris Jackson) was suspended and blackballed by the NBA for refusing to stand during America's national anthem, which was too much protest for status quo (Ridenhour 201; Rhoden 216). Jay-Z stays on the music-industry conveyor belt, but that is not intended to down play his skill as a rapper or to down play the quality of his music. (The reverse is also true: it did not make Mahmoud Abdul-Rauf a better athlete nor will it make a rapper better if they are not on the conveyor belt.) In fact critics will often criticize him for his dumb-downed music without acknowledging his talent as an artist, meanwhile listening to his music in their stereo system. Furthering his self-reflection he finishes the first half of the verse with a statement that acknowledges the lyrical ability of artist Talib Kweli.

This idea reinforces what Jay-Z has already stated, he juxtaposes his career to an artist considered lyrically complex and political, even though Talib Kweli does not claim this title for himself. He continues this juxtaposition to another artist, Common Sense (known now as just Common) and in this comparison he describes how much money he makes when he raps in a less complex way which makes more sense to someone who has been poor for his entire life.

Here Jay-Z then provides his listeners with his very tangible motivation — money: neither Talib Kweli nor Common are as financially successful as Jay-Z, yet Jay-Z acknowledges that they are more lyrically skillful. He then moves gracefully into the idea that an artist should ignore what critics say or think and do what makes the most sense. Jay-Z also argues that he must be rich to help people and that "giving back" is his solution. Many rap artists give back to their communities and according to Russell Simmons, "The rap community gives back to their community more than any music group that you can think of" (qtd. in Green 81).

The idea of giving back after getting rich is one of the reasons that Jay-Z and rappers in general fall into Rhoden's paradox. To get rich, you must uphold the system to a certain degree. Jay-Z and other rappers are the sole attraction, the reason that companies are making money yet have almost no decision-making power. While they are well paid compared to most people rappers actually make very little in relation to the company for which they work, but are expected to be happy about their paychecks. Even when Jay-Z moves from rapper to CEO, this essential paradox does not change; he stays within the system and ultimately does not and cannot challenge it.

The music industry is a well-oiled and efficient profit-making machine, making it almost impossible to challenge. It is difficult to discern a typical percentage that an artist will make in royalties but sources use seven percent as a gauge (Weissman 69). If a label can get away with an even more profitable contract, they will. Jay-Z recalls when it happened to him: "I had a messed-up contract. And everyone knew. But we didn't know. We was like, 'Why were we...?' But they was like, 'Why you so offended? It's just business.' To them it's good business; to us it was deceit" (VIBE 256). In *The Music Business,* a book to help aspiring musicians deal with the industry, Dan Weissman states, "you should never sign a deal with a record company without consulting a competent music business attorney" (65). However, many of the artists are not from affluent families and many are happy to sign because some money is better than no money. It is widely known within the industry that, starting out, an artist should not expect too much by way of royalties: but, an artist can make good money by touring and putting on shows. This is particularly troublesome in the rap industry because another set of power brokers; venue owners and people who control booking are all involved when an artist decides to tour. They have almost carte blanche to decide who plays and who does not (Rose 134). Often they will simply not book a rap act because of stigma surrounding rap concerts (Ridenhour 108–11). If the venue does decide to allow a rap group to play, they are often faced with exorbitant fees and extremely high insurance costs. "For example, Three Rivers Stadium in Pittsburgh, Pennsylvania, tripled its normal $20,000 permit fee for the Grateful Dead. The insurance companies who still insure rap concerts have raised their minimum coverage from about $500,000 to between $4 and $5 million worth of coverage per show" (Rose 133). The insurance companies are a major hurdle when touring because it is possible that an artist will book a show, the venue will get away with large fees, but the artist could not find an insurer and effectively ends up unable to do that show (Ridenhour 114; Rose 131, 133). Chuck D of Public Enemy says, "A heavy-metal band could play at a venue and the insurance would be like twenty-five to thirty cents a ticket ... on our 1990 Def Jam tour our insurance was damn near two dollars per person" (Ridenhour 114). Big-name artists like Jay-Z might not have as much trouble booking a show because of how much money he will generate but, again, he is the exception that proves the rule.

The Exception: Shawn Carter, CEO

In 2005, Shawn Carter, a.k.a. Jay-Z, took over as CEO of Def Jam Records, defying all odds of an artist becoming a CEO. In the *Rolling Stone* article "The Book of Jay," Touré analyzes the rarity of Carter's CEO role, as well as the rapper/CEO relationships. Carter's humble beginnings allow him to be an even more effective CEO due to his rapper credibility: "Having Jay says that the legacy continues. If you're a 16-year-old rapper in Brooklyn or Atlanta or Houston, and you know that Jay-Z carries on the legacy of hip hop, then Def Jam becomes your preferred destination," L. A. Reid states in Touré's *Rolling Stone* article. Touré also points out that "many people think Jay's presence at Def Jam is more important for Def Jam than for Jay," which becomes apparent because Jay-Z "won a five-label bidding war and signed the Roots to Def Jam." According to Ahmir (lead drummer for The Roots), "If the bidding war was based on money, Sony won ... 'but it wasn't about money. Jay's offer was less than Sony's but I really needed someone that answers phone calls.'" Rhoden interviews Robert Johnson in *Forty Million Dollar Slave* and Johnson explicitly acknowledges wanting to use his external affiliations (that of race in his case; vocation and race in Jay-Z's) to get more out of his property, his players. "I'm a black player playing for a black man. I can't let him down.... My hope is that it translates into a little bit more hustle, a little bit more aggressiveness, a little bit more behavior modification" (qtd. in Rhoden 252). In an effort to counter the lopsided power relationships, Rhoden describes a call for black ownership, by the black community. Rhoden then uses Johnson to demonstrate that black ownership does not change the power relationships of owner exploiting athlete. There have been similar calls for change in ownership in the music industry and while Jay-Z was not the owner, he held major decision-making power (Kelley 233). As CEO, Jay-Z was able to sign sought after rap groups with less money and no change in the power relationships. Jay-Z had the power to change the power relationship but he did not; therefore, his role as CEO was more important, or financially rewarding, than the other values he also maintains. At the end of the day the artist is still at the mercy of the record company.

Tricia Rose, in *Black Noise*, looks at how the industry deals with smaller labels: she observes, "Instead of competing with smaller, more street-savvy labels for new rap acts, the major labels developed a new strategy: buy the independent labels, allow them to function autonomously, and provide them with production resources and access to major retail distribution." The labels that manage to keep a larger degree of autonomy, the ones not bought up, still have to set up a distribution deal through one of the major companies, limiting their independence (Kelley 8). Kevin Powell, in a *Newsweek* article, "My Culture at the Crossroads," reinforces the idea of corporate dictation: "In other words, Jay-Z's 'Big Pimpin'' would not bother me so much if Dead Prez's 'Mind Sex' received as much notice." "Big Pimpin'" is a funky song that glorifies pimping whereas "Mind Sex" is a stereotype-busting song about male/female relationships. The stereotyped rapper deals with male/female relationships in their songs only with gratuitous sex, while "Mind Sex" is about the male/female conversation. Powell's statement is particularly poignant because the industry financially rewards and promotes artists who do not challenge status quo (in unsafe ways), like Jay-Z, more so than a group like Dead Prez, which explicitly operates outside of the conveyor belt and speaks specifically about dismantling the current system. Jay-Z's Horatio Alger tales leave him in a better financial situation than Dead Prez's revolutionary ballads, but in addition to the finance, his conveyor-belt ride affords him better general recognition and more fame.

Conclusion

The lure of fame and big money caused Jay-Z to "dumb down" his lyrics for his audience. The industry has it set up that lyrical skills do not sell and that challenging the industry often leads to a pay cut or no record deal. Even with the artists being the sole attraction, music industry expert Carlton Ridenhour (Chuck D) argues that "record company executives' lawyers and accountants in the business go through long tenures and million-dollar bank accounts while the artists, because of a lack of schooling and a lack of concern for the art form, end up broke and penniless most of the time, misdirected, and dependent upon foundations for their existence" (105). While many artists of other genres use touring as a means to supplement their royalties, rappers have to deal with fewer tours and less money due to the perception of rap being dangerous. Jay-Z demonstrated he was an excellent CEO but because the industry is such a well-run machine, he ended up doing little to shake up the status quo. Steve Stoute, the head of *Translation Consultation and Brand Imaging*, stated in Touré's article, "On 'What More Can I Say,' there's a line ... that put Reebok's NFL jersey business back to fans, removed it from fashion. He [Jay-Z] can move the cultural needle because his listeners believe his honesty." With this type of influence in popular culture, possibly the strongest influence, Jay-Z also has the highest potential to be an agent of change.

In order for Jay-Z or hip hop to make systematic change, to truly "give back," he, and rappers in general, need to focus more on making challenging music along the lines of his "Minority Report," which speaks about the injustices of Hurricane Katrina. In Tricia Rose's *Journal of Negro Education* article, "'Fear of a Black Planet': Rap Music and Black Cultural Politics in the 1990s," and Jeff Chang's *Can't Stop Won't Stop,* both make the case that the "golden" era of hip hop (in the late 1980s to early to mid–1990s) contained much more socially critical and politically conscious music than that of today. During this time, modes of resistance to societal pressures were more pronounced. (I am not arguing here that rap is the reason for this but it is worth exploring.) If trend-setters like Jay-Z made music that contained more socially critical and politically conscious messages, it could send a ripple effect through the music industry and, more importantly, through society. If artists realize how much power they have, they could collectively change their contracts. If artists are able to reap most of the money from their art, they will transform society in the process because they could focus more on making transformative music rather than worrying about corporate interests. Articles like Rachel E. Sullivan's "Rap and Race: It's Got a Nice Beat, but What about the Message?" published in *Journal of Black Studies*, demonstrate how rap's listeners are affected by the message in the song. The article also provides evidence that songs can serve as an act of empowerment and resistance due to their content; so rather than be cogs in the industry, albeit big cogs, rappers should continue to make music that empowers people. "Hip hop's true significance for the community activists and leaders I have worked with resides in its ability to encourage young people to believe that they have the power to make a difference" (Watkins 255). In *The Hip Hop Generation* Bakari Kitwana documents scores of situations when hip hop has used its remarkable talent for change (206, 207, 208, 209).[4] Potent lyrics laced with criticism of society would be more effective to make system-wide change than uncritical lyrics or black (or rapper) ownership. With lyrical skills like Jay-Z's rappers have such potential to challenge the status quo and empower people to resist injustice. Songs such as "Minority Report" or "Mind Sex" shatter stereotypes about rappers and empower people to continue fighting for justice. Songs that make heads nod yet retain socially empowering lyrics is what I call a win, win.

For Further Consideration

BOOKS AND ARTICLES

Coates, Ta-nehisi. *A Beautiful Struggle: A Father, Two Sons, and an Unlikely Journey to Manhood.* New York: Spiegel and Grau, 2009.
McWhorter, John. *All About the Beat: Why Hip-Hop Can't Save Black America.* New York: Gotham, 2008.
"Who Gets Paid," *Ebony Magazine,* July 2007, p. 84.

QUESTIONS

1. In Byron Hurt's award winning documentary, *Beyond Beats and Rhymes,* he initiates a conversation with aspiring rappers who are interesting in obtaining a record deal. In short they have a conversation about their proclivity toward *gangsta* rap vs. conscious rap. With a collective sigh, the young aspirants reply that record companies aren't interested in "that" (conscious rap). In fact, one young man states, that "if you go to a label with self destruction you will self-destruct." Was this encounter an isolated incident, or are most aspiring rap artists conscious about the need to dumb down their lyrical sophistication? Can you think of examples from other rappers who engage in this process other than Jay-Z?

2. The author suggests that "trendsetters like Jay-Z made music that contained more socially critical and politically conscious messages, it could send a ripple effect through the music industry and, more importantly, through society." First, do you agree with the implicit assumption that Jay-Z and other "trendsetters" lyrics are devoid of political content? Also, should why should we continue to ask musical artists to do the job of civic, social, and political leaders?

Notes

1. For lyrics, please see CD sheets or the numerous websites available online.
2. For lyrics, please see CD sheets or the numerous websites available online.
3. The term "hustler" refers to someone who sells things without paying taxes, and a "booster" is someone who uses other businesses' goods as their source of profits
4. Kitwana discusses the Haitian refugee crisis, Mumia Abu-Jamal, the Million Man March, East Coast/West Coast conflict settling, and many social programs and foundations.

Works Cited

Chang, J. *Can't Stop Won't Stop: A History of the Hip-Hop Generation.* New York: Picador, 2005.
George, N. *Hip Hop America.* 2d ed. New York: Penguin, 1998.
Green, J., ed. *Rap and Hip Hop: Examining Pop Culture.* Farmington Hills, MI: Greenhaven, 2003.
Jah, Y., and C. Ridenhour (Chuck D). *Fight the Power.* New York: Bantam Doubleday Dell, 1997.

Kelley, N., ed. *R&B Rhythm and Business: The Political Economy of Black Music.* New York: Akashic, 2002.

Kitwana, B. *The Hip Hop Generation: Young Blacks and the Crisis in African-American Culture.* New York: Basic Civitas, 2002.

Light, A., ed. *The Vibe History of Hip Hop.* New York: Three Rivers, 1999.

McWhorter, J. *All about the Beat: Why Hip-Hop Can't Save Black America.* New York: Penguin, 2008.

Mitchell, T., eds. *Global Noise: Rap and Hip-Hop Outside the USA.* Middletown, CT: Wesleyan University Press, 2001.

Powell, K. *Who's Gonna Take The Weight? Manhood, Race, and Power in America.* New York: Three Rivers, 2003.

Ramsey, G.P. *Race Music: Black Cultures from Bebop to Hip-Hop.* Berkeley, CA: University of California Press, 2003.

Rhoden, W.C. *Forty Million Dollar Slaves: The Rise, Fall, and Redemption of the Black Athlete.* New York: Crown, 2006.

Rose, T. *Black Noise: Rap Music and Black Culture in Contemporary America.* Middletown, CT: Wesleyan University Press, 1994.

Tanz, J. *Other People's Property: A Shadow History of Hip-Hop in White America.* New York: Bloomsbury, 2007.

VIBE Street Lit. *The Vibe Q: Raw and Uncut.* New York: Kensington, 2007.

Watkins, S.C. *Hip Hop Matters: Politics, Pop Culture, and the Struggle for the Soul of a Movement.* Boston, MA: Beacon, 2005.

Weissman, D. *The Music Business: Career Opportunities and Self-Defense.* New York: Three Rivers, 2003.

9

Hip Hop's Prospects for Womanist Masculinity

Melina Abdullah

The approach that hip hop artists take with regard to gender is not necessarily static. While several artists are fairly consistent in their sexism, others have clearly grappled with questions of gender and have opened themselves up to the evolutionary process. Several factors combine to encourage stagnation and compliance with a predominant view that treats women as objects and commodities, or opens them up to being more thoughtful in their treatment and, as a result, permits their evolution and growth. These factors include broader societal trends, the messages pushed by hip hop gatekeepers, how the artist views hip hop "knowledge," the artist's own personal experiences, and the relative power of the artists themselves. For Jay-Z—who has been widely criticized for presenting some of the more degrading images and messages about women in tracks like "Money, Cash, Hoes" (1999), "I Just Wanna Love U" (2000), and "Girls, Girls, Girls" (2001)—there has been the general misperception that his treatment of women has been stagnant. However, upon closer examination of three key measures—song lyrics, music videos and public image—a process of evolution, where women become more (though not completely) humanized, is revealed.

Hip Hop, Black Masculinity and Sexism

In its original form, hip hop emerged as an African American political expression that, while male-dominated, leaned more towards womanism in its open discussion and inclusion of women than the classic sexist tendency to present women as voiceless objects with no agency of their own (Abdullah). In fact, women and the womanist principle of collective ownership were central in the very founding of hip hop.[1] The communal nature of hip hop is widely credited to the sister of one of hip hop's "founding fathers"—Kool Herc (born Clive Campbell). It was Herc's sister who encouraged him to DJ in open spaces like the recreation room of their housing development in the Bronx (Chang 2005, 67). In its early years, hip hop was a conversation that was open enough to offer space for women's voices. Most illustrative of this was the Roxanne battles beginning with UTFO's 1984 release of "Roxanne, Roxanne" which quickly brought one of the most widely heralded answer tracks from — then 14-year-old Roxanne Shante — and ignited what is perhaps the most extensively recorded hip hop conversation in history, which happened to center around gendered relationships and sexuality, involving, not only UTFO and Roxanne Shante, but the Real Roxanne, Sparky D, and a host of others.

Despite this openness, hip hop has always been a black male-centered art form (Perry 2005, 118) and my analysis focuses primarily on black male roles in hip hop sexism. For black men who stand at the juncture of oppression based on race (and, often, class) and sex-based privilege, the treatment of women — especially black women — is complicated. We must recognize that hip hop does not exist in a vacuum and that, while often targeted by feminist organizers, sexist messages and images in hip hop are largely part of a broader societal treatment of women. Sexism[2] places women as the oppressed and men as the oppressor and pervades society, standing as the default treatment of women in all areas of life, from personal (i.e., expectations during marriage), to the formal political sphere (i.e., the neglect of reproductive health in healthcare policies), to representations in visual media (i.e., constant presentations from the perspective of the male gaze). For black women, sexism in broader society has taken hold in particular ways which shape her according to three classic stereotypes: the mammy, the jezebel, and the sapphire (Bogle 2001, West 1995, Guerrero 1993). Thus, sexism and misogyny, both broadly applied and in its specific application to black women, both predate and predominate a world that is much larger than hip hop. Moreover, larger societal sexism interacts with specific hip hop forms, making the source of sexism experienced by black women particularly difficult to identify as it often derives from two separate, but interlocking sources: white patriarchal society and black men (hooks 1996). Both forms impact the treatment of women in hip hop, and one might contend that it is the former that bears primary responsibility in that it holds the real power in the industry. However, the role of black men — especially black male artists—cannot be completely neglected. Even when used as tools to forward a white patriarchal agenda, we must question the extent to which black men are compliant with this effort and reap some residual benefits.

Imani Perry offers one of the most thorough and thoughtful analyses of black men's treatment of black women through hip hop to date. Perry contends that "Black male hip hop artists do not simply assert power over women's bodies in a kind of effort to create imaginative patriarchy; they also use [B]lack women as a kind of commodity expression of wealth and sexual power in the face of racialized economic powerlessness" (Perry 127). In other words, black male artists are not simply buying into white conceptions of sexist domination, but engage in their own form of patriarchy as a very warped form of resistance to their own oppression.

Corporate Control and Hip Hop Sexism

The predominance of the unilateral presentation of women as objects is concomitant with the corporate takeover of hip hop. As the collective ownership of hip hop gave way to a small business model in the early 1980s, much of the political messaging and open dialogue remained intact, as evidenced by the pivotal role played by Sylvia Robinson (co-owner of Sugar Hill Records and co-producer of tracks like "The Message"). This period also included women in hip hop crews, like Sha' Rock in the Funky Four Plus One and Roxanne Shante in the Juice Crew. By the mid–1980s, however, once the profitability and longevity of hip hop music had become somewhat apparent, corporate interests began to hone in on hip hop music as a "capitalist tool" (George 154). As Nelson George argues, rap was viewed, not only as a potentially profitable commodity, but also as a marketing tool through which other products could be sold. By the mid–1980s, artists like Kurtis Blow, Run–DMC, and The Fat Boys drew from their popularity as hip hop artists to peddle everything from soft drinks, to tennis shoes, to watches. I contend that a third and more long-term use for hip hop as a capitalist tool was also identified by corporate interests — the conditioning of the largely working-class, urban, black hip hop community. Central to this process was the entrenchment of a consumerist mentality and an updated take on the "classic" black stereotypes that cast women as mammies, sapphires, and jezebels and men as toms, coons, and bucks. Under corporate controlled hip hop, black women as jezebels took center stage under the perceived control of black men as bucks.

The subjugation of women in hip hop has been encouraged by corporate gatekeepers who have come to lock out women's voices that had earlier been central to gendered dialogues. These same corporate interests work to amplify the most oppressive of male-centered messages. This is not to say that such a shift occurred in one fell swoop. In fact, the ten year period from the mid–1980s to the mid–1990s, known as hip hop's "golden age," was marked by tremendous breadth in hip hop messaging, including radical political messages, along with gendered perspectives led by a critical mass of women artists. This period was also marked by an increasing corporate interest in rap music (Cobb 47). Corporations that began to buy out rap music did not immediately push out all women artists and shut down conscious rap ... it was a process. By the close of the golden age, both goals had been all but achieved, but how did corporations and capitalism more broadly benefit from this process? It is clear that corporations benefit from a depoliticized urban populace; radical messages like the ones advanced by Public Enemy, KRS-ONE, and Sista Souljah could push hip hop from political expression to be the spark for a political movement — a movement that could potentially destabilize the capitalist structure. But why would corporations have an interest in advancing a sexist frame? How might they reap a profit from the oppression of women — especially black women?

Without delving into a full discussion of capitalism and its relationship to sexism, it can be simply stated that sexism, like racism and other oppressive forces, has been used as a tool of the capitalist class to divide the working class and make a proletarian uprising less likely (Eisenstein). Rather than understanding class position, factions of the working class are pitted against one another through socially constructed and amplified differences like gender. Oppressive conditions are blamed on those who share working class positionality rather than on a structure that keeps the entire class down. In hip hop, this means that black men are cast as the oppressors of black women — and while they do hold some relative power over women, they serve largely as a buffer for white patriarchal capitalist interests, which reap the vast majority of the profit from black women's commodification. This is most apparent in the pimp/whore relationship that pervades corporate controlled hip hop and was a central theme in Jay-Z's early work.

Big Pimpin': Corporations, Artists and the Re-Creation of the Whore in Hip Hop

Under the pimp/whore structure, black men adopt an updated buck persona — retooled as the pimp — with a voracious sexual appetite, becoming the quintessential "bad man," (Judy 108–109). As the pimp, his sexual insatiability is topped only by his quest for profit, which comes from the subjugation and oppression of women as whores (Sharpley-Whiting 2008). The whore persona in hip hop, again, is a retake on the classic stereotype of black women as jezebels and is the most common way in which women are presented in corporate-controlled hip hop. Variations of this persona include the video vixen, the gold digger, the stripper, the party-girl, and the prostitute. Nowhere is this pimp/whore identity presented more clearly than in Jay-Z's 2000 hit "Big Pimpin'" (a collaboration with Pimp C and Bun B). In this highly commercial song, Jay Z romanticizes or bespeaks a life of disregard for women. The use of their bodies, as objects to love and leave after sexual and, potentially physically abusing, while self-identifying as cold hearted and emotionless, is consistent in the pimp/whore paradigm.

The brutality of the lyrics is topped only by the presentation of women in the accompanying video. Hundreds of bikini clad women fill a yacht and dance, gyrate, and frolic for the pleasure of male onlookers who pay them occasional notice only to rub up against them — usually more than one at a time — pour champagne on them, and point to them as objects. The yacht shots are interspersed with similar interactions at a beach, a carnival, and a party. Women greatly outnumber the men and vary in ethnicity — with most either black, Latina, or racially ambiguous. While the "clean" version of the track is played along with the video, the hook belies the true mission of a pimp — to make money through the sale of women as sexual commodities. Thus, while Jay-Z claims to be "big pimpin'" he actually assumes a position as a consumer (or "john") rather than owner (or pimp) of the commodified woman (the whore). Such a theme continues in other tracks, including "I Just Wanna Love You" (with Pharell), in which Jay-Z initially states that he refuses to spend money on women, but then admits he is willing to succumb if she can prove her sexual prowess. Even more telling than the verse is the hook's use of the original Rick James riff positions Jay-Z as asking women for sex and is even willing to pay for it if the sex is "worth" the price. Just "Give it To Me [Baby]" as Jay Z retells the Rick James line. Such an approach is consistent with john rather than pimp behavior, but continues to move forward the insatiable black male buck persona and firmly entrenches women as objects with a singular value in that they provide sexual pleasure to men.

Whether Jay-Z is in fact a pimp or a john is less important, however, than how either persona casts women. Under both scenarios, women occupy positions as whores. While the "Give it to Me" video features Lil' Kim in a fairly prominent role as a sort of Jay-Z sidekick, she appears to condone and, in a sense, legitimize Jay-Z's behavior and treatment of the bevy of women who fill his mansion and gyrate around for the pleasure of the male party attendees who have their way with these women on the dance floor, in the bedrooms, and in closets. Such images are a part of the mass commodification of women that subtly points to as being endemic in music videos; it presents women as nymphomaniacs who are a collection of body parts that enjoy nothing more than being used for the pleasure of men.

So how do such depictions connect with corporate profitability? Commodification means the molding of an object (or an objectified person) into a product from which profit can be derived. By making women whores, they are no longer human beings, but commodified objects ... as such, they are not simply labor, but things that are bought and sold. They become superexploitable entities from which profit has no limit. The depiction of women as whores in music videos and song lyrics both contributes to sexist conditioning and brings actual corporate profit, as it is these images that are purchased for mass consumption. The presentation of such images encourages a process of internalized sexism among women where women begin to view themselves as objects whose value is based on the level to which their commodification can rise. Contemporary women artists like Trina (2000) and Lil' Kim (2003) serve as key examples in hip hop in their quests to be the "Baddest Bitch" and "Queen Bee," based on how fly they are and how much a man is willing to pay for them as products. Such identities make relationships between men and women trans-actional, with women becoming participants in their own oppression and false power being derived from commanding the highest price for her own sale. Men — as either the john or the pimp — become the oppressor, acknowledging women only as commodities. While some profit is derived by artists who par-ticipate in the commodification process by pimping women as video vixens and whores in their lyrical messages, the real pimps (those who derive the bulk of the profit) are the corporations who package and sell not only the women as whores, but male artists who think that they are pimps as well.

The corporate structure that controls the music industry, including rap, is comprised of three industries: the recording industry, the music video indus-try, and the radio industry (including the burgeoning area of internet radio). What is notable is how few corporations dominate each of these industries. While urban radio was once locally owned and represented the diverse locales of their particular markets, this has become less the case over the last decade as major media conglomerates have gobbled up smaller, locally owned stations (Chuck D). In addition to the rapid rise of satellite radio (owned almost exclu-sively by Sirius/XM), traditional radio, which remains the primary way in which people listen to music, has been largely bought out by a few major corporations. Clear Channel, Radio One, and Emmis Broadcasting dominate the urban mar-kets. The major music video stations— BET, VH-1, and MTV — are owned by a single corporation: Viacom. Even the recording industry, which at first glance appears to be much more open in its ownership base with almost every artist having his or her own "label," is actually owned and run by the "big four"— Sony Music Entertainment, Universal Music Group, EMI, and Warner Music Group.

Artists like Jay-Z who have typically aligned themselves more with owners than workers have made significant inroads into these corporate structures. To many in the hip hop community, Jay-Z's former position as CEO of Def Jam and role as co-founder/co-owner of Roc-A-Fella Records attests to his prowess in the boardroom and affirms Jay-Z's place as a "pimp" rather than a "whore" in the recording industry. What is less understood, however, is that neither Def Jam nor Roc-A-Fella are stand-alone corporations; both are subsidiaries of Uni-versal Music Group. Nevertheless, as CEO, Jay-Z has the responsibility of ensur-ing that the strategic vision of the company is being implemented by the production of the music and images within the brand. As such, he holds much more power in the industry than do most artists, but not as much as those who stand at the very top of the industry. His relative power, however, has afforded Jay-Z the opportunity to both nurture new artists and command creative control over his own work. Such freedoms place Jay-Z at a crossroads in terms of gender. Corporate structures stand as less of a barrier to his evolutionary process—opening up the way for him to explore his own beliefs and take a stance that is not predicated on corporate dictates. How he navigates this space is an essential piece in understanding his evolutionary process.

During the three-year period from 2004 to 2007 that Jay-Z served as president of Def Jam, we witnessed a tremendous shift in Jay-Z's own work as well as his public image. Jay-Z released a single album during this span —*Kingdom Come* (2006)—which marked somewhat of a departure from previous releases in terms of both its politicism and its treatment of women. While Jay-Z did not completely abandon his affinity for objectified, commodified women, his pimp persona or his affinity for high-end material possessions (as illustrated in tracks like "Show Me What You Got" and "Anything"), tracks like "Lost One" and "Beach Chair" are both self-reflective and reveal a much more humanized treatment of women. "Lost One" represents one of the first tracks where Jay-Z presents himself as vulnerable to a woman and capable of being hurt by her. If taken at face value, he agonizes over relinquishing a narcissistic need to be the center of this particular woman's universe and empathizes with her need to work as a means of self-development and expression.

Many have attributed this verse to Jay-Z's relationship with Beyonce, which brings in an added element of personal experience in the shaping of his treatment of women. While all artists, undoubtedly, have a life outside of their entertainer personas, those within corporate controlled media are often confined by the dictates of the corporations who push particular messaging, with the freedom to be vulnerable often reserved for independent artists. Jay-Z's rise to power offers an alternative model where relative power in the corporate structure allows him — as an artist — to more fully explore and present his own range of experiences in his music.[3]

In some ways, Jay-Z presents an oppositional model to the prospects for creative freedom in hip hop. It has been widely acknowledged that underground and independent artists like dead prez, The Coup, and Immortal Technique have much more freedom to step out with radical, politicized messages, confront corporate structures and critically analyze gender in ways that corporate-owned artists have been both unwilling and unable to do (in part from the lack of record company independence). However, the prospect that Jay-Z presents is one where he has risen to such power within the corporate structure that some (though not all) of that same freedom has been realized. This is not to say that there is room at the top of these corporate enterprises for any critical mass of artists or that this is the manner in which a more gender-conscious hip hop is most likely to be ushered in. I contend that corporate-owned hip hop will always drown out the more conscious and radical voices if they stand a real chance of mobilizing people and that the real potential in hip hop as a political movement lies in the underground. However, what the Jay-Z model presents us with is the role that relatively powerful artists can play in beginning to shift things. While these gatekeepers who control record companies, radio stations, and video music stations bear primary responsibility for the commodification of women, the role of more powerful artists must also be challenged — especially of those artists who share partial ownership of the industry.

Womanist Pushback

Despite the corporate ownership of the vast majority of the rap music that we are exposed to, hip hop remains a cultural and political form that a working class black collective, comprised of both men and women, gave rise to and of which we still claim ownership. For an entire generation of women, hip hop is something that we once loved and thought loved us back. The betrayal that took hold in the mid–1990s, when sexism and misogyny began to pervade hip hop, still pains us. For some, we opted out — hip hop journalists regularly discuss the mass exodus of women, both as artists and members of the hip hop community, that occurred in the mid to late 1990s (Creekmur). Other women either remained a part of the culture and functioned within its limited parameters or returned after our initial exit to reclaim what we see as rightfully ours.

My own hip hop journey is illustrative of what many black women experienced. As a child of the hip hop generation, I grew up in Oakland, California, one of the most politically conscious cities in the nation. I was in elementary school when rap music found its way to the West Coast, and like every other little black girl or boy in my neighborhood, I spent entire weekends rockin my Biggie tape til it popped in the cassette deck (Notorious B.I.G. 1994), diligently writing down every (often wrong) word to tracks like "Rapper's Delight" and "The Message." By the seventh grade, we had formed the Ladies of Lace; we wrote our own lyrics over beats like "Egypt, Egypt" and battled on the school yard. In high school, we went to every rap show that came to town, from the "Fresh Fest" to the "Rock the Bells" tour, and while we sang along with our eyes closed to "I Need Love" and screamed incessantly at LL's shirtless body, we also pumped our fists at "Fight the Power" and understood hip hop to be more than entertainment, but a part of who we were and how we were to move forward in the world.

By the late 1980s and early 1990s, we had become so entrenched in hip hop culture that we understood NWA's "Fuck the Police" (1988) for its political meaning and fought with our parents who were appalled that we could possibly be fans of a group that so degraded women. We bought the notion that they "were not talking about us" when they referenced bitches and hoes. We relied on MC Lyte, Monie Love, YoYo, and Queen Latifah to push back against the degradation of women, but as their voices quieted by the mid–1990s, we could no longer claim a corporatized rap music as our own. Some were brave enough to stay and fight — artists like Eve and Remy Ma attempted to balance womanist messaging with the requisite sexuality, while Foxy Brown, Trina, and Lil' Kim claimed that by owning and selling their own sexuality they were actually empowered. I was one of those who retreated and found a refuge in me'shell ndege ocello, Erykah Badu, and Lauryn Hill. I eventually discovered underground hip hop and fell in love with The Coup and Paris; it was only in my moments of nostalgia that I would rock an old Too Short record and largely from a sense of loyalty that I remained a Tupac fan. I am not alone in my position; this sense of betrayal and search for a womanist space in hip hop has been widely discussed by women like Shani Jamila, Gwendolyn Pough, Joan Morgan, and Tricia Rose. The opening up of such discussions has served as a means by which we hope to reshape hip hop — to push back against the white patriarchal capitalist forces that have claimed control over what was once ours and to challenge the men who were once our partners in struggle to again stand alongside us, to fight for open spaces where our voices can be heard, and to be the womanist voices, themselves, when ours are drowned out.

For many of us who define ourselves as womanists—as women who recognize and experience the simultaneity of racist, sexist, and classist oppression and work to end it—hip hop sexism is deeply personal. The betrayal that we feel by black male artists who advance sexist and misogynistic images of black women represents the severing of a partnership that was once sacred. Jay-Z emerged in the mid–1990s just as so many of us were exiting hip hop. It is interesting to note that his early representations of women were not exclusively sexist. His first music video, "I Can't Get with That" (1994), featured crowd scenes that included women peppered in as a part of the hip hop community rather than as objects or commodities. However, as his career moved forward, he rode the wave of hip hop sexism which was made apparent in the DVD release *Streets Is Watching*, which featured gratuitous woman-on-woman sex for the pleasure of male onlookers, full frontal female nudity, pornographic scenes, and misogynistic lyrics (1998).

Even with such lyrical content and imagery, Jay-Z was not a departure from much of the messaging of his mainstream contemporaries. What set him apart was such content coupled with his public image. Ironically, it was through a dispute with another man, fellow hip hop artist Nas, that Jay-Z committed what may be his greatest offense to women. In their competition for the hip hop crown in the wake of the Notorious B.I.G.'s death, Jay-Z relied much less on his lyrical ability than personal assaults on Nas, which used the mother of Nas' child and Nas' daughter as canon fodder.

In an ongoing battle that found its way onto several albums, onto mixtapes, and onstage at concerts, and was broadcast on New York's Hot 97 from 2001 to 2005, Nas engaged by demonstrating his tremendous lyrical ability and creativity, targeting Jay-Z's looks, questioning his sexual orientation in a very humorous manner, and attacking his lyrical ability. Rather than engaging in the same, Jay-Z named the mother of Nas' child, Carmen Bryan, as promiscuous. Not only was she sexually wanton but Jay, in "Super Ugly," went so far as to explicitly describe occasions in which he had has sex with the mother of Nas' child.

Eventually, Jay-Z's mother pushed her son to issue a public apology to Nas and Carmen Bryan. While the use of women as collateral damage is not new (the same theme arose in the infamous feud between the Notorious B.I.G. and Tupac), Jay-Z's engagement in such a blatantly disrespectful, dehumanizing, and public manner sparked protest and pain among women in the hip hop community. However, womanist pushback is different than the feminist form. Where feminists, or those who engage in the fight to end sexism and sexist oppression (hooks 2000), target men as the oppressor, womanism, which focuses on interlocking sexism and racism, views the role of black men more complex. In the case of Jay-Z, at the very same moment that he was targeting a black woman, rehashing the jezebel stereotype in both his music and his public image, he was also fighting for public school funding for black children, challenging mandatory drug sentencing laws, and leading New York City protests. Thus, womanist pushback entailed developing a strategy whereby his sexism could be challenged at the same time that his work for racial and class-based empowerment was praised.

How, then, do womanists engage in pushing back against hip hop sexism? Because womanists, and I will contend the majority of black women, recognize their racial and gender identities simultaneously, the push back against black male sexism looks very different than that of mainstream feminists who prioritize gender identity. Rather than making black men an opponent that needs to be conquered, womanists often seek to engage black men in discussions around gender and sexist oppression. Such gendered conversations, which have occurred in hip hop forums (including the Feminism and Hip Hop conference at the University of Chicago), in writings (like the seminal volume *Home Girls Make Some Noise*), as a part of informal discussions, and even on wax (recorded by independent artists like Jean Grae, Cihualt-Ce, and Mystic), are particularly important to womanists who hold on to the hope that hip hop might again revert to a more open form. Jay-Z has been confronted with gendered questions in interviews, most recently with Oprah Winfrey, who challenged him on both gender and his use of the "n" word. While he made no firm commitment and stated his disagreement with regard to the "n" word, he demonstrated some willingness to engage. Such an openness to talks with non-elites is unclear. However, what can be documented is a willingness by Jay-Z to evolve.

Mr. Knowles? Jay-Z's Gender Evolution

When Jay-Z emerged as an artist in 1994 — prior to the release of his first album, *Reasonable Doubt*— his treatment of women was fairly consistent with that of most mainstream rappers. In the video for "I Can't Get with That" there was some inclusion of black women as members of the hip hop community as well as some objectification of women — where they were presented as things to be watched through the male gaze. Key here is that women were not exclusively objects; some were also human beings. By 2000 with the release of *The Dynasty*, Jay-Z had devolved to present women only as commodities, presenting them as whores in the pimp/whore relationship. He teamed up with Snoop Dogg (the quintessential pimp persona of rap music) and Roc-A-Fella artist Memphis Bleek to present the "pimp game" on the track "Get Your Mind Right Mami." The album maintains this theme in tracks with women presented exclusively as whores in tracks like "I Just Wanna Love You" and "Holla.'"

Beginning with the *Kingdom Come* album in 2006, Jay-Z does wrestle with a more complex treatment of women. Tracks from his most recent three albums maintain references to women as whores, including "Anything" and "Show Me What You Got" on *Kingdom Come*. There is "Party Life" on *American Gangster.* But with the release of *Blueprint 3* in 2009, Jay-Z all but abandons the whore references, instead referring to the exceptionalism of his "girl" in tracks like "Jockin'" and "Venus vs. Mars." Such an evolutionary process might be attributed, in large part, to his marriage to Beyonce and out of respect for that relationship. However, other factors no doubt played in, as Jay-Z had begun to move away from the exclusive presentation of women as whores in years prior. As early as 2002, he attempts to delineate between "Bitches and Sisters" with a track of that name on the *Blueprint 2* album. In the continuum of popular rappers "Too Short" and "Tupac," who also penned similar "explanatory narratives," such tracks point to the path of the exceptional possibility — where some women transcend the whore identity.

This notion of exceptionalism is, in itself, problematic in that it presents the norm for women as being the whore persona, while admitting the possibility that a few might "rise above" such an identity. It is essentially the "he is not talking about me" phenomenon — the notion that while most women are whores, there are a few that are not. Such a mindset remains oppressive in that it places the onus on women to prove their exceptional status. However, despite the deep problems with Jay-Z's presentation of female exceptionalism in recent years, it does represent a forward shift for him and signals his willingness to evolve.

It seems that his current focus is on this exceptional woman, in the form of Beyonce as his ideal. While this does not place him in the sphere of a black man who embraces womanist principles, it does point to his willingness to accept women as human beings and openness to the evolutionary process in gendered terms. Such an evolution is also apparent in his more recent music videos which replace the bulk of the bikini clad women scenes with more artistic presentations and thoughtful story lines. Similarly, in his public persona, he has been very public in his position against domestic violence in his treatment of artist Rihanna following the very public domestic violence case with Chris Brown. These presentations and acts work together to make the prospects for womanist masculinity a very real possibility. While Jay-Z has not arrived at this yet, he presents the possibility for movement in that direction.

In a sense, Jay-Z serves as a shining example of the conflict between oppression and privilege embodied in black manhood. He is simultaneously the oppressed and the oppressor: the worker and the owner, oppressed by race while privileged by gender. Womanist masculinity recognizes the privilege that all men reap as a result of their gender identity; however, it also challenges men to work vigorously to depose the sexist structure from which they benefit. For black men, challenging this structure can be linked to struggles for racial equality. As discussed, black men stand at the intersection of oppression and privilege — oppressed by a black racial identity and a largely working class position, but privileged by their standing as men in a sexist society. Even as there is some privilege that comes with manhood, each identity interacts and influences the other. As such, black masculinity and male identity is not the same as that of white men.[4] Such a position also opens up space for black men to more fully understand oppression than white men. It is what allowed black men, historically, to serve as true partners to black women and accept her leadership.[5] The unique position of black men and the history of black male/female relationships makes the prospects of womanist masculinity more likely for black men than for men of, perhaps, any other racial group. When applied to the context of hip hop, with its early communal nature, this becomes even more of a possibility. Womanist masculinity recognizes that men can never embody a woman's gendered identity. However, he can adopt a framework that is conscious of how racist, sexist, classist, and all other oppressions converge, and he can work diligently towards their elimination. Womanist masculinity challenges men to essentially give up the privilege that comes with manhood in order to work to end all forms of oppression — including sexism. It is my assertion that artists like Jay-Z might be moved in such a direction. However, this will not happen without pressure.

Womanists must continue to engage in the process of challenging Jay-Z, and other artists, to view women (not simply those deemed exceptional) as full, complete, and equal human beings and black women, particularly, as partners in the struggle for universal freedom. Additionally, we must continue our struggles against oppression in society more broadly, recognizing that much of the sexism that pervades hip hop is reflective of the sexism that circulates in overall societal power relations. In that world of hip hop, Jay-Z has demonstrated a willingness to evolve. His personal experiences have set him up to move forward in this process—especially his marriage to one of the most powerful women in the music industry. However, he must also be willing to challenge the corporations that attempt to woo him into believing that their interests are his interests. What has become clear in womanist attempts to challenge hip hop to return to the openness and collective ownership from which it hails is that black women cannot win the battle alone. Our partnership with black men must also be restored; there is some momentum building among underground and conscious artists. However, a huge swing would take place were a powerful mainstream artist like Jay-Z to embrace womanist masculinity—it is this swing that is necessary for mainstream hip hop to undergo an evolutionary process.

For Further Consideration

BOOKS

Chase-Riboud, Barbara. *Hottentot Venus.* New York: Doubleday, 2003.
hooks, bell. *Ain't I a Woman.* Boston: South End, 1981.
Pough, Gwendolyn, ed. *Home Girls Make Some Noise! Hip-Hop Feminism Anthology.* Mira Loma, CA: Parker, 2007.
[B] Television and Film
Brooks, Philip. *The Life and Times of Sara Baartman.* Icarus Films.
Hurt, Byron. *Hip Hop Beyond Beats and Rhymes.* Northampton, MA : Media Education Foundation, 2007.
Jeff Johnson & M.C. Lyte: Hip Hop vs. America II. Black Entertainment Television.
Kitwana, Bakari. *Does Hip Hop Hate Women?* Rapsessions. West Lafayette, IN: C-SPAN Archives, 2008.

QUESTIONS

1. How do you assess the "sex as power" element found in hip hop? What and how do men facilitate and promote such behavior? To what extent has America fostered this blatant disregard for black bodies (especially women)?

2. The author admits that, though Jay-Z's utilization of sexist language and imagery has diminished, he is still subject to a critical interpretation. In what ways does the author track his change? Do you agree with the assessment? And to what do you attribute this continuum?

3. Female rappers like Lil Kim, Khia, Trina, Missy, Diamond and Shawnna all speak a language of power through sexuality that seek to shatter the phallocentrism that has been dominant within the culture. How would you respond to the claim that these

women either, (a) self-loathe and create a sexualized disconnect between their bodies as subject and their bodies as object; or (b) they attempt to strip a historically superior position of power claimed by men and reappropriate language, attitudes, and actions to avoid being "used" by men? See Michael Eric Dyson's term "misogynistic ventriloquist." Provide your argument for or against these positions.

Notes

1. The principle of collective ownership is tied to group-centered leadership in womanist praxis— meaning that no single individual owns a movement or stands as its solitary leader. Rather, sustainable movements require collective investment, ownership, and derived benefit. (See Abdullah and Freer.)

2. When referencing sexism, I am defining the term as oppression based on sex, which is experienced by women and not men. Oppression extends beyond the realm of prejudice, which can be defined as the assignment of stereotypical characteristics based on identity. It is also more than simple discrimination, which implies action based on prejudices. Both prejudice and discrimination can be experienced by both sexes. Oppression is the ongoing, constant, and continuous subjugation of a less powerful group by one that is more powerful. Thus, sexism is imposed on women (as the oppressed) by men (as the oppressor).

3. Jay-Z's career trajectory begins with his position as an artist, or worker, one who sells his labor to corporations, earning a small percentage of the profit made from his labor (his music). In his transition from the stage to the boardroom, he takes on a managerial role where he reaps greater profit from his own labor, as well as profiting from the labor of other workers (artists), still amassing the bulk of the profit for the ownership class. While Jay-Z himself is not a full-fledged member of the ownership class, it is with this class that he is most fully aligned and from this class that he derives his power. In a sense, Jay-Z serves as a buffer between the ownership class and the worker and is rewarded both in terms of capital and prestige.

4. For example, it is at the convergence of these identities that the stereotype of the buck emerges. It is also in this space that black men are targeted by and disproportionately affected by the criminal justice system.

5. See, for example, slave narratives that cite the leadership of Harriet Tubman (Harrison, et al.), writings on Ida B. Wells (Giddings), and writings on the willingness of SNCC members to be mentored by Ella Baker (Grant).

Works Cited

Abdullah, Melina. "Hip Hop as Political Expression: Potentialities for the Power of Voice in Black Urban America." In *The Black Urban Community: From Dusk Till Dawn*. Ed. Gayle T. Tate and Lewis A. Randolph. New York: Palgrave, 2006.

_____ and Regina Freer. "Towards a Womanist Leadership Model." In *Racial and Ethnic Politics in California*. Vol. 3. Ed. Bruce E. Bass and Sandra Cain. Berkeley: University of California Press, 2008.

Bogle, Donald. *Toms, Coons, Mulattoes, Mammies, and Bucks: An Interpretive History of Blacks in American Films*. New York: Continuum, 2001.

Chang, Jeff. *Can't Stop, Won't Stop: A History of the Hip Hop Generation*. New York: Picador, 2005.

Chuck D. *Fight the Power: Rap Race and Reality.* New York: Delta, 1998.

Cobb, Jelani. *To the Break of Dawn: A Freestyle on the Hip Hop Aesthetic.* New York: NYU Press, 2007.

Creekmur, Chuck "Jigsaw." "I Miss Women in Hip Hop." *www.allhiphop.com.* 2009. 29 January 2010. *http://allhiphop.com/stories/editorial/archive/2009/09/22/21948553.aspx.*

Eisenstein, Zillah R. *Capitalist Patriarchy and the Case for Socialist Feminism.* New York: Monthly Review, 1979.

George, Nelson. *Hip Hop America.* New York: Penguin, 2005.

Giddings, Paula. *Ida: A Sword Among Lions.* New York: Harper, 2009.

Grant, Joanne. *Ella Baker: Freedom Bound.* New York: Wiley, 1998.

Guerrero, Ed. *Framing Blackness: The African American Image in Film.* Philadelphia: Temple University Press, 1993.

Harrison, Beth, Donna Brown Guillaume, Jacqueline Glover, Juliet Weber, and Donna Garland, producers. *Unchained Memories: Readings from the Slave Narratives.* HBO Studios. DVD.

hooks, bell. *Feminism is for Everybody.* New York: South End, 2000.

_____. *Killing Rage: Ending Racism.* New York: Henry Holt, 1996.

Jay-Z. "Anything." *Kingdom Come.* Roc-A-Fella Records, 2006.

_____. "Big Pimpin'." *The Dynasty.* Roc-A-Fella Records, 2000.

_____. "Bitches and Sisters." *The Blueprint 2.* Roc-A-Fella Records, 2002.

_____. "Get Your Mind Right Mami." *The Dynasty.* Roc-A-Fella Records, 2000.

_____. "Girls, Girls, Girls." *The Blueprint.* Roc-A-Fella Records, 2001.

_____. "Holla." *The Dynasty.* Roc-A-Fella Records, 2000.

_____. "I Can't Get with That." Independent single, 1994.

_____. "I Just Wanna Love U." *The Dynasty.* Roc-A-Fella Records, 2000.

_____. "Jockin.'" *The Blueprint 3.* Roc-A-Fella Records, 2009.

_____. "Lost One." *Kingdom Come.* Roc-A-Fella Records, 2006.

_____. "Minority Report." *Kingdom Come.* Roc-A-Fella Records, 2006.

_____. "Money, Cash, Hoes." *The Hard Knock Life.* Roc-A-Fella Records, 1999.

_____. "Party Life." *American Gangster.* Roc-A-Fella Records, 2007.

_____. "Show Me What You Got." *Kingdom Come.* Roc-A-Fella Records, 2006.

_____. *Streets Is Watching,* DVD. 1998.

_____. "Venus vs. Mars." *The Blueprint 3.* Roc-A-Fella Records, 2009.

Jhally, Sut. *Dreamworlds 3: Desire, Sex and Power in Music Video.* Media Education Foundation, 2007. DVD.

Judy, R.A.T. "On the Question of Nigga Authenticity." In *That's the Joint! The Hip Hop Studies Reader,* ed. Mark Anthony Neal and Murray Forman. New York: Routledge, 2004.

Lil' Kim. "Can't Fuck with Queen Bee." *La Bella Mafia.* Atlantic Records, 2003.

Notorious B.I.G. "Juicy." *Ready to Die.* Bad Boy Records, 1994.

N.W.A. "Fuck the Police." *Straight Outta Compton.* Ruthless Records, 1988.

Perry, Imani. *Prophets of the Hood: Politics and Poetics in Hip Hop.* Durham, NC: Duke University Press, 2004.

Pough, Gwendolyn, ed. *Home Girls Make Some Noise! Hip-Hop Feminism Anthology.* Mira Loma, CA: Parker, 2007.

Sharpley-Whiting, Tracy. *Pimps Up, Ho's Down: Hip Hop's Hold on Young Black Women.* New York: NYU Press, 2008.

Trina. "Da Baddest Bitch." *Da Baddest Bitch.* Atlantic Records, 2000.

UTFO. "Roxanne, Roxanne." Select Records, 1984.

West, Carolyn. "Mammy, Sapphire and Jezebel: Historical Images of Black Women and Their Implications for Psychotherapy." *Psychotherapy* 32.3 (September 1995).

PART III

The Classroom Freestyles

10

Complicating
Shawn Carter

Race, the Code, and
the Politics of School

DAVID STOVALL

Beyond the iconography of Jay-Z as MC, recording industry mogul, and entrepreneur, the following chapter seeks to deconstruct his popular narrative and shift towards the nuanced and complex narratives of African-American males in K-12 schools. Seeking to excavate the dialectic between Shawn Corey Carter the person and Jay-Z the icon, this chapter seeks to accomplish several tasks. First, I seek to provide an analysis of the lure of street economies in relationship to schools that are sometimes deemed irrelevant by young people. Second, by taking into account Jay-Z's educational narrative as ninth grade dropout, I want to pay specific attention to his lyrics that run counter to popular narratives of African-American males as innately destined to become criminal social deviants. In this sense, these iterations operate as a "code," providing intelligently astute, but subtle, messages of resistance and critical consciousness to the listener. These particular lyrics are referenced as code because some people, upon first listen, may not recognize the underpinning of the verse. Because the claims of critical consciousness often appear amongst proclamations of material wealth, drug sales, and female objectification, the code becomes questionable at best. However, for those who have similar experiences to the instances relayed in Jay-Z's music, the message is less subtle, identifying the contradictions and struggles many African-American males endure in their maturation from young person to adulthood. For the purpose of this account, I'm making a similar argument concerning the plight of African-American males in urban schools—because the code is intricate and complex, some understand, but many still don't. For those of us who may not understand but are willing to engage, I pose that a portion of Jay-Z's music may provide useful insight. In the same light, the following comments are not meant to excuse destructive actions or derogatory commentary. The code, like our lives, is often wrought with contradictions that deserve attention. To constructively address the situation, we must take into account the ways in which the code is realized in the lives of these young men. Never to pathologize them, but to take into perspective their realities, while recognizing the interplay between context, choice, and relationships.

In K-12 schools, many African-American males embody this code in thought and action. However, lack of constructive outlets for expression and our unwillingness to engage them often lead to further misinterpretations of their actions. In many cases, often due to these misinterpretations, we find African-American males disproportionately overrepresented in special education classes, suspensions, expulsions, and in the criminal justice system. Instead of centering my discussion solely on the clever wordplay of Jay-Z's lyrics, I seek to place them into a framework, simultaneously interrogating and critiquing what Jay-Z the icon has become in the eyes of many while continuing to identify the critical underpinnings (read: code) of his lyrics. Again, the issue is to delve into the complexities, as they may provide us ways in which to constructively ask questions concerning our relationship to African-American males. As an educator, this becomes critically important to me, as my actions as an African-American male student were often misinterpreted, leading me down a path of being unnecessarily categorized in school as "troubled," "deviant," or "angry all the time."

Because Jay-Z is not grouped with "conscious," "backpacker," or "underground" hip hop,[1] the subtleties revealed in his lyrics are reminiscent of the "code" embedded in the African-American musical sub-genres of negro spirituals, blues, work songs, and bebop. Simultaneously, because popular hip hop music warrants critique in reference to its propensity for misogyny and excessive material consumption portrayed in much of its lyrics and celluloid imagery, this document seeks to include Jay-Z in the dialogical tension between critical consciousness and material fetish. Through the investigation of said complexities, the hope of the chapter is to provide further insights on the need to acknowledge, develop, and provide constructive critique to African-American males with the purpose of creating relevant and viable places of learning for them and their classmates.

Why Shawn Corey?

Minus the material wealth and excess, many of us grew up with a number of "Shawn Carters" in our neighborhood. Reflecting on my own life, there were those whom I grew up with who were intelligent beyond measure and didn't believe in the utility of a place they found demeaning and irrelevant (in this case, school). Never to ascertain that all urban public schools were dens of madness, but it's important to understand that many inner-city schools in the early to mid-eighties were caught in the throws of the decade's decline. In 1983, Secretary of Education William Bennett referred to Chicago schools as the "worst in the nation." New York City disinvested in its school system, citing state budget cuts as the primary culprit. For those inner-city students who weren't able to attend boarding or private schools like children from affluent or middle-class families, if school wasn't working for you, many times the options were the military, low-wage service sector work (e.g., fast food, tele-marketing, receptionist, loading dock, warehouse, etc.), maybe a trade school, or the dope game.[2] As deindustrialization entered its second phase, factory employment was scarce, and trade apprenticeships were hard to come by unless you had a family member who could get you into the guild. Coupled with the Reagan Administration's elimination of programs designed to provide low-income families with livable incomes, the eighties were tough times for many families in urban areas. Compounding these tragedies were the savings and loan crisis and the emergence of crack cocaine on the Eastern Seaboard, soon to spread to the Midwest, South, and the West Coast. Many urban public school districts were either being de-funded or drowning in a sea of budgetary scandal. Major cities like Chicago and New York were host to several teacher strikes, often in protest of ridiculously low pay and deplorable conditions. Worse off than the teachers were the students, who had to navigate the possibility of a teacher not caring about their wellbeing and tried to engage in learning when the building could be crumbling above their heads and beneath their feet (Chang, Rose, etc.).

Captivated by the lure of the drug game and disenchanted by the realities of school in Brooklyn, Shawn Carter decided to drop out of the ninth grade. Discussed in detail in later sections, this lure and dissatisfaction was not uncommon for many urban youth. The difference, however, lies in the outcome. Jay-Z should not be lauded for his ascension. Instead, it should be understood as a set of nuanced choices, which include the influence of social forces and the ability to survive the contradictions of personal decisions. Crucial to this discussion is the fact that most of Jay-Z's contemporaries never made it out of the drug game and did not achieve wealth and stardom. Nevertheless, there were those who felt they had a chance to bask in riches and the ability to leave their surroundings. Where few were practical in creating a plan to get out, there were some, who with careful planning, were able to achieve minor success, by converting monies gained in drug sales into legitimate businesses. Unfortunately, the majority of participants never attained such dreams, no matter how reachable they seemed in the beginning.

For many, the aforementioned comments may appear to be generalizations, but in order to make sense of the life of Shawn Carter pre–Jay-Z, context is critically important. Like the situations many young people find themselves in currently, context provides insight to the ideas and material realities that could serve as a major influence to a young person's decision-making process. If you're living in a world where critical analysis is scant and it's a struggle to get to the next day, there's great potential for your life-decisions to work to your detriment. Nevertheless, when folks like Jay-Z "make it out," it becomes a testament to human will and the ability to succeed despite the odds.

Missing from this equation, however, is the fact that many Shawn Carters do not "make it." Instead, most die young or are never able to get their lives in order due to elongated jail sentences and felony disenfranchisement.[3] In this sense, "success" is simply individual and rarely accounts for the devastation that has occurred in inner-city communities of color. Similar to the *Superfly* pimp protagonist Priest, the lines between self and community are blurred when steeped in "the game."[4] For those who achieve, the rewards are sweet. For those who fail, death comes physically or spiritually.

For these reasons, I think it becomes important to identify the complexities of the life of Shawn Corey Carter, his ascension to Jay-Z the icon, and the subsequent connection to African-American males in schools. At first glance, the lure of his "rags-to-riches" story makes good copy for popular media outlets. What I am interested in, however, is how Jay-Z's story and music speaks to the code enacted by young people of color, revealing their dreams, aspirations, and day-to-day struggles. In between the material accomplishments of Jay-Z lies a story we need to pay attention to. As many young people communicate in a similar code, their affirmations of self and cries for support often fall on deaf ears. At the same time, I agree that hip hop and young people deserve to be viewed with a critical and constructive lens. By paying attention to young people, we are able to offer the necessary constructive critique, with the purpose of building solidarity with them to positively impact our conditions. In order to do this, we must begin to unpack the code.

Interrogating the Code

Jay-Z's famous line from his 2000 record "H to the Izzo" is important in recognizing the code. An investigation into the complete song allows us to view the frustrations and subsequent contradictions that speak to the life of someone engaged in the record industry. Similar to songs created by Africans in bondage during the days of chattel slavery in the United States, the idea of the "happy slave" was a misnomer. Instead, slaves participated in subtle and overt acts of resistance that spoke to the frustration of their plight while affirming their longing for better days. Noted by Kinser, in Abrahams' anthropological study of corn shucking by slaves in the plantation South, "slaves ... did not content themselves with effusive thanks, but performed sly, satiric songs and skits about the lords' and ladies' behavior" (qtd. in Abrahams 87). The assumption, in both instances, is that the song creators are considered to be happy in their plight. As code, the message to the critical listener could determine anything from meeting in the slave quarters to plan a rebellion to warning a young person in the present day to beware of imminent danger. Sometimes overt, the code allowed for those who knew to deliver the message to those who needed to know. Because "H to the Izzo" was a top ten hit, this one-verse critique of the record industry serves as an example of the subtleties that often go unnoticed in the verses of a song deemed to be party music by the majority of its listeners. One would have to know the history of the Cold Crush Brothers in New York City in the late '70s to understand Jay-Z's frustration with the exploitation of the hip hop pioneers and the need for recognition of one of the foundational groups to the genesis of hip hop music and culture. Even without the Cold Crush reference, a listener can understand Jay-Z's irritation with the music industry.

Another song that enacts the code comes from his critically acclaimed album *Reasonable Doubt.* Considered by some to be his opus, the album delves deeply into his life in the dope game while painting vivid images of his struggles on whether or not to leave his situation as someone who is constantly deemed a target. His lyrics from "Politics as Usual," provide insight into the realities self-definition and introspection of his circumstance.

Where numerous lines speak to the code, the entire verse reveals the apparent conflicts, while simultaneously delineating his choice to take the call from the streets. Deeper in the code, Jay-Z speaks to the curse he feels has been placed on him despite his recognition of the life he has chosen. Although he left this life behind for a career in music, his recollections of his former life appeal to those who experience and view the daily realities of the street. For those who aspired to live the lifestyle that Jay-Z depicts, many did not listen to the narrative of trial and tribulation. Many still ignore the code, often blinded by the imagery of materialistic excess. Even deeper in the contradiction lie the fact that many consumers of hip hop are those who exist outside the stereotypical "urban" demographic of the inner city (e.g., white suburban males).

However, much like the contradictions observed in one's life after a period of self-discovery, Jay-Z's rise to super-stardom has a learning curve of its own. After years of teaming with Damon Dash to create Roc-A-fella Records, Jay-Z became the president of Def Jam Records in 2004, becoming the industry person he so famously vilified in earlier records. While his taking of the position should not be categorized simply as a contradiction, it should be noted that his shift from recording artist to label president was not without fallout from artists on the label. After experiencing injustice, the plan by many to rectify the infraction is to either destroy the person(s) that brought forth the injustice, or to destroy the very structure itself. In simple capitalist terms, this type of behavior between companies is referenced as a hostile takeover. In the case of individuals who have similar aspirations, the move is usually subtle, as an individual "climbs the corporate ladder." For Jay-Z, it appears as if he took time to observe the form and function of the operations that controlled his movements, and when the time presented itself, he took the opportunity to control it. To his dismay, it doesn't appear as if it was all he dreamed it would be.

Def Jam, as one of the original hip hop imprints, became saturated in the economics of the music industry and made a collective decision to incorporate artists from genres other than hip hop. Although viewed by many as a sound business decision, hip hop purists thought the move further devalued the label's standing. The business decision of incorporating R&B singers Ne-Yo and Rhianna through the Def Soul subsidiary proved lucrative for the company, but it seems that Jay-Z's departure after a three-year tenure denotes his displeasure with the role. I only surmise his dissatisfaction in observing his desire to record post-resignation. Additionally, while retaining control of his master recordings and publishing rights as vehicles to secure financial longevity, he maintains some connection to the code, now as a judicious participant-observer of the business of music.

In this instance the relationship to the code is a bit mysterious. One could surmise that Jay-Z was unhappy with his decision to become label president. On the other hand, we could interpret his business savvy akin to former Def Jam co-founder Russell Simmons in that he made a decision to "move on." As corporate business-speak, the loose rhetoric of "moving-on" could signal anything from dissatisfaction to an actual desire to pursue new interests. Whether his venture into retail (through his Rocawear label) or alcoholic beverage distribution (Armadale Vodka) reveals a desire to maintain a foothold in business, his retirement and re-entry from recording could be considered a change of heart. As every human being is allowed to change their mind, interrogating the code allows us to delve deeper into where Jay-Z's thought process may rest in relationship to his maturation.

From the Chi to N-Y: Block Business and the Code

Returning to the more definitive aspects of the code, my reflections as a young person growing up in Chicago has particular relevance to the depictions in Jay-Z's album *American Gangster*. Inspired by the movie of the same title starring Denzel Washington and Russell Crowe, the drama is a loose historical account of the rise of drug kingpin Frank Lucas in New York City during the early to mid–'70s. Lucas was an anomaly in that he made his fortune in heroin through the process of controlling a distribution network from Southeast Asia to New York City. Jay-Z, whose story could also be considered somewhat of an anomaly, was invited to a screening of the movie and decided to pen an album. Because Jay-Z was still a toddler in the time of Lucas' rise, the songs for the album spoke to the era he was most familiar with — the early to mid-eighties when crack cocaine hit the East Coast and spread throughout the continental U.S. In a sense, the album speaks to his sense of history, as songs on the album oscillate between tales of the trade from Lucas in the seventies to his own involvement as a drug dealer traveling from New York to Virginia in the next decade.

Similar to Jay-Z's situation in New York City, in Chicago, the 1980s were of particular significance to me. Many of my formative memories occurred in that decade as I finished grade school (1986) and almost all of high school (1990). Encapsulating those times, the lyrics from "American Dreamin'" provide a glimpse into what happened on many blocks in cities across the country. Jay-Z critically examines the options provided to inner-city specifically, and poor people in general. He calls for an affirmative action (of sort) as he calls for a chance, a place, to take part in the American Dream, The verses captured a moment I vividly remember upon graduating from high school. From the beginning of eighth grade to my senior year of high school, I had become deeply acquainted with the reasons why some of my friends chose the streets over school and legal employment. As some of us went away to college, some of us remained in the city. All of us were trying hard to figure out what our next steps in life would look like.

During that summer, between part-time jobs and whatever we would do to pass the time, many hours were spent at neighborhood barbeques relaxing and enjoy each other's company. At those gatherings, there were always these awkward moments. We'd recall some of our friends who decided to choose the dope game, leading them to relocate from Chicago. This was of particular significance to me because ten people I grew up with made a collective decision to work with a particular crew in downstate Illinois.[5] Word had gotten back to us that there was lots of money to be made and there was little chance of getting caught. We would see the fruits of the enterprise when some of the people who were older than us would visit their families in the city. They usually would show up in an extravagant car, with loads of cash in their pockets. On my block alone, three friends decided to go this route, taking the short-term lure of quick and easy cash. Like Jay-Z, all three never finished high school. All were exceptionally intelligent, but felt that high school wasn't working for them. Because the aforementioned options of factory work, military service or fast food were not in the scope of what they were trying to accomplish, relocating downstate provided the most viable solution to getting out from under their parents' roof.

Because we all stayed in touch, I would run into some of them during winter and summer breaks. We would catch up on the happenings downstate and in the neighborhood since I had been away. On one particular occasion, I got some of the worst news. The three friends from my block got caught in a drug raid and were all sentenced to significant jail time. One of them was the first person I ever met outside of my immediate family. Another graduated from a prominent Catholic grade school and dropped out of high school during his sophomore year. We have known each other since I was eight years old. The third person was a former honors student with whom I had developed a bond due to our love for sports. In one conversation, I contemplated how their lives would be significantly changed forever.

As I got older, due to relocations and life changes, many of the people I would catch up with moved away from the neighborhood. However, there were some friends who returned, as some had families and were gainfully employed. I would still see the parents and relatives of my friends who were incarcerated, and they would tell me how things were going. When I was still in graduate school, some friends alerted me to a homecoming celebration for one of my friends from the block. He was being released after serving eight years of a fifteen-year sentence for drug trafficking. As we relaxed in the backyard of his grand-parents' house and reminisced about happier times, he told me what happened to the people who joined the crew from the neighborhood. The other two friends from the block had relocated. One moved away to upstate New York, while the other stayed in downstate Illinois. The one who stayed downstate started a family, enrolled in a local college and worked at a factory. The one who went to New York entertained the idea of going to college, but couldn't resist the lure of the dope game. Since then, he's been in and out of jail and drug treatment programs, never being able to establish a foothold in life while battling addiction.

Soon after that summer, I received news that the one friend who remained downstate was killed in an altercation stemming from an association in his past life as a drug dealer. Because volatile situations often exacerbate grudges, his run-in with an old acquaintance proved deadly one evening outside his house. At 29 years of age, he was recently engaged and was expecting his second child. After attending his funeral, I thought of how his dreams of using money from the dope game to establish legitimate businesses never came to fruition. Unlike Jay-Z, right as he started to get his life in order, it was tragically cut short. In this sense, Jay-Z's verse evokes a painful memory of how choices can have cruel consequences. The message in its code is one I know painfully well.

Death of Auto Tune: Bringing the Code to the Schoolhouse

Returning to the usages that young people have for the code, my current position as an educator has particular significance in how I try to make sense of it in my current work. In addition to holding a position as a professor at a research university, I also operate as a volunteer social studies teacher at the Lawndale/Little Village School for Social Justice (SOJO). My participation on the design-team for the school morphed into a volunteer teaching position, where I team-teach classes with other SOJO staff. Because SOJO is an African-American and Latino/a school, it behooves me as an instructor there to pay attention to the myriad of positions occupied by African-American and Latino/a males in school and in life outside the building.

In teaching, it is impossible to ignore the tensions that can sometimes exist between students, teachers, administrators, parents, and community members. Especially in the high school setting, where young people are constantly navigating the space between the thoughts and opinions of their parents, peers, teachers, and themselves. In order to create a conducive space for learning, I share the position with many critical pedagogues that

> educators should create a critical counter-culture in their classrooms and programs. This should be a culture that mounts a deliberate attack on any and all forms of low expectations and social, political, and economic exploitation, replacing them with a culture of excellence and justice. These efforts should begin by confronting the immediate material conditions of the community where the teaching is taking place. However, the developing counter-culture should also work to connect the local struggle for freedom to larger state, national, and global struggles over similar issues [Duncan-Andrade and Morrell 172].

For my own classroom, in order to create a progressive counter-culture, I must first find out where my students are. Not in terms of performance on standardized tests and responses to writing prompts, but where they are in terms of their thinking. Because school has operated as a confrontational space for many of my students, my purpose is for them to understand that education is my concern, not necessarily the arbitrary standards set forth by the state that supposedly measure academic progress. The aforementioned counts strictly as "schooling" in that it is only meant to maintain the current status quo as opposed to challenging it.

To achieve the previous task is not an exact science. Instead, educators must engage a lot of "give and take" in the classroom. This means paying attention to what your students are saying and providing constructive feedback with the purpose of encouraging learning. As an educator, I have to take into account that the social, political and economic context of their lives is considerably more intense that it was for me in high school 20 years ago. The advent of high stakes testing, zero tolerance discipline policies, and stricter sentencing for minor criminal infractions mean that it is much easier for my students to go down the path of my friends I grew up with. To interrupt the potential of this happening, I must take into account the various learning styles of my students while pushing them towards reaching the goals they have set forth for themselves. In this sense, teaching is an art and science that requires constant reflection on your practice, for the purposes of improvement. In reference to the code, Jay-Z offers the constructive feedback to current hip hop recording artists in his song "Death of Auto Tune (DOA)." Upon first listen, the vitriol of telling another assumed to be male hip hop artist to "man up" comes off as fighting words. Additionally, the direct call to incite violence may make you wonder what does this have to do with the aforementioned code. As some hip hop artists thought Jay-Z was blatantly disrespecting them and aggressively responded to the song, I offer an alternative.

With deeper introspection, we can argue that Jay-Z was challenging the current monotony of popular music. As the popularized audio program popularly known as auto tune adds a computerized sound to the human voice, a number of artists in hip hop, R&B, pop, and rock music have used the program on their albums. It has been critiqued by industry insiders and the popular media as a program used to disguise the fact that the artist can't really sing. Coupled with the reality of radio playlists that repeat the same sets of songs at what appears to be every twenty minutes, people are inundated with the auto tune sound. Pushing for originality, Jay-Z is challenging his contemporaries to think differently while developing a sense of history. Similar to his stance in "H to the Izzo," he understands this as another form of an industry standard that needs to be challenged.

Nevertheless, in relationship to the code, the verse warrants some dissection. Imani Perry is correct in stating that "Black men as gendered and racial beings occupy a specific, constructed and oppressed role in society, one from which they must be liberated with a sophisticated political understanding of the grounds of their oppression" (Perry 119). Jay-Z, in occupying said spaces, embodies these complexities in his Sinatra reference. Much like his contemporaries, imitations of Italian mobsters or icons speak to a problematic connection to lifestyles that many of his listeners never will experience. At the same time, one could argue that the same reference could be code-speak to his younger colleagues in the music business to grow-up and recognize the responsibility to your craft as an artist. Again, the code sometimes sends conflicting messages, but our ability to demonstrate the utility of use of his lyrics remains the most important task.

In similar fashion, I challenge my students to engage a broader perspective of their world as young people. Minus the confrontational aggression expressed in *DOA,* I have students use a writing prompt answering the following questions: What does the world think about me? How am I portrayed in mainstream media outlets? Where the questions at first may seem simple, they operate as an introduction to the concept of hegemony. They offer the images of the common stereotype of baggy jeans, do-rags, plain white t-shirts, and boots. Marching on the same continuum, they offer that mainstream society positions them as drug dealers, dead-beat fathers, gang-bangers, and murderers. Following their offerings, I explain hegemony as a totalizing force, eliminating variance or creativity. After a brief discussion of Antonio Gramsci and how he used a code to write to his fellow organizers from prison, we begin a discussion on how they use codes. Students offer up slang as a code to prevent outsiders from figuring out the intent of the word. From there, they offer their examples of hegemony. The most common answers are television, radio, and print media in relationship to popular images of themselves. Continuing the conversation are the final two questions: What examples do we have of interruptions to hegemony? How can we interrupt hegemony personally and collectively? According to the state standards for high school language arts, I have engaged the students in expository writing and introduced vocabulary through use of a practical example. More importantly, I have trusted my students to engage material often believed to be "beyond" their capacity. All of it is centered in recognizing and deciphering a code.

Conclusion

In closing, it should be understood that the document offered for this collection is incomplete. Missing from this discussion is the ways in which African-American males dissect, consume and attempt to perpetuate the rampant materialism, misogyny and excess portrayed in some of Jay-Z's music. I maintain that hip hop, as the creation of young African-Americans and Puerto Ricans in response to urban renewal in the South Bronx, deserves a critical and constructive lens. Because this edited volume is intended to interrogate the work of Jay-Z, I wanted to remain responsible to the scope set forth by the editors.

However, as much as we need a critique of what's happening in hip hop and how Jay-Z contributes or challenges the pathologizing of people of color, the scope of my contribution is narrow at best. Where I cannot make excuses to absolve him from this reality, I must understand Jay-Z as human being, brother, and fellow African-American male. Recognizing him as a wordsmith of sizeable proportions, I cannot claim a "holier-than-thou" stance on his approach to the music industry or his particular craft as MC. Instead, like the situations with my students, I have to engage in some "give-and-take." My critique is intended to be constructive, recognizing his varied uses of the code. In the end, I hope I have allowed readers some insight as to how we can begin to listen to our students and make school a viable place where young people feel they are being educated. The code, as complex and simple text, is worth our time if we take our responsibility as educators seriously.

For Further Consideration

BOOKS

Ahearn, Charlie, and Fricke, Jim. *Yes Yes Y'All: The Experience Music Project Oral History of Hip-Hop's First Decade.* Cambridge, MA: Da Capo, 2002.
Chang, Jeff. *Can't Stop Won't Stop: A History of the Hip-Hop Generation.* New York: Picador, 2005.
Fashola, Olatokunbo. *Educating African American Males: Voices From the Field.* Thousand Oaks, CA: Corwin, 2005.
George, Nelson. *Hip Hop America.* New York: Viking, 1998.
Jacobson, Mark. *American Gangster: And Other Tales of New York.* New York: Grove, 2007.
Kelley, Robin, D.G. *Yo' Mama's Disfunktional! Fighting the Culture Wars in Urban America.* Boston: Beacon, 1997.
Kitwana, Bakari. *The Hip Hop Generation: Young Blacks and the Crisis in African American Culture.* New York: Basic Civitas, 2003.
Powell, Kevin. *Who's Gonna Take the Weight: Manhood, Race and Power in America.* New York: Three Rivers, 2003.
Shujaa, Mwalimu. *Too Much Schooling, Too Little Education: A Paradox of Black Life in White Societies.* Trenton, NJ: Africa World, 1994.

QUESTIONS

1. What is the connection between the ability to translate the "code" and the high placement of African American male in special education programs and high dropout rates?
2. What are some of the dangers of Jay-Z the "icon" and Shawn Carter "the man" and the portrayal of a drug dealer's lifestyle on other African American males?
3. How has Jay-Z both challenged the status quo and participated in maintaining it throughout his career?

Notes

1. "Backpacker," "underground," or "conscious" hip hop is in reference to artist's work that is reflective of a conscious decision to refute the suggestions of the mainstream, often posing alternatives and critiques of materialism and excess.
2. The dope game is referencing drug trafficking or drug sales. It's often referred to as the "game" due to the high stakes consequences if a participant is accused, tried and sentenced for any of the crimes associated with the sale and distribution of narcotics or controlled substances.
3. Felony disenfranchisement refers to the inability of formerly incarcerated persons to exercise his or her civil rights upon being released from prison. This most notably comes in the form of not being able to vote once released or hold certain occupations in certain states (e.g., baker, carpenter, barber, etc.) Many have argued that felony disenfranchisement contributes to high rates of recidivism in prison populations.
4. *Superfly* was a 1972 film directed by Gordon Parks Jr. that told the story of a drug dealer named Priest who was attempting to leave his life as a drug trafficker. The movie is famous for its soundtrack and protagonist.

5. "Dope crew" references groups of people who compromise a collective of individuals that have organized a system of drug sales and distribution. These are often highly organized operations that have specific responsibilities for each of its members.

Works Cited

Abrahams, R.D. *Singing the Master: The Emergence of African-American Culture in the Plantation South*. New York: Penguin, 1992.

Burnim, M.V., and P.K. Maultsby, eds. *African-American Music: An Introduction*. New York: Routledge, 2006.

Duncan-Andrade, J.M.R., and E. Murrell. *The Art of Critical Pedagogy: Possibilities for Moving from Theory to Practice in Urban Schools*. New York: Peter Lang, 2008.

Fisher, M.T. *Writing in Rhythm: Spoken Word in Poetry in Urban Classrooms*. New York: Teachers College, 2007.

Forman, M., and M.A. Neal. *That's the Joint! The Hip-Hop Studies Reader*. New York: Routledge, 2004.

Perry, I. *Prophets of the Hood: Politics and Poetics in Hip-Hop*. Durham, NC: Duke University Press, 2004.

11

Oedipus-Not-So-Complex

A Blueprint for
Literary Education

A.D. CARSON

Two roads diverged in a wood, and I—
I took the one less traveled by,
And that has made all the difference.
— Robert Frost, "The Road Not Taken," 1915

I credit my success as a first year teacher to many qualities, the most valuable of which was my ignorance about what was permissible in class, rivaled only by a dogged determination to make sure that all my students left my classroom with an understanding that classical literary traditions have some relevance in their real lives—during *and* after high school. Bloom's taxonomy freshly burned into my brain, I set out to light the torches of my students, many of whom were considered uneducable by my colleagues. I was determined to teach plot, point of view, setting, figures of speech, characterization, and other fundamentals to my students, but I knew I would somehow do this differently. I knew that literary personification never meant so much to me as it did the day I heard Common Sense's "I Used to Love H.E.R.," in which the rapper likens hip hop music and culture to a woman that he fell in love with as a 10-year-old kid. I wasn't much older than the song's protagonist when I first encountered "I Used to Love H.E.R.," which lent Common's figurative use of language credibility and inspired the future literature teacher in me to listen up. To this day I use this song as both a springboard for conversation with students about hip hop history and as an extraordinary example of personification as a literary device. Later I would realize that Eminem's wordplay rivaled that of many of the great poets I'd read in my college classes. I knew that poets like Gwendolyn Brooks, Nikki Giovanni, and Sonia Sanchez recognized the artistry of some of my favorite rappers. All this inspired me to use hip hop to teach literature.

172

Clearly a talented teacher can make use of the many rap artists like Tupac, Nas, Mos Def, Talib Kweli, and Jay-Z, who allude to classical texts. These rappers are not originators in this sense, but their popularity makes their instances of intertextuality more accessible to students who come to class having memorized their lyrics. Taking that as a given, we teachers must better educate ourselves to the teaching possibilities existent within hip hop culture. Jay-Z's catalogue alone contains numerous examples from which students might glean literary enlightenment. Aside from instances of simile, metaphor, irony, exaggeration, analogy and comparison, double entendre, punning, and wit that can be found throughout his lyrics, specific examples include repetition and parallel structure as found in "22 Two's," hubris as found in "Song Cry," identity in "There's Been a Murder," hyperbole in "Girls, Girls, Girls," and mood in "Minority Report." In addition, several of Jay-Z's songs, such as "December 4th," "Hard Knock Life," and "So Ambitious," when taken together, comprise a kind of Bildungsroman.

That classical texts inform Jay-Z's lyrics should be unsurprising given that many believe there are no original stories left, only retellings of the same stories across cultures and generations. Editors M.B. Clarke and A.G. Clarke use this understanding as the foundation of their comparative textbook *Retellings: A Thematic Literature Anthology.* They state in the introduction:

> The comparative approach is, of course, quite an old one, as a glance at early scholarship on sources and analogues for Shakespeare's and Chaucer's works makes clear. We are not, then, claiming to break new ground. Instead, we are hoping to encourage students to think more deeply along the lines that already inform much of their thinking. All of us often think comparatively [x].

Similarly, I am not claiming to break new ground, but simply to widen the scope of comparison performed in texts like *Retellings* to include the works of writers like Jay-Z. Using rappers like Jay-Z to teach the likes of Shakespeare, Chaucer, and Sophocles empowers students who bring to the classroom extensive knowledge of the relevant themes (passion, betrayal, love gained and lost, envious friends, and dishonorable foes) through their love of rap music. Employing Jay-Z's lyrics in my teaching effectively demonstrates, as asserted in *Retellings,* that contemporary artists do indeed "pay homage to earlier stories and reinvent them for a new time and audience" (ix).

The path to my position as a teacher was a fairly unique one. By the time I began student teaching I had recorded two albums and performed countless shows as "A.D. The Great." My dream was to become a famous rapper; teaching was my back-up plan. When the time came for me to present my first lesson for observation during practicum I was up for the challenge — and I wanted it to be just that. My observing teacher, a veteran in the Decatur Public School District, let me know that I would present my own lesson over the course of my practicum. Naturally, I thought poetry would be the ideal subject for me to present, given my former career as a rapper. I could simply teach a short lesson on a poem, or how to write a poem and be done with that portion of the practicum. My thoughts, however, were more focused on what would make both a lasting impression on the students and best prepare me as an educator. A riskier lesson was in order. I would teach Jay-Z and Sophocles. The lesson I created led to many rich discussions of Jay-Z, Sophocles, and *Oedipus Rex* in my classes.

I'd read *Oedipus Rex* when I was in high school and thought it was a decent story. I'd even learned along the way that "Aristotle considered *Oedipus Rex* the masterpiece of Greek drama and used it to illustrate the perfection of tragedy" (Clarke and Clarke 847). All the things I needed to gather from the reading I understood from when I was a student, except back then I wasn't so much interested in the story as I was interested in maintaining my place on the honor roll. My challenge was finding a way to make the story relevant to the group of teens that I would be facing while teaching all the skills my observing teacher wanted them to learn — the transferable skills that extended beyond the walls of that classroom and the school building: critical thinking, effective argumentation, the joy of reading for fun.

Jay-Z's *The Blueprint: The Gift & The Curse* was released on November 12, 2002. At the time I was working on a rap career of my own, which meant that I listened to as much music as humanly possible and read whatever I could get my hands on to ensure I was doing all the right things with regard to my craft. I was also toying with the idea of going back to school to finish the education degree that I deferred to record and promote my first album. I felt that I needed a legitimate backup plan, and teaching was what suited me best. Listening to *The Blueprint* from the perspective of a fan I was satisfied, even amazed, at Jay-Z's deftness as an emcee and businessman, proud that he was continuing to propel rap's popularity with what I deemed "good music." From the perspective of an artist I was awed by the complex simplicity, or simplistic complexity, of the lyrics of many of the songs. Lyrically, there was fodder for critics and fans alike. A song like "Excuse Me Miss" would definitely burn up the charts, appealing to the commercial market Jay-Z conquers with each outing, simple enough to be widely liked and understood, yet appealing to those who look for lyrical depth in places most consumers don't — between the lines. "Bonnie & Clyde" would resonate with the purists who accuse Jay-Z of dumbing down his lyrics so much that they can't stomach his rhymes though they recognize his potential, and it probably would get extra special consideration because of the inclusion of a sample from Tupac's "Me and My Girlfriend" from 1996's *The Don Killuminati: The 7 Day Theory*. These were singles, so it was expected that they would be highly marketable, enjoyable to both the avid hip hop consumer and the ordinary top-ten radio listener.

However, there was more — track four on *Disc Two: The Curse* is "Meet the Parents." At first listen, it's a gritty tale of street life and the perpetuation of the vicious cycle created when boys grow up without their fathers' presence.

A closer examination of the lyrics reveals much more. This is a retelling — "Meet the Parents" is a story about fate, free will, and pride, and it closely mirrors the backstory of *Oedipus Rex*.

Oedipus' parents, Jocasta and Laius, receive a prophecy that their son will grow up to kill them. Attempting to prevent this from coming to pass, Laius instructs Jocasta to kill the child. Jocasta assigns the task to a servant who binds the child's feet together with a pin and abandons him in a field. A shepherd finds the baby and names him Oedipus, which literally means "swollen feet," intending to raise the child as his own. Oedipus is given to another family who cannot care for him, and he ultimately winds up living in Corinth with the childless King Polybus and his wife, Merope, who raise him as their own. Curious about his parentage, Oedipus asks Polybus and Merope if they are his biological parents, but is unconvinced by their assurances. He asks an oracle the same question and is told he is doomed to "marry his own mother, [and] shed his father's blood/ With his own hands" (872, Ode 2, Scene 3). To avoid the prophecy's indication that he would mate with Merope and kill Polybus—the only parents he knows— Oedipus leaves Corinth. During his travels Oedipus meets King Laius on the road to Thebes and becomes involved in a quarrel over whose carriage has the right of way. Oedipus throws Laius from the carriage, killing him, and continues on his way unaware that he has fulfilled part of the oracle's prophecy. Later in his trip he solves the riddle of the Sphinx, causing the Sphinx to throw herself off a cliff and ridding the people of her incessant riddling. Since the king of Thebes has been recently killed, the people offer Oedipus their queen, Jocasta, and the title formerly held by his biological father, King of Thebes, setting in motion the fulfillment of the rest of the prophecy.

This backstory sets the stage for the action that takes place in *Oedipus Rex*. I wanted my students to discuss themes such as free will versus fate, pride, and determination with regard to *Oedipus Rex*. Does Oedipus ultimately have any choice in the outcome of his circumstance since it is said to be his fortune by the oracle? Does his pride as King of Thebes mixed with his determination to find the murderer of King Laius ultimately doom him, or is his fate something that he could have avoided by abandoning the search when instructed to do so? I wanted my students to think critically about whom the hero of the story is, the main conflicts, and the circumstances under which they could possibly see the outcome being different.

I knew I could use the tragedy in Jay-Z's song "Meet the Parents" to help modernize the tragedy of Oedipus and his family. I anticipated that the students' response to Jay-Z would be much more favorable than their initial response to Sophocles. Jay-Z has the ability to engage them in a way that Sophocles simply cannot — Jay-Z is one of the voices of their, of my, of *our* generation. Jacobus' claims in his introduction that "[s]ome writers inform us about how the world works and what is important ethically, but no reader will pay much attention if the writing is not engaging" (3). I wanted to use Jay-Z as a bridge, a way for my students to engage critically with Sophocles despite the difficulties they might have with his language, not simply to be provocative. This was my means of teaching tragedy to this group of students, with the knowledge that "tragedy is, above all, serious in tone and importance. It focuses on a hero or heroine whose potential is great but whose efforts to realize that potential are thwarted by fate: circumstances beyond his or her control" (*Glencoe Literature* 845).

My methodology was simple. My pre-teaching would consist of engaging the class in a discussion about fate, free will, pride, and how they are relevant to young people like themselves. The conversation was typical of a group of high school students, but effective in that it primed them, if only a bit for the next step, which was actually playing the song. I first had to find an edited copy of the song so as to not get myself in trouble with my participating university or the administrators in the school building.

This was the moment of truth — handing out copies of the lyrics and being told, "I thought we were talking about a play, Mr. Carson. Are you sure you gave us the right thing? This says 'Jay-Z' on it."

My response: "We are. I am. And it does."

Before playing the song I told the students to underline parts that were either confusing unclear or just needed more explaining. They were also instructed to underline any phrases or sections that were particularly interesting to them, or they wanted to discuss when the song was finished playing. I wrote the word "archetype" on the board, and I had a student find the definition from his book — "a thing, person, or pattern of circumstances that appears repeatedly in literature" (*Glencoe Literature* 825) — and read it to the class. I instructed the class to keep this definition in mind because it would be pertinent to their reading and assignment for the night. And then I played "Meet the Parents."

Jay-Z's "Meet the Parents" opens in a cemetery on a rainy day with the speaker reminiscing and making a claim about fate, stating the lament of yet another early death of a good kid. The speaker enacts the ghetto ritual of pouring a drink on the grave of a fallen brotha (sic), which far too often occurs at the end of a young black life. This is a statement about the multitudes of young black men dying violently at an early age. Though society regards the subject of the memory in Jay Z's *Blueprint 2* narrative as simply a thug who caught a random slug from a random gun, the narrator relates to him, asserting that he is loved due to his commonality with those in the hood. The narrator continues, giving us background information about the kid, stating that his mother's name is Isis, but that the child never knew his father's name. The kid leaves home at a young age, with his mother telling him he acts just like his father. The narrator foreshadows tragedy by rapping, in chilling irony, that the same .38 caliber pistol one carries throughout life will serve as the proverbial "gift and curse" (the subtitle of the *Blueprint 2* album) and be the cause of death before you reach your 38th birthday. The narrator then informs the listener of the circumstances under which Isis came to have her son, using a flashback Isis has after retreating into a land of fantasy while viewing his body at the city morgue. Faced with the never palatable reality of burying her son, she laments as he is the fruit of her womb. His father's name is Mike, a "hardhead" whose seedy lifestyle proved intoxicating to him and to her as she gravitated to the danger and instability of his lifestyle. When he saw the child at birth, the only time he ever saw the kid, the father didn't take responsibility. He gave only a cursory glance to the infant, articulating the cultural idiom of parental irresponsibility, "momma's baby, poppa's maybe." Fourteen years later, Mike, now age thirty-two, still has a life of the streets and carries the .38 caliber pistol. When he approaches a younger street thug with a "mean mug" (which characterizes the face and spirit of a hardened and non-emotional reality), an argument ensues between Mike and the younger street "cuz," as he is (non)affectionately, but familiarly called. The elder tells the younger to vacate his street. The boy has an advantage over Mike, but the proximity of his foe's gaze startles the boy; it's as if he saw a ghost. Seeing the teen's hesitation, Mike doesn't think. He simply uses his street instinct and kills the teen — who was, in fact, his disavowed son. The lyrics thereby complete the cycle Jay-Z indicates is caused by fathers being absent from their sons' lives. Jay-Z's allegorical tragedy not only reminds us of the adage "the sins of the father revisit the son," but also suggests that the absence of fathers literally and figuratively kills children.

It was easy to get the students to follow the story; they were engaged by the grim music of the introduction, the buzzing guitar, and Jay-Z's nasal vocal introduction. We went over the details of the story to make sure we were all on the same page, discussed inconsistencies in their interpretations of the narrative, talked about particularly striking portions of the story, and pondered the themes they believed Jay-Z was presenting in his story. We then discussed our initial questions about fate and how it relates to them and people their age, and how it relates to the story. Additionally, we talked about free will, pride, and how they pertain to this and similar situations. They were eager to discuss all these elements of Jay-Z's story and, as we got nearer to the end of the hour, I let on that the story of Oedipus was very similar, and Jay-Z's story shares many archetypes present in Sophocles' story. Their homework was to find the similarities and differences in *Oedipus Rex* and "Meet the Parents."

The stage was set. I had a group of students eager to read Sophocles, and it was literally because of a blueprint laid out by Jay-Z. Free will versus fate, pride, and determination are easy to see as themes in both texts. Is Oedipus more comparable to Mike or Mike's son? Does the son ultimately have any choice in the outcome of his circumstance since it is said to be his fortune by the narrator? Does his pride mixed with his determination to "live by the gun" doom him to "die by the same fate," or is his fate something that he could have avoided by not going into the life his mother warned him about when she "said he act just like her husband," alluding to the young man headed toward the same path as his father? Who is the hero of Jay-Z's story, what are the main conflicts, and under which circumstances could the outcome have been different? These are a few of the questions my students had to consider in their examination of "Meet the Parents" as a retelling of *Oedipus Rex*, but there are a multitude of educational possibilities that can be explored here.

Educators attempt to engage students with literature, in part, because the stories of each generation provide glimpses into the conflicts that society faced, and what they valued as a people. According to Jacobus,

Literature ... does all these things—

- It gives us a special awareness of what we already know.
- It tells us what we don't already know.
- It moves our feelings.
- It gives us pleasure.
- It puts us in another world.
- It uses language in especially powerful ways [2].

One thing I surmised, before I ever presented a lesson on my own, was that I would never teach English literature the way it was taught to me in the Decatur Public Schools. That was probably not much different from how it has been taught in many other places. We talked about the themes in the text to build (or build on) background knowledge; read silently, as a class or in small groups; answered questions at the end of the text; and did a group project or wrote an essay. This bland repetition worked for me; by the time I was in high school, language *qua* language meant something special to me, and I knew that my career, no matter the ultimate destination, would be somewhere within the world of words. But for most students, the hurdle, rarely overcome, was the painful feeling of irrelevance and desynchronization that atrophies creative development.

Rita Dove retells the story of *Oedipus Rex* in *The Darker Face of the Earth*. I found, that when I employed these two texts in class, "these pairings [led] to a richer discussion of both the retelling and the original text, a more complete understanding of how an author's decision about setting character, and theme are made and transmitted" (Jacobus 2). Rappers are the bards of this generation — the griots, as they have often been called. Using their telling and retellings of stories in literature classrooms is a natural progression.

In my teaching career thus far, it has made all the difference that my path to the teaching profession was via the road less traveled. It is especially important that I continue to teach by the philosophy of "The Road Not Taken," employing the writers of this generation to help make relevant to the students of this generation the literature of previous generations. "Meet the Parents" and *Oedipus Rex* are but one of the many pairings that exist in the realm of hip hop. The lyrics of Jay-Z alone are rich territory for a literature course — eleven number-one albums' worth. Likely, students are more familiar with *Reasonable Doubt, The Blueprint* (the first, second, and third iteration), and *The Black Album* than they are with much of what I'm charged with teaching them in just a year's time. Similarly, on "Thieves in the Night" rappers Mos Def and Talib Kweli paraphrase a paragraph from the conclusion of Toni Morrison's *The Bluest Eye,* deepening the potential for discussion between the original text and the retelling while bringing her message to a new generation of listeners. Utilizing our common love of hip hop, I make the teaching of literature more relevant to my students. I suspect that there are many other teachers whose sensibilities as educators are hovering — like mine — somewhere between Jay-Z and Robert Frost. My advice: listen to Jay-Z when you come to that fork in the road, and go straight. It will make all the difference.

For Further Consideration

BOOKS

Dove, Rita. *The Darker Face of the Earth.* Brownsville, OR: Story Line, 1994.
Ellison, Ralph. "Hidden Name, Complex Fate." Washington, DC: For the Library of Congress by the Gertrude Clarke Whittall Poetry and Literature Fund, 1964.
Sartwell, Crispin. *Act Like You Know.* Chicago: University of Chicago, 1998.
Smitherman, Geneva. *Talkin that Talk: African American Language and Culture.* New York: Routledge, 2000.

QUESTIONS

1. The author assumes that his students are familiar with the conventions of rap music. In fact he anticipates and exploits their familiarity with the conventions of one art form — hip hop — to ground their knowledge of another, more formal art form — classical literature. What are the benefits and drawbacks to this approach?

2. Artists are often credited as representatives of inspiration and originality. How does an artist retelling or updating an earlier story effect your opinion of their creativity? Is originality still a valid criterion for assessing art?

Works Cited

Clarke, A.G., and M.B. Clarke, eds. *Retellings: A Thematic Literature Anthology.* New York: McGraw-Hill, 2004.
Glencoe Literature: Course 4 Student Edition. New York: McGraw-Hill, 2009.
Jacobus, Lee A. "Introduction." In Jacobus, ed., *Literature.*
_____ ed. *Literature: An Introduction to Critical Reading.* Upper Saddle River, NJ: Prentice Hall, 2002.
Sophocles. *Oedipus Rex.* In Jacobus, ed., *Literature.*

12

The Culture Industry

Mainstream Success and Black Cultural Representation

GIL COOK

As Todd Boyd points out in his 2002 book *The New H.N.I.C.: The Death of Civil Rights and the Reign of Hip-Hop*, one of hip hop's defining aspects is the constant negotiation of its roots as a transgressive social movement with its current assimilation into mainstream culture[1]— not only as a form of music, but also as a marketing tool to sell everything from vitamin-enriched water to mobile phones. The field of media and cultural studies contains longstanding discourses that illuminate how/why hip hop's cultural leap was possible. Much of the language contributing to such an analysis of hip hop surrounds Theodor Adorno and Max Horkheimer's theory of "the culture industry" and the resultant mass versus popular media/culture debates it continues to inspire. When viewed within the context of the social machinery Adorno and Horkheimer posit as defining the culture industry, we see how hip hop's artistic and cultural machinations are indicative of an ongoing struggle to balance mainstream success with the problematic race ideologies that contemporary popular culture represents. As the record holder for number-one albums sold by a solo performer, Jay-Z, as a hip hop artist, serves well as the subject for our examination of the music's delicate balance between racial awareness and commercial achievement.

As is standard in black studies, this project assumes that race — as most of us understand it in the contemporary Western world — is a socially constructed category invented for the purposes Jacob Pandian and Susan Parman describe in their 2004 publication *The Making of Anthropology: The Semiotics of Self and Other in the Western Tradition*:

> Beginning in the 16th century, an elaborate mythology of race with multiple semiotic significations came into being.... Along with such a development of racial mythology

and racial science, which were created to serve the economic and political interests of Europeans and Europe in the New World, there came into being a body of knowledge that depicted sub–Saharan Africa as an undeveloped, wild country, peopled by inferior or sub-human forms of humanity [159–60].

Following this race myth's dissemination from Africa to the nations now constituting the African Diaspora via the slave trade, centuries of iniquitous laws and social practices were established to prevent Africans and their descendants equal access to education, economic opportunity, and basic civil rights. These factors all served to provide observable cultural proof of black inferiority. With the continued perpetuation of these myths through media, including hip hop, we see the root of Boyd's point concerning the balancing act artists like Jay-Z must perform.

Hip Hop in the Culture Industry

Horkheimer and Adorno's *Dialectic of Enlightenment* introduces the concept of culture industry in its penultimate chapter, "The Culture Industry: Enlightenment as Mass Deception." Here Horkheimer and Adorno argue "culture today is infecting everything with sameness" (94). This sameness results from processes of standardization within the production of media for distribution to consumers who resemble the mechanical reproduction seen in industrial factories. This assertion posits culture as being largely defined by the values, practices, and beliefs transmitted to and adopted by members of society via the media they consume. Horkheimer and Adorno articulate their point concerning this industrialization of culture in the following manner:

> Interested parties like to explain the culture industry in technological terms. Its millions of participants, they argue, demand reproduction processes which inevitably lead to the use of standard products to meet the same needs at countless locations. The technical antithesis between few production centers and widely dispersed reception necessitates organization and planning by those in control. The standardized forms, it is claimed, were originally derived from the needs of the consumers: that is why they are accepted with so little resistance. In reality, a cycle of manipulation and retroactive need is unifying the system ever more tightly. What is not mentioned is that the basis on which technology is gaining power over society is the power of those whose economic position in society is strongest. Technical rationality today is the rationality of domination. It is the compulsive character of a society alienated from itself [95].

For Horkheimer and Adorno, this forced standardization of the themes, images, and values culturally transmitted for the pacification, manipulation, and delight of the masses has resulted in the omnipresence of films, music, and art of far inferior quality to those "great bourgeois works of art" that predate the industrial reproduction of culture necessitated by capitalistic urgings (99).

The latent elitism of such an assertion is partially responsible for some of the criticism that has been leveled against Horkheimer and Adorno, and their notion of the culture industry, by media and cultural studies scholars both before and after them.[2] The work of renowned cultural studies scholars like Stuart Hall and John Fiske, whose work contradicts the tenets of the culture industry, largely find it unappealing due to its seeming disavowal of any agency for the consumer or producer in culture's meaning-making processes. Where Horkheimer and Adorno spoke of mass media/culture in detailing the effects of the culture industry, their succeeding cultural studies scholars—here represented by Hall and Fiske—theorize the relationship between consumers and the media they consume as popular culture/media.

Fiske characterizes the distinction between mass and popular media/culture in his seminal 1988 study *Television Culture*, where he defines popularity as "a measure of a cultural form's ability to serve the desires of its customers" (310). He continues by stating: "For a cultural commodity to become popular it must be able to meet the various interests of the people amongst whom it is popular as well as the interests of its producers" (310). This counters Adorno and Horkheimer's presentation of consumers as one indistinguishable mass to whom culture is uniformly imparted by multi-national corporate forces in that it foregrounds the multiplicity of individual tastes among consumers and producers as paramount to the meaning-making processes of culture. Hall's acclaimed essay "What is this 'Black' in Black Popular Culture?" builds on this formulation of the popular in its attempt to enumerate what makes the contemporary social moment a unique one for considering the state of black popular culture. Here, Hall explains how "in one sense, popular culture always has its base in the experiences, the pleasures, the memories, the traditions of the people" (25). Hall's expression of this notion of culture as being "of the people" captures the fundamental ideology shift that takes place in media/cultural studies away from Horkheimer and Adorno's notion of culture as a mass industrial complex devoid of individuality and driven solely by market interests.

Though contemporary observers of media/cultural studies' history and evolution acknowledge the value of the field's ideological paradigm shift from "mass" to "popular," there remains some reluctance to completely throw the culture industry's baby out with the bath water. Denis McQuail points to this apprehension on the part of contemporary scholars of cultural studies in the 2005 fifth edition of his groundbreaking study *McQuail's Mass Communication Theory*:

> Despite the re-evaluation of popular culture that has occurred and the rise of postmodernism, several charges of the kind made by Frankfurt School critics remain on the table. Much of the content offered by media that is both popular and commercially successful is still open to much the same objections as in more elitist and less enlightened time.... Its production is governed by a predominantly commercial logic,

since most popular culture is produced by large corporations with an overriding concern for their own profits, rather than for enriching the cultural lives of people. Audiences are viewed as consumer markets to be manipulated and managed. Popular formulas and products tend to be used until threadbare, then discarded when they cease to be profitable, whatever the audience might demand in the "cultural economy." There is not much empirical support for the theory that media texts are decoded in oppositional ways [119].

McQuail's specific reference to Hall's decoding theory — where, as he puts it, "the same cultural product can be read in different ways, even if a certain dominant meaning may seem to be built in"— serves to simultaneously elucidate both what differentiates mass and popular media/culture and what inextricably binds them (118).

Hall's notion that the meaning of cultural products is largely determined by the multiplicity of readings ascribed to them by consumers and producers, regardless of whatever initial meaning may have been intended by the system, demonstrates the foregrounding of individual's agency found in popular culture studies. However, as McQuail points out, this does not free us of the culturally prescriptive powers of the culture industry:

> The content of media with the largest audiences does appear broadly supportive of reigning social norms and conventions (an aspect of socialization and of cultivation). Fundamental challenges to the national state or its established institutions are hard to find in the mass media. The argument that mass media tend towards the confirmation of the status quo is thus based on evidence both about what is present and about what it missing in media content [495].

Even in recognizing the multiplicity of voices that are allowed to be heard in our contemporary popular cultural paradigm versus the few elite voices allowed access under more elitist paradigms, we must acknowledge that the seemingly overwhelming uniformity of social beliefs, values, traditions, and normative transmitted to consumers is no less prevalent now. So how do these two things exist in the same space at the same time? It would appear the processes of mechanical social reproduction characterizing Horkheimer and Adorno's concept of the culture industry are very much at work in some fashion in popular media/culture.

The contemporary popular cultural media consumed on the global market certainly does not seem to incorporate contentious ideologies as much as it assimilates them into the industrial reproductive machinery responsible for the cultural sameness of the sort Horkheimer and Adorno describe. Political, racial, sexual, economic, national, and religious movements that have sought to promote agendas counter to those uniformly prescribed by the majority of existing cultural product have seemed to undergone the process Horkheimer and Adorno call standardization:

> The general designation "culture" already contains, virtually, the process of identifying, cataloging, and classifying which imports culture into the realm of adminis-

tration. Only what has been industrialized, rigorously subsumed, is fully adequate to this concept of culture [104].

All cultural products, including those originating from countercultural ideologies, are transmitted — or administered — to consumers in such a way as to fit neatly into prescribed roles in keeping with a reinforced cultural identity. It is a boiling down of diverse and divergent components into an indistinguishable mass of uniformity: what black studies discourse would call "essentialism."

Once standardized, or essentialized, these products are catalogued for distribution to the masses as informative of their "(enter your self-identifier here) culture." Culture has therefore become subsumed as an industrial commodity in that these constructed cultural identities are transmitted and reinforced via media sources driven by the corporations' desire to manipulate and profit from consumers. When specifically applied to a discourse on race, this functioning of the culture industry illuminates how hip hop — as the most prominent black cultural product in the world — has been assimilated into popular cultural ideologies.

In a January 23, 2005, article published in the British newspaper *The Guardian*'s online music and culture section, acclaimed hip hop scholar Nelson George reflects on hip hop's meteoric rise as a cultural phenomenon:

> Hip hop is the new international definition of the contemporary black experience. ... My point is that what was once a folk expression has since matured into a multimillion dollar industry encompassing an array of products that sell across the spectrum of race, class and nationality. Advertising images have accelerated the acceptance of hip-hop imagery as powerfully as any music videos. Aside from Oprah Winfrey's ubiquitous TV talk show, images of black people around the world are now dominated by hip hop figures or symbols associated with it. ... To watch hip hop grow from black America's bastard child to its current central place has been an object lesson in the power of culture.

This description of hip hop's explosion is emblematic of the culture industry's prevalence in contemporary popular media/culture. Though the popular media/culture model allows more space for marginalized voices to emerge than in elitist social paradigms, the cultural products those voices create — like hip hop — are just as subject to processes of industrial reproduction on the global market as anything else.

As an art form born of the black community, the popular cultural system industrially standardized and incorporated hip hop in the manner all black culture has been assimilated into Western culture since the slave trade: through perpetuation of the race myth. As George points out, this assimilation has resulted in the hip hop that is most readily available on the global market being that which contains coarse lyrical content, rapacious capitalism, casual misogyny, and disdain for education. As a result of "hip hop [becoming] the establishment — a monolithic enterprise that stifles opposing voices and sustains the like-minded," its power to define how African descendants across the globe view themselves and are viewed by others has functioned to imbue Westerners with notions of black inferiority in keeping with established race ideologies (George).[3] Despite this, as Boyd notes, hip hop has as much capacity to destabilize these ideologies as it does to reinforce them due to its straddling of the culture industry and popular culture/media models.

As a style of music originated to provide traditionally marginalized populations with access to meaningfully engaging their society, hip hop stands as a paradigmatic example of the anti-elitist character Hall and Fiske ascribe to media and culture. Hip hop simultaneously serves the systematic sameness foundational to the culture industry's elitism in that it standardizes these marginal voices into a race monolith that is constantly reinforced in society through the interests and marketing budgets of multinational record corporations. However, the culture industry's engulfing of popular culture into its inescapable ubiquity means that the individual's capacity to transgress cultural industrialization — popular culture's defining characteristic according to Hall and Fiske — persists as a constituting element of the system's design.

Hip hop's cultural and artistic makeup as a hybrid between the culture industry and popular media/culture models is the root of its capacity to simultaneously function in the mainstream and transgressive manner Boyd claims. We most readily see this simultaneity take shape in hip hop when looking at the career of its most successful participant: Jay-Z. The unprecedented achievement of Jay-Z on the global music market, it can be argued, is attributable to his mastery in portraying and navigating hip hop's dual nature. While examples of Jay-Z's musical reinforcement of mainstream race ideologies are abundant, the more interesting aspect of his work — for this project — revolves around his ability to simultaneously offer means of reconfiguring and transcending those strictures.

Jay-Z, Black Liberation Pedagogy, and What's Really 'Hood

As hip hop's dominant figure, Jay-Z has often ventured to set the music's artistic and political agenda with his work. It is often in these instances where we see Jay-Z most directly embody hip hop's dual role as mainstream cultural force and social transgressor. On the third track of his 2001 release *The Blueprint*, "Izzo, H.O.V.A.," Jay-Z directly addresses this aforementioned duality. While attempting to solidify his name as not solely an artist but a "mover and shaker" within the business of hip hop, the sentiments Jay-Z expresses here function on several levels. His willingness to engage the mainstream music industry in efforts to "talk mo' bucks," despite his awareness of its "hoeing" his culture, seems emblematic of purely capitalist motivations in keeping with the negative representations George earlier described as dominating hip hop culture. Though these motivations are undeniable, Jay-Z's use of a hip hop track to criticize the hip hop industry is quite transgressive. This transgression has less to do with the criticism's medium than it does with Jay-Z's stated reasons for expressing them.

In the second verse of this pop hit, he devotes the entire verse to serve as a mouthpiece and representation of those artists in the past whom the industry ripped off. He uses the Cold Crush Brothers, a pioneering hip hop group of the late 1970s, as a cultural representation that underscores a pedagogical element of his engagement with hip hop's dual nature. His willingness to put himself through the music industry's cultural "roaster" and handle his business while the parasitic crows and vultures attempt to devour the weak seemingly underscores his repeatedly expressed desire to uplift other members of his culture by later forewarning them of the social pitfalls he has successfully navigated during his experiences. Jay-Z says as much in the next verse of "Izzo, H.O.V.A.," as he reminds us listeners that he is somewhat of a hip hop patriarch, doing the dirty work so that the future generation can merely benefit from his blood, sweat, and trials of fire. With "Izzo, H.O.V.A," Jay-Z engages the mainstream in order to later undercut it in an attempt to educate black listeners about the pitfalls of standardized racial identity and calls for a social realignment toward equity. As such, Jay-Z engages in a discourse of what I call black liberation pedagogy.

Black liberation pedagogy, as a concept, stems from Paulo Freire's theory of "pedagogy of liberation"—which he most famously and cogently describes in his masterwork *Pedagogy of the Oppressed*. Here, Freire posits that education should be the path to permanent liberation for members of oppressed populations. He describes education's contribution to liberation as occurring in two stages. The first stage is a process Freire calls "conscientization," or becoming "conscientized," which refers to the process of oppressed peoples coming to consciousness or awareness of themselves as oppressed. The second stage calls for a building upon the conscientizing process wherein members of oppressed populations use their raised awareness concerning their social circumstance as motivation to actively combat inequity through social and cultural action. Black liberation pedagogy, then, is the carrying out of Freire's pedagogy of liberation stages for the express purpose of conscientizing black peoples in particular in order to facilitate their eventual attainment of social liberation.

When I say Jay-Z engages in a discourse of black liberation pedagogy, I am saying that he attempts to specifically raise the black audience's awareness of themselves as socially oppressed and offers his engagement with the hip hop industry as one example of transgressive libratory action. This, of course, does not mean that all of Jay-Z's music does this or that his methods for achieving his goal are infallible — his musical offerings are much too varied and complex to be defined uniformly — but what it does mean is that there is a large enough sampling of these ideas appearing in his work to make his pedagogical project perceptible and noteworthy. We especially see this drive to educate and uplift black culture in the manner Jay-Z works later in his career to directly disavow and reconfigure the prominently reinforced negative images of black culture transmitted via popular media. This occurs in his appearance with Oprah in Brooklyn, his recurring public image in suits, and even as he blasted news commentators Bill O'Reilly and Rush Limbaugh in "Off That," in which he announced that long is the day of pigeon-holing and racial classifications of blacks versus whites. In making this proclamation on his latest album, Jay-Z signals his career-long political and artistic interest in using his music to undercut existing perpetuations of racial divide in popular media. This interest in reconfiguring popular culture's imaging of race identity has even resulted in Jay-Z's music factoring into the field of Spatial Studies.

In proposing "the city" as a fourth addition to the three "repertoires of black popular culture," John Jeffries in his essay "Toward a Redefinition of the Urban: The Collision of Culture" works to "emphasize the significance of the place, defined both in geographic and political economy terms, in which these repertoires of black culture are born and remixed" (154). Defining a spatial component for the examination of black cultural production leads Jeffries, and other scholars doing similar work, to conceptualize "the city" or "the urban" as a racialized space bearing particular representational stakes for its black inhabitants. Jeffries articulates this point by describing how American methods for socially constructing race during the eighteenth and nineteenth centuries correspond with the rise in the number of urban centers taking shape in America during the same period. This correlation between race and urban space is one Murray Forman builds upon in his 2002 publication, *The 'Hood Comes First: Race, Space, and Place in Rap and Hip-Hop.* Here, Forman posits that "the ghetto"— a term expressing America's pejorative view of urban areas racially signified as black — has been replaced in common social parlance by the concept of "the 'hood." This shift has taken place, Forman argues, largely due to the mainstream influence and success of hip hop music.

Where Jeffries and Forman provide spatial analyses of the 'hood and — in the case of Forman — link the urban landscape to developments in hip hop, Jay-Z's work represents how hip hop has come to represent the ideological integration of the spatial 'hood into the social, political, racial, and economic consciousness we know as "being 'hood." Though discussions of 'hood existences are common throughout hip hop, Jay-Z serves well as our focal point due to his continued citing of his hood consciousness as factoring heavily into the monumental success he has experienced on the global mainstream music market. In this sense, Jay-Z's conception of hood is in conversation with the spatial 'hood Forman describes:

> The point here is that although ghetto regions and so-called inner-city neighbor-
> hoods frequently conform to the images and expectations of officials and the wider
> public, they also provide the site for a rich array of cultural creativity, social propriety,
> and nurture. As lived experiential environments, these spaces are invested with value
> and meaning by those who inhabit them. Seen in this light, a shift to an alternative
> discourse based on the 'hood's revised spatial frame introduces a potentially empow-
> ering conceptual transition for those who call its narrowly circumscribed parameters
> "home" [64].

With lyrics saying he'll be hood forever, Jay-Z offers one example of his engagement with a discourse on being hood — and being of the 'hood — resembling
what Forman describes ("Empire State of Mind").

In this lyric, Jay-Z presents his hood-ness as containing enough versatility
to facilitate his simultaneous existence between disparate worlds — represented
by Tribeca (an affluent lower-Manhattan neighborhood) and the 'hood. This
assertion relates to Forman's in that Jay-Z presents being hood as an empowering concept he has endowed with value and meaning. For Jay-Z, it seems, his
interaction with the 'hood — and his resulting hood consciousness — has prepared him to successfully establish a mainstream presence that allows him to
comfortably navigate the disparate worlds of mainstream culture and black
urban culture. Being hood, then, represents cultural hybridity for Jay-Z. The
urban space from which hip hop was born, therefore, epitomizes the same
hybrid social character as the music it birthed.

The cultural stakes of such a claim relate to those of Jeffries' essay in that
Jay-Z's conception of hood consciousness demonstrates the diversity of cultural
representation within the 'hood's spatial parameters, and among its inhabitants.
As such, Jay-Z's formulation of the 'hood — and its adjoining consciousness —
answers Jeffries' call for black urban popular culture to redefine the urban in a
manner in keeping with the cultural hybridity that defines our contemporary
moment:

> Late-twentieth-century cities have been transformed into vast depositories for the
> culturally hybrid. These other-than-modern, "postmodern," and socially constructed
> pairings give rise to a constant collision of human beings engaged in cultural (and
> economic) practice — it is these collisions and their hybrid by-products that dictate
> a redefinition of the urban. For urban black popular culture, there is no hip way to
> escape these collisions and the resultant call for redefinition [163].

Jay-Z's reconstruction of the urban serves to answer this call for change in black
popular culture, while also demonstrating how his success on the mainstream
media market can serve to offer a transgressive representation of the black cultural environment responsible for hip hop — whose representations in mainstream culture traditionally serve to perpetuate our pathological race
associations. In so doing, Jay-Z offers a blueprint for how hip hop can function
as an agent for black cultural fortification despite its participation in an iniquitous media system.

For Further Consideration

BOOKS

Cashmore, Ernest. *The Black Culture Industry.* New York: Routledge, 1997.
Kitwana, Bakari. *Why White Kids Love Hip Hop: Wankstas, Wiggers, Wannabes and the New Reality of Race in America.* New York: Basic Civitas, 2006.
McLaren, Peter, and Christine Sleeter. *Multicultural Education, Critical Pedagogy, and the Politics of Difference.* New York: State University of New York Press, 1995.
Price, Emmett, G. *Hip Hop Culture.* Santa Barbara, CA: ABC-CLIO, 2006.
Rose, Tricia. *Black Noise: Rap Music and Black Culture in Contemporary America.* Middletown, CT: Wesleyan, 1994.
Watkins, S. Craig. *Hip Hop Matters: Politics. Pop Culture, and the Struggle for the Soul of a Movement.* Boston: Beacon, 2006.

QUESTIONS

1. Has a culture lost its authenticity once it has become commercialized?
2. What strategies does Jay-Z use to reconcile his cultural authenticity and his mainstream appeal?
3. What does the transformation of the "hood" from an inner city location to a consciousness allow artists like Jay-Z to do?

Notes

1. The term "mainstream" in media and cultural studies discourse denotes the systematic cultural projection of a cohesive majority value system through the use of mass media. As we'll discuss, this socially constructed sense of consensus runs counter to the tenets of popular culture while simultaneously encompassing them in its design.

2. Rolf Wiggerhaus' 1994 publication *The Frankfurt School: Its History, Theories, and Political Significance* offers a thorough consideration of Horkheimer and Adorno's notion of the culture industry, with an equally thorough detailing of the often negative response it garnered from scholars and critics following its introduction.

3. Where, in our contemporary racial environment, it is almost understandable to see why predominantly white-owned multinational corporations that control the vast majority of record distribution would see it as profitable to sell a standardized pejorative image of blackness to the predominantly white consumers of hip hop on the global market — it should also stand to reason that African descendants who have learned from the same cultural system as all other Westerners would share in its resulting pathology. Individual hip-hop artists, therefore, share agency and culpability in the music's design and transmission.

Works Cited

Boyd, T. *The New H.N.I.C.: The Death of Civil Rights and the Reign of Hip Hop.* New York: NYU Press, 2004.
Fiske, J. *Television Culture.* New York: Routledge, 1988.

Forman, M. *The 'Hood Comes First: Race, Space, and Place in Rap and Hip-Hop.* Middletown, CT: Wesleyan University Press, 2002.

Freire, P. *Pedagogy of the Oppressed.* 1970. 30th anniversary ed. Trans. M. B. Ramos. London: Continuum, 2000.

George, N. "Rhymin' and Stealin'." *The Guardian.* 25 January 2005. Retrieved from *http://www.guardian.co.uk/music/2005/jan/23/popandrock.llcoolj.*

Hall, S. "What is This 'Black' in Black Popular Culture?" In *Black Popular Culture*, ed. G. Dent. New York: New, 1992. 21–33.

Horkheimer, M., T. Adorno, and N. Schmid. *Dialectic of Enlightenment.* 1947. Ed. G. S. Noerr. Trans. E. Jephcott. Stanford, CA: Stanford University Press, 2002.

Jay-Z. "Izzo, H.O.V.A." *The Blueprint.* New York: Roc-A-Fella Records, 2001.

_____, and A. Cook. "Empire State of Mind." *The Blueprint 3.* New York: Roc Nation, 2009.

_____, and A. Graham. "Off That." *The Blueprint 3.* New York: Roc Nation, 2009.

Jeffries, J. "Toward a Redefinition of the Urban: The Collision of Culture." In *Black Popular Culture*, ed. G. Dent. New York: New, 1992. 153–63.

McQuail, D. *McQuail's Mass Communication Theory.* 5th ed. London: Sage, 2005.

Pandian, J., and S. Parman. *The Making of Anthropology: The Semiotics of Self and Other in the Western Tradition.* Pitampura, New Delhi: Vedams, 2004.

13

The Self-Reliant Philosopher King

Shawn Carter Exonerated

SHA'DAWN BATTLE

Both casual observers and established critics charge hip hop's mogul, Shawn Carter, or Jay-Z, with the "crime" of delivering hokum lyrics—lyrics that question his authenticity and disclose his feigned "hood representation." And to some extent, their claims are absolutely legitimate. Between *Reasonable Doubt* and his most recent effort, *Blueprint 3*, Jay-Z has undergone a much-needed, gradual metamorphosis. It is not my purpose to apologize for Jay-Z, but to see him through the perspective of a modern Philosopher King. And so I draw from Plato, Emerson, and post-modernists.

Jay-Z's entrance into the hip hop arena, in 1996, was characterized by a proud hood mentality that was a reflection of the ghetto from which he emerged. He was not ashamed to proclaim Marcy Projects as the kennel that groomed him into the Frank Lucas of Brooklyn. In fact, in his first album, *Reasonable Doubt,* he announced in his lyrics many of the sacrosanct, unspoken codes of the hood. Jay-Z poetically declared war on anyone who impeded his road to riches in "Can't Knock the Hustle." He used his hood dialect to express his devotion to those within his circle of trust in "Feelin It," where he affirmed that collective uplift is the code of his clique, and that no one will fall as long as they stay together. Moreover, Jay-Z articulated the inevitable disjointing effects of greed and envy in the viscerally-charged track, "D'Evils." Thus, *Reasonable Doubt* and the other earlier albums not only disclosed his hood consciousness, but also gave him the green light to be the moral voice for the various cultures that Marcy beheld, and cultures alike around the world, and to chant these realities to a beat.

Jay-Z was then held to the titles of spokesman and leader of the hustlers, the proletariats, and the have-nots. The single-parent moms, the high school dropouts, the hopeless teens all relied on Shawn Carter — the modern-day Brooklyn griot — to retell their tales. However, the world witnessed a palpable shift in Jay-Z's lyrics and demeanor. As Jay-Z reached new heights as an artist, trendsetter, and businessman, he could not ignore his ascendency. He transcended being looked upon as solely "hood rich," an individual who maintained his allegiance to the hood only. The world began to recognize his intellectualism and his articulate nature as a substantial aspect of his character and complexity as a person and artist. Jay-Z, unlike many of his contemporaries, could operate within the parameters of standard American dialect, infusing African-American vernacular with what is known as the "Double Voice" — an ability Alice Walker, Zora Neale Hurston, and Toni Morrison are often praised for. His witty metaphors, his lexical and syntactic ambiguity, and his anecdotal abilities set him apart from other rappers. His rhetoric broadened his audience and allowed him to coexist within other cultures. His music was no longer limited to "the hood."

Jay-Z's multicultural consciousness began to develop consequences, though. His cultural allegiance was now determined by proximity. He had soared to new heights and, of course, his lyrics had to reflect his positioning. His lyrics became exclusive and his language esoteric, it seemed, to those he had previously represented, but to whom he could no longer relate. Consequently, the excluded audience who identified with the Marcy culture began to resent him, suggesting that his ascendency and exclusive lyrics denied him re-entry into the hood culture, and they ultimately called into question his authenticity as a rapper. This accusation had rippling effects. Critics used it as a segue to charge him with various other "crimes" such as being an all-around "phony" and a walking contradiction, imitating others, and refusing to share his wealth.

As Socrates discusses in Plato's *The Allegory of the* Cave, the Philosopher King is the individual who emerges from the cave of darkness to seek enlightenment and ascribe forms and truth to the shadows they thought were realities (*Republic VII* 388). The Philosopher King would rather coexist with other Philosopher Kings; nevertheless, Socrates proposes that implementing social order in society requires the Philosopher King to return to the cave to lead the disillusioned prisoners to the sun, for Socrates considers "the journey upwards to be the ascent of the soul into the intellectual world" (389). The question then is not, "Is Jay-Z an authentic member of the culture which he used to represent, since his lifestyle, lyrics, and paychecks have changed?" Better questions are: "*Should* his authenticity even be called into question just because he has opted to leave the cave? And does he still have a broader responsibility with his music now that he has escaped darkness? Is Jay-Z being forced into this role of leadership through this urge to return to darkness just to reassert himself and lead those who remain imprisoned toward the light?" Ralph Waldo Emerson would say that Jay-Z's responsibility is to himself first, because he is the embodiment of the Emersonian individual who relies on the self and not the impulse to accommodate others. Thus, Emerson's ideal individual redefines the Platonic Philosopher King in the sense that while he must embrace enlightenment, he must not succumb to the compulsion to return to the cave. Endorsing this Western philosophical belief would exonerate him of all "charges" of inauthentic representation and/or allegiance.

Intentions and Authenticity Questioned

Andrew Murfett, editor of EG, *The Age*'s music section, interviewed the erudite revolutionary artist Lupe Fiasco, who expressed his contentment with being able to contribute to the improvement of sociological issues in the world. Fiasco declared, "I don't have necessarily the celebrity success they [his label] want me to have but it's more social success and being able to speak at a college about world affairs. That's a success, to me." He maintained, "I don't want to be Jay-Z and be worth $400 million and perform on every awards show. It's getting in touch with somebody who needs to improve their self-esteem. As opposed to driving a Bentley and putting some chains on [sic]." Thus, Fiasco implicitly criticized Jay-Z for his apathy toward the human condition and his lack of social consciousness, and he is not the only artist who objects to Jay-Z in this sense.

Beanie Sigel is Roc-A-Fella's most ruthless brute and potent "hot head," and arguably, he was at one point Jay-Z's self-appointed successor. Jay-Z asserted that if one was to make a round two of his life, Sigel would be the sequel to it (Sigel, "It's On"). But nowadays, Sigel frequently expresses his disavowal of Jay-Z's new aura and his disconnectedness from the hood. During a DJ On&On interview, Sigel responded to a prison letter that asked him to comment on Jay-Z's "gangsta" being "put on trial." Sigel apparently saw Jay-Z's character as not comparable to his own: "I don't have no blemishes in my character at all. I will never be the dude that switched up or changed or fronted on my people. I can still go to my hood and walk down the street, go to the corner store, chill with the young boys, or whatever, and I still got that respect in the hood." DJ On&On then forced Sigel to specifically comment on Jay-Z's hood credibility. Sigel said the following:

> He [Jay-Z] got respect as far as his talent, not as the individual he is.... When you got a person who states at the beginning, "I wore the doo-rag on MTV; I made them love you"—you talking about the people in the street the ones you represent. Then once you obtain the amount of success you get to, you tell people "I used to carry knots like that; now it's Black Cards and good credit and such." So you tell people who out there who hustle, who make their money, who can't fathom having a Black Card, their money's under the mattress or whatever, he ain't cool for that. You got

the Maybach and all of this. If you ain't got a Maybach your SS Impala ain't shit; your Charger ain't shit.... How you turn your back on the shit that helped supported you to get to that Maybach and to get them Black Cards? ... A lot of people caught up in a façade of materialistic things.... Now you're turning your back on the things that got you there. How can y'all accept that? *Jump the Turnstyle.*

Thus, Sigel not only placed Jay-Z's street credibility on trial, but he charged him with the "crime" of declaring his allegiance to high society and neglecting the hood, the hustlers, and the Beanie Sigels around the globe, and, falsifying his affiliation with this latter culture.

Millionaire rapper 50 Cent also expressed his intolerance of Jay-Z's "disloyalty" in a recent duet with Beanie Sigel entitled, "I Go Off." He not only openly criticized Jay-Z for no longer representing Marcy, but also underlined Jay-Z's new class consciousness, referencing "Grey Poupon," which, incidentally, is not a condiment commonly found in the ghetto.

Even hip hop magazines and blog sites have questioned Jay-Z's loyalty to the Marcy culture. Preston Jones, writer for *Slant Magazine,* admitted that " it's kind of hard to cling to street cred [sic] when you've got shareholders on your mind," in his rejection of *Kingdom Come,* Jay-Z's "come-back" album after his short-lived retirement. Additionally, blogger J.C. Arenas recently posted a blog about Jay-Z's accessibility to President Obama, suggesting that the mere idea of his proximity and fellowship with the president is indicative of his detachment to the hustlers and have-nots. He called Jay-Z a "sell-out," and he said Jay-Z "loses credibility for a seat in the White House Situation Room." Arenas posited, "Through his music, he's continuously flaunting his accessibility to the president — who has an average monthly approval rating from Blacks exceeding 90 percent — which serves as a reminder of just how far he's come from Brooklyn's Marcy Projects." His argument, however, is a hasty generalization because it supposes that anyone who accepts gifts from executive leaders is no longer of the "plain folk" because he or she has "sold out." However, Jay-Z was invited to the White House because, for one, Obama is a fan of his music; second, it was a gift to help support his campaign to raise money for the victims of "9/11." A third grader from an unknown town could write a poem that inspires the president and receive an invitation to the White House. Thus, Jay-Z's appearance in the White House does not disassociate him from the community, but it is clear how it can be interpreted that way if all facts are not presented.

On Another Level?

These critics' claims can be validated, however. Jay-Z's language awards him acceptance into the world of intellects; his net worth is proof that he exists on another level; his peers and former confidants understand his positioning; and his lyrics imply transcendence.

Many artists attribute their "self-proclaimed" greatness to their inclusion of oversimplified metaphors. An example of this can be found in "The Way," which rapper Fabolous simply conflates a nine-millimeter handgun, which he claims remains on his person, and the number nine on the Philadelphia Seventy Sixers, Andre Iguodala. However, Jay-Z's language is a testament to why many accept, recite, and deconstruct his lyrics. More often than not, his language allows his lyrics to penetrate the realm of academia. In a composition classroom, lexical ambiguity, for example, can be taught by simply listening to a Jay-Z album. An example when Jay-Z incorporates lexical ambiguity, or an instance when his words and phrases have multiple interpretations, occurs in "Lost One." Here he uses vocal deflection to highlight the ambiguity within the use of the words "be" and "B." Surely, he could have placed more emphasis on the second "be" used as an echo, in order to highlight the fact that he is, presumably, referencing his girlfriend (now wife) and musical counterpart, Beyoncé, whose pseudonym is "B." Another example of ambiguity lies in a line about "white lies" in his opus, "My President is Black." The phrase "white lies" is ambiguous because, in its political context — Barack Obama's inauguration — the black world no longer has to suffer the injury of being lied to by the highest government official. Jay-Z could have been referring to a way of "stretching" the truth, or telling a not-so-harsh fib. Furthermore, he is conscious of the way that language and pronunciation differ according to culture.

Jay-Z's lyrics are also a combination of cultural consciousness *and* word play. Consider the line in "Dear Summer" where he is making reference to the allegiance that young people have for him, by playing on the term "blasphemy." Because in black culture the colloquial pronunciation of "for" is sometimes "fuh," and a rapid enunciation of "blast for me" is easily mistaken for "blasphemy." For Jay-Z, this desirably leaves room for both interpretations: "blast for me" or "blasphemy." Jay-Z's awareness of how language is a construct of culture allows him to incorporate lexical ambiguity here. Many rappers do not possess this type of language consciousness, and so their music has a "piece-of-cake" ring to it and lacks hermeneutical depth. In this respect, Jay-Z's music places him on an almost insurmountable pedestal in hip hop because his language separates him from most of his contemporaries.

A look into his earning power suggests that Jay-Z has consciously chosen a fairly expected trajectory. He had no choice but to separate himself from his previous lifestyle and correspondents as he rose to prominence. *Foxnews.com*, reporting from *Forbes.com*, reveals that Jay-Z grossed an estimated $34 million in 2006. *Best Life Magazine* reports that Jay-Z's net worth as of 2009 was $350 million, grossing approximately $82 million annually. Moreover, his success does not stop at making music. Jay-Z was not stretching the truth when he frequently exclaimed that to reduce his life to being a businessman is too limited. He wants us to recognize that he, Jay-Z, is a business (Kanye, "Diamonds from Sierra Leone"). The capitalist crusader, according to *Best Life*, has a business empire that includes clothing, fragrances, the New Jersey Nets, sports bars, liquor, and hotels. And this list is not the breadth of his success. In fact, he reminds his doubters of how he juggles running 16 businesses while simultaneously writing 16 song bars, frequently ("Reminder"). Jay-Z is not on dubious grounds for his disassociation with the hood and for proclaiming it in his music, because he is now held to a different set of expectations in order to complement his achievements.

Even Beanie Sigel has admitted that he understands Jay-Z's transcendence. In an interview with Charlamagne Tha God, posted on *WorldStarHipHop (WSHH)* in October 2009, Sigel announced:

> I understand, Jay, you're somewhere else in your career.... And it's certain things, where he at, everybody can't go. And I understand that. Like, he somewhere else. You don't need Beanie Sigel in the building with the preperception [sic] that people got of me — this crazy dude liable to do anything or whatever — or Emilio Sparks liable to say anything out of his mouth. You know what I'm saying? He's in records saying "L'chaim" and things like that. So he dealing with Jewish people.... Ain't nothing wrong with that but then you got Freeway, Muslim, with the beard.... So it's certain things that — we taint his image, State Property — and the places he's at.

Sigel thus alluded to clashes of cultures, cultural gaps, and irreconcilable differences that would inevitably put a halt to Jay-Z's race to wealth and stature, in that a person is ultimately judged by the company he maintains. He understands that Jay-Z cannot be enmeshed in the members of State Property, the label he gave Sigel, and their dealings. He has become a positive emblem of success, and they are the antithesis of Jay-Z's transformation.

In addition to Sigel's admission, Jay-Z acknowledges in his rhymes that his reticence and disengagement with the Marcy culture is due in part to his financial portfolio. In *The Black Album*, for example, Jay-Z reveals his class consciousness when he reminds listeners of the rarity, even in 2003, of a black man's mere appearance and appraisal in esteemed magazines, whose sales amount to almost $500 million ("What More Can I Say"). He may seem pretentious when he reminds his critics of his worth by warning a dominant class of rich Americans that there is a guest on the landscape of corporate wealth who is the black community's version of the Jewish Martha Stewart ("What More Can I Say"). But his self-appraisal is unfathomable to the average black man in Marcy's dungeons.

Kingdom Come also contains lyrics that connote Jay-Z's welcomed arrival to upper-class society. In the song "30 Something," he acknowledges this transformation as maturation, but it is more than that. Jay-Z has relinquished the Marcy mindset, and he has embraced the privileges as well as the codes of conduct of high society. He sings about how he has refrained from putting rims on luxury cars, how his cars are made with curtains, which means he no longer purchases tinted windows, and how he no longer buys expensive, diamond-filled jewelry that is not of quality. He no longer flexes his ability to "buy out the bar," because he now invests his money in entire night clubs. He now sings about stocks and stockbrokers instead of drugs and gaudy jewelry. Here, he is not bragging about his material possessions. He is demonstrating his investment I.Q., and the importance to him of quality and class. Jay-Z knows he has become a paradigm of investment strategizing.

The completion of Shawn Carter's evolution from rags to riches appears in his lyrics in *Blueprint 3*. The language is matter-of-fact and conspicuous. He is now comfortable with proclaiming his transformation and separation from the hood. Throughout the entire album, he makes it his business to announce his distinctiveness. In "Already Home," for example, he states that, while listeners already know H&R Block is no longer a potential tax preparer for him, his wealth has placed him in a different tax bracket or *league* of the *game*. Jay-Z is now the gentleman one can find in the opera balcony, dawned in culturally exclusive tuxedos ("Thank You"). Jay-Z maintains, in this album, that he is a suave individual who frequently sits courtside in Madison Square Garden, so close that he can touch a referee or give New York Knicks players high fives ("Empire State of Mind"). Even his attire and agenda have evolved from throwback jerseys to tailored suits—the look of an owner ("On to the Next One"). Jay-Z metaphorically explains the degree of his surpassing regularity when he says that he has now ascended to a galaxy level of explorations, because to be relegated to earth is mundane ("Already Home"). So, Jay-Z *is* on another level, and his life as a perpetual vacation ("Beach Chair") is warranted.

A Platonic Response

Plato's *Allegory of the Cave* is a dialogue that exists between Socrates and his older brother, Glaucon. The conversation itself mirrors Plato's own thoughts. It deals with men dwelling in a dark cave since their childhood, facing the back of the cave, in restrictive shackles that prohibit any type of movement that would allow them to turn away from the wall. There is a blazing fire behind them that causes their shadows and shadows of things to appear on the wall they are facing. They cannot describe the things that have cast shadows in their true essence because all they know are shadows created by the fire. They do not complain about their condition because they know nothing else. Socrates says they need to be introduced to the sun, which symbolizes enlightenment. But they will be afraid to embrace the light at first, because their only realities were shadows. When they do face the sun, this transformation will be painful (388).

In *Blueprint* 3, Jay-Z suggests that he appreciates enlightenment. He announces his transcendence in this album, even though he used to reject it on previous albums by centering his lyrics on the darkness from which he emerged. In *Kingdome Come*, for example, he titles a song "Can't Knock the Hustle"; in it, he discusses dealing drugs to acquire property, enemies who plot one's demise, and all the realities of the hood — a culture, as of 2006, that Jay-Z had long bade farewell to. No doubt this transformation was difficult. But as Socrates proposes, after turning away from this light and refusing it, and after seeking "refuge in the objects of vision which he can see" (388), Jay-Z, like the prisoners, will eventually come to embrace the light and understand what the truths actually were. But this only occurs after he has adjusted his vision to the glare of enlightenment (388).

Plato's Philosopher King thinks of his old dwelling place and those still imprisoned, and he will "pity them" (389). Similarly, Jay-Z empathizes with the human conditions of poverty and tragedy in "Minority Report." He makes reference to a war on racism, to social injustice, and to unequal access to education, especially in *The Black Album*, which demonstrates his concern with "his old habitation" (389). He laments the poor conditions of the masses, but his return to these conditions is unimaginable. Socrates says that the Philosopher King will be willing to "endure anything, rather than think as they do and live after their manner" (389). If he did return to darkness and was then asked to define the shadows in the cave after being exposed to light, he would not be able to. Socrates insists that the prisoners will "say of him that up he went and down he came without his eyes; and that it was better not even to think of ascending; and if one tried to loose another and lead him up to the light, let them only catch the offender, and they would put him to death" (389). Thus, the prisoners will not be able to fathom what the emancipated individual knows to be truth, or that he could even want to advance toward the light. Obviously, his vision no longer correlates with theirs. The prisoners offer no complaints to their situation and are content with darkness. Similarly, the hood cliché is to become "hood rich" and to re-invest your earnings right back into that same society because to do otherwise is incomprehensible.

The Philosopher King will not want to return to darkness: "those who attain to this beatific vision are unwilling to descend to human affairs; for their souls are hastening into the upper world where they desire to dwell; which desire of theirs is very natural" (389). Jay-Z demonstrates his unwillingness to return to darkness on the "Ain't I" hook, when he declares that he is never going back, referring to the lifestyle that deals with acquiring things with dirty money, being the primary target of interest of the FBI, and scorning the so-called American Dream. He also asserts in "Minority Report" that although he was able to produce a million dollars for the Hurricane Katrina efforts, he did not donate his time, which for him equated to him having done nothing. He felt guilty on two levels: one, because he only gave his money to the relief effort without ensuring its effectiveness; and two, because his financial assistance landed in the hands of the very politicians and bureaucracy that stranded thousands of New Orleaneans. The point is that although the song talks about the Katrina disaster, no one expected Jay-Z to go to New Orleans and help rebuild the levies. Emerson would say that he is not even required to donate his money. And Jay-Z declares that he has no intention to return to poor and unfortunate conditions.

But Socrates compels the Philosopher King to revert to his previous conditions. Now he is admonished to "descend again among the prisoners in the den, and partake of their labours and honours, whether they are worth having or not" (390). Obviously, Socrates would have disagreed with Du Bois's concept of the "Talented Tenth," the idea that not everyone is suitable for higher education. Socrates believes that the prisoners can become great intellects "later by habit and exercise" (390). Likewise, Jay-Z's refusal to take responsibility for Sigel after being given the opportunity by a judge suggests that he understood he could not simply transfer his enlightenment to Sigel. Sigel's disposition was incongruent with Jay-Z's new cultural affiliations and realities. Since the prisoners offer no complaints, does this imply that they are satisfied with what they consider reality? Does "the power and capacity of learning exist in the soul already" (389–90)? If so, then it is innate and cannot be implanted later on. So why burden the Philosopher King by forcing him into this role of leadership? Why burden Jay-Z with the roles of leader, supplier, and escort to Sigel and other prisoners into enlightenment?

Plato essentially believes that society must have rulers who are intelligible thinkers. Socrates states, "neither the uneducated and uniformed of the truth, nor yet those who never make an end of their education, will be able ministers of State" (390). Not a farfetched notion! If literacy influences reasoning, then a more than literate and/or knowledgeable person should be entrusted with the affairs of the State. However, his reasoning is flawed. Socrates argues that those who are not philosophers will only act "upon compulsion, fancying that they are already dwelling apart in the islands of the blest" (390). He is wrong for positing that a philosopher is uniformed or uneducated if he exhibits compulsion. The world itself is not harmoniously constructed; dissonance is a part of normalcy. Disagreement is inevitable. But to consider acquiescing to others' ways of thinking, even after they contrast with what you hold to be true, requires compulsion. If one is forced to act a certain way against one's will and one acquiesces, it is only because of a compelling notion to do so. Of course, it is true that after being exposed to paradise, there will be no interest to return to that deprived state, and if one does, it is only because one has been pressured to do so. This is the nature of compulsion, and the Philosopher King must be liberated from not only darkness, but also predicaments that necessitate compulsion.

Plato's *Allegory of the Cave* is legitimate and paints a much-needed picture to those who remain in the cave and have no desire to emerge and embrace enlightenment. But forcing the Philosopher King to return to the cave to redefine realities and to disclose possibilities further confines him. He must be granted the opportunity to converse and travel with his equals. There should be no moral obligation for Philosopher Kings to be stewards of enlightenment. Being interspersed with those still imprisoned would limit them and their consumption of knowledge. Thus, the Platonic Philosopher King must be redefined in opposition to Platonic expectations.

The Emersonian Individual

Seeing Jay-Z through the lens of individualism leaves little room for anyone to question his devotion to group thought and the communal. It also challenges Plato's ideal Philosopher King and his role(s). Emerson's theories on individualism allow Jay-Z to roam freely on this new plateau, without being subjected to accusations of inauthentic representation, desertion, imitation, and desired solitude; it also liberates him of the obligation to return to "darkness" to reassert or redefine himself. Emerson's lengthy essay "Self-Reliance" points out three crucial concepts that exonerate Jay-Z of the aforementioned charges: self-trust, nonconformity, and divorcing consistency.

According to Emerson, it is dreadfully important to believe in your own intuitions and inner thoughts. He despises the notion of welcoming the convictions and truths of others. He asserts, "To believe your own thought, to believe that what is true for you in your private heart is true for all men, — that that is genius" (420). In addition, he states, "A man should learn to detect that gleam of light which flashes across his mind from within, more than the lustre of the firmament of bards and sages" (420). In our context then, Jay-Z must trust the words that arise from within, which is why he insists that whenever he possesses the urge to write, he should be granted the room opportunity to say that which comes to mind, whatever it may be ("Change Clothes"). Whatever appears in black and white on the page must represent his truths, even if those truths reveal the new, loathed Shawn Carter. He must trust in himself and dislodge the opinions of others, for this is the nature of individualism.

As Emerson suggests that the individual is afraid to allow his thoughts to manifest themselves, he must be ready to accept someone else's laying claim to ideas that were rightfully his. Emerson posits, "Else, to-morrow a stranger will say with masterly good sense precisely what we have thought and felt all the time, and we shall be forced to take with shame our own opinion from another" (420). Sigel, during his interview with Charlamange Tha God, lamented that Jay-Z stole an idea from him and included it in "Already Home" on *Blueprint*

3. He explained how he was late for a photo shoot because he did not have a car. The manager asked Sigel if we wanted a pricey vehicle, and he proudly declined. He wanted the label to teach him how to reach the status that would afford him such a vehicle, instead of simply providing it for him. He thus declared, "Them lines when Jay say bout '... fish for em'—now they want me to cook, clean, and do a dish for em,' I told him that" (*WSHH*). Unequivocally, Sigel is referring to the popular line in Jay-Z's "Already Home." Emerson would say that Sigel can hardly be angry because he failed to allow his own idea to turn into palpable success like Jay-Z did. He must shoulder the guilt of not allowing this idea to come to a reward beyond the confines of Marcy.

Emerson also proposes that self-trust involves refraining from envy and imitation of others: "envy is ignorance; ... imitation is suicide" (420). In other words, it is imperative to trust in your own ingenuity instead of relying on the knowledge of other great thinkers who predate you. Jay-Z is frequently accused of imitating the late Notorious B.I.G., who was arguably the most esteemed hood figure and whose death was the mere reflection of the troublesome life he lived—the life Jay-Z has escaped. His critics oppose Jay-Z for recycling Biggie's lyrics in his own rhymes, but his rebuttal is this: when he recites a Biggie verse, he is only "biggin' up" (which is a popular phrase for showing respect) his brother, or evoking his memory or lyrics that left a lasting impact, and he is bodacious enough to do this. He declares that his periodic use of Notorious B.I.G. adages and lyrics are, by no means, imitating Biggie because of his own lack of ingenuity. He boastfully asserts in "What More Can I Say" that it is all in a spirit of love and respect, which he is man enough to acknowledge; but he also reassures those naysayers that his lyrical flow is great in its own right.

Apparently, Jay-Z's intentions here are to immortalize the great "Biggie Smalls" and to keep his legacy thriving. This is self-gratifying for him. Perhaps preserving what Biggie stood for means that although Jay-Z has transcended the realities of Marcy, he can maintain ties with that culture through his art. He is therefore not reciting Biggie's lyrics because of sloth or the inability to trust in his own creativity. The real issue is that these critics do not want him falsifying his association with someone who was the embodiment of the culture which Jay-Z is no longer associated. Their argument is red herring. It has nothing to do with imitation; rather, Jay-Z has taken an idea and allowed it to evolve into something greater. Jay-Z has given form to a perilously nebulous concept, while Sigel chooses to remain in the cave of disillusionment.

Emerson said that a person must not only trust in his abilities, but must allow them to surface assertively and daringly, because "God will not have his work made manifest by cowards" (420). Jay-Z's similar assertiveness is evident when he affirms that he is simply talented and courageous enough to give love to a fallen lyrical and cultural hero. He trusts in his own inventiveness and shuns any fears of being taunted or rejected for his actions. In "What More

Can I Say," he explains his intentions by reciting another Biggie rhyme. Pompous? Perhaps, but Jay-Z's conviction is rooted; neither envy nor imitation is a possible motive. He is spearheading a rebellious regime based on individualistic principles here.

For Emerson, "Whoso would be a man, must be a nonconformist" (421). One cannot be vulnerable to the expectations thrusts upon him. An individual must have a strong constitution: "For nonconformity, the world whips you with its displeasure. And therefore, a man must know how to estimate a sour face" (423). Similarly, Jay-Z must not consider any of his actions a transgression against another, and he must not embrace "universal" truths. He endorses this way of thinking in "Say Hello," when he directly addresses the esteemed Al Sharpton, stating that he does not need Sharpton to be his spokesperson — that he will stop using the word "bitch" in his lyrics when Jena 6 is no longer an issue, and when there no longer exists disparities in the school systems in America. Jay-Z refuses to accept society's denunciation of the word "bitch" as demeaning women and as misogynistic. Although he offers an ultimatum, his accentuation of the word at the end of the rhyme is a forewarning that he will not abstain from its use. Jay-Z refuses to conform to Sharpton's ideologies, as the world does. He does not care that Sharpton is an intimidating civil rights activist whose words many embrace.

Jay-Z is much too ambitious to conform. His aspirations to succeed, as has been discussed earlier in this chapter, are rooted much higher than the typical trajectory of the eye. In "So Ambitious," Jay-Z enters the philosophical through a post-structural lens, because with any set of binary pairs, one must be privileged over the other. As such, everything is partially defined by what it is not. Jacques Derrida argues that "we can subvert these oppositions and show that one term relies on and inheres within the other" (qtd. in Sarup 38). It is thus commonly expected for a black male not to identify with his binary opposite, the white man, in class or economic status. However, Jay-Z dismisses this belief of black ineptitude when he explains white society's disdain of his progression and his living in penthouses as their neighbors. Jay-Z references authenticity when he recognizes that his class status has changed, and that he can no longer physically dwell in darkness. Still, he is reluctant to divorce the relationships formed with many of that culture, which is why he states, in "Diamonds are Forever," that he hosts his friends from his past to the new home as they get high and watch chandeliers. This juxtaposition of location and culture and normative values are what makes Jay-Z a unique subject for inquiry into the question of authenticity. However, this song is from *Blueprint 2*, which was released in 2001. Jay-Z had not yet completely transcended the Marcy culture and lifestyle, and he was battling having to do so. This represents the Philosopher King's need to turn away from the light and seek "refuge" (388) in the darkness, because he "is unable to see the realities of which in his former state he had seen the shadows" (388). Moreover, in response to nonconformity, he does not accept the status quo, which would rather deny him and others alike equal economic representation and a chance to coexist equally with members of the privileged class. This is shown through his literal and metaphoric allusions: "watching chandelier ceilings high as fuck." His ascendency is thus proof of nonconformity. Sigel and others expect Jay-Z to sign over his liberties, as Emerson argues (421), and accept the denial of ascendency instead, which Sigel seems to be content with.

The self-reliant man, under these terms, must also do only what creates his own euphoria. "What I must do is all that concerns me, not what people think" (Emerson 423). One argument against Jay-Z is that his music has changed: it no longer embodies the cries of struggle; it no longer reflects the downtrodden subcultures of the hood. Yet, Jay-Z's response to reverting to that sound is, "Why would I go back to my old music when this new music is constantly elevating my status?" ("What We Talkin' Bout"). His music and lyrics indicate what stimulates his own interest. Socrates even admits that the Philosopher Kings would rather "remain in the upper world" (390) and "spend the greater part of their time in the heavenly light" (391) because that is what concerns them. Hence, doing the opposite would strip the Philosopher King of his private concerns. The argument then is whether Jay-Z's responsibility is to pacify his audience only. What about personal interests? His responsibility is to the image he sees when he gazes into a mirror.

Sigel complains that Jay-Z has failed to take on the responsibility of carrying him, as well as the other members of State Property, financially. "If you had to go through hardships and struggles in your life," Sigel explained in an interview on Philadelphia's *Power99 Hot Boys Radio*, "and then you get to the point where you are out of that, why let your brother go through that pain too?" Sigel was angered by Jay-Z's statement to him, "I got you, no matter what," and how he fell short of that promise in his refusal to help Sigel and the other State Property members through their economic hardships.

Part of Jay-Z's obligation as an Emersonian individual is not to adhere to others' misfortune. He cannot return to the cave to ameliorate social, economic, and political problems. If he is to become this self-reliant individual, he must ignore the impulse to compensate others for what they lack; he must exercise self-control. And for this reason, Emerson believes a man does not have to provide an explanation for why he may choose to climb heights in solitude: "Expect me not to show cause why I seek or why I exclude company" (422). He maintains, while infusing subtle sarcasm, "Then again, do not tell me, as a good man did to-day, of my obligation to put all poor men in good situations. Are they *my* poor?" (422). That is, Jay-Z must resist the impulse to shower the poor — granted pennilessness does not apply to Sigel — with the wealth that he has rightfully earned. Furthermore, Emerson reminds readers that a man's duty is not to liberate men of their poor conditions because of the plethora of institutions already designed to aid the poor, like "the thousandfold Relief Societies" (422). Jay-Z thus owes no compensation to Sigel and his cronies, and he must exhibit self-reliance through indifference and resistance to this impulse. Some may say this is selfish and undermines altruism. Nevertheless, Jay-Z seems to be annoyed with these expectations when he asks members of Roc-A-Fella, in "Already Home," why it is so difficult for them to reach the peak of their success when he has provided them with the necessary tools. In other words, he is saying, I emerged from the cave and advanced toward the light and sought truth in objects and ideas that existed before my arrival. I seized these things independently, through intellectualism, and it is not my responsibility to make sure you follow the "blueprint" after I have distributed it. He has equipped them with the necessary tools to expand, but he denies obligation to Sigel. His stance on this is apparent when he says that he owes no one anything and adult men should not expect him to be Santa Claus when they can stand up on their own and get off his lap of accommodation ("What We Talkin' About?").

No one is saying Jay-Z is perfect. Jay-Z is walking a tightrope because many disagree with the contradictions that appear in his lyrics. Jay-Z makes occasional references to the criticism of him snubbing his affiliation with the culture from which he emerged. Such responses are suggested by him asserting that he will forever being linked to the hood ("Empire State of Mind"), or when he even invites listeners to show respect to the bad guy ("Say Hello"). Furthermore, Jay-Z shuns the gangster mentality in the very next album when he begrudges those who pose with firearms in front of computers, posting the pictures to social networking sites. He tells them to drop that attitude, because he has, and to accompany him to the White House dressed in professional attire instead ("What We Talkin' About"). Jay-Z's lyrics also present polemical interests in that he sometimes sings about relentless loyalty to "La Familia" ("The Dynasty"), and then his music will, too, reflect the selfish, privatized goals of gangster capitalism. He has boasted as late as 2006–07 about being able to "break bread" with his companions and ensure that his wealth is distributed amongst them all ("Do You Wanna Ride"). However, Jay-Z is now at a place where he openly objects to feeding everyone who feels a part of his music and life. Consider how in "What We Talkin' Bout" Jay-Z sneeringly responds to Sigel for blaming him for his own lack of production and for not supplying his financial needs. When Jay-Z tells him "Get of my lap / I don't have a beard and Santa Claus ain't black," he belittles him by implying that Sigel and the host of others, with their hands outstretched, are childlike and expect Jay-Z to reach inside of his little red bag and award them with gifts. But Jay-Z totally objects to this.

Emerson would respond to this allegation by referring to what he terms "foolish consistency" (424). Emerson argues that being consistent is unnecessary and becomes mundane: "With consistency a great soul simply has nothing to do. He may as well concern himself with his shadow on the wall" (424). He insists that it is perfectly normal to declare a belief one day, and then state the exact opposite the next, because it is imperative to "live ever in a new day" (424). "Speak what you think now in hard words," he insists, "and to-morrow speak what to-morrow thinks in hard words again, though it contradict every thing [sic] you said to-day" (424). Contradiction is welcomed, then, for memory is a slippery faculty: "It seems to be a rule of wisdom never to rely on your memory alone" (424). If memory is a slippery faculty that tells a man his beliefs are wedded to certain deities and institutions of the past, must he reconsider them in the face of a new day? Emerson would think so. The notion then is to detach from the cave. Emerson further instructs, "Leave your theory, as Joseph his coat in the hand of the harlot, and flee" (424). He leads us to believe that complex consistency invites being misunderstood: "To be great is to be misunderstood" (424). We might say that Jay-Z is right to challenge his old affinities; his divergence means he is living in the moment and is not caged in by a mundane, "foolish consistency."

Emerson would critique the Philosopher King. He would say that he must be self-reliant. He must rely on his thoughts and personal concerns instead of placing others at the forefront of his missions. He must not concern himself with returning to the cave to assert what he now understands as truth.

Consequences of Enlightenment

I will not dismiss the fact that the Philosopher King will endure consequences for seeking enlightenment. He is forced into the role of leadership, and his language and ideals become esoteric to the masses.

According to Socrates, the Philosopher Kings are "bought into the world to be rulers of the hive" because they have the capacity to comprehend the truths of the world and thus attain higher knowledge (390). He does not want to account or speak for the masses still imprisoned. However, compelling the Philosopher King to return to darkness is forcing the role of leadership upon him.

Consider Paul Beatty's narrator, Gunnar Kaufman, in his novel, *The White Boy Shuffle* (1996). Gunnar is a black basketball superstar, a genius, who spends most of his childhood in a predominantly white society, but who is then forced to move to an urban ghetto in Los Angeles, called Hillside. He develops multicultural consciousness as he is exposed to black cultural customs. Because Gunnar is a gifted poet and intellect, the people of Hillside expect him to be a spokesman for all of the subcultures of Hillside: the "welfare cheats," "panhandlers," "baseheads," dealers, recovered addicts, Hispanics, and blacks (220).

This leadership role even follows him when he attends Boston University. He rejects the role assigned him, but he is forced to give several speeches because of his superlative oratory skills. But each time, he digresses from the desired subject and speaks about unrelated issues, or he exhibits a rebellious attitude.

After being asked to deliver a speech protesting the school's advocacy of an Uncle Tom–like "black Statesman" and his rule in South Africa, and after being introduced as "accomplished poet, black man extraordinaire, voice of the nation, Gunnar Kaufman" (198), Gunnar instead opts to discuss suicide or martyrdom as a means of refusing to surrender to the status quo (196). Gunnar disappoints an anxious crowd in Hillside that wants him to offer himself as a sacrifice to commemorate the death of his best friend, who commits suicide after listening to his speech about believing in something enough to die for it. However, while the world is watching, Gunnar decides to cut his finger off instead of immolating himself in efforts to become the "nigger stamp of approval" (196) in the cause for martyrdom. Gunnar never expects everyone to endorse his beliefs. He advocates individual consciousness rather than group thought which allows one voice to represent the whole. This is demonstrated when he tells the media that he will commit suicide when he is "good and god-damn ready" (202). In the prologue, he states, "On the one hand, this messiah gig is a bitch, on the other I've managed to fill the perennial void in African-American leadership" (1). He is only able to accomplish this because the messiah role and the "voice-of-the people" title are practically shoved down his throat. He tries to rebel against their demands, but ultimately cannot.

Jay-Z and Gunnar have much in common. Jay-Z is articulate and infuses standard American dialect with African-American slang in his lyrics, swinging the pendulum back and forth from one culture to another. His role becomes burdensome because he is expected to always voice the concerns of black culture in his music. In essence, forced leadership is a consequence of enlightenment.

A major consequence of enlightenment is that while it advances a person, it also ostracizes him. His language becomes elusive and even foreign to those still inside the cave. Jay-Z's lyrics become exclusive to minorities he used to represent. Consequently, these lyrics warrant indictment. Because the under-privileged no longer identified with or understood his music, they began to unfairly critique him as an inauthentic member of this culture. How else can they feel about the statement in "Already Home" where he creates distance by bragging that he made it out of a place where his steady diet of dodging bullets and incarceration has now been replaced with eating quail? These lyrics are exclusive because if an inhabitant of Marcy, or any other project, was inter-viewed and asked if he or she had ever eaten quail, the answer would probably be no. Quail is for the upper class. The Marcy culture prefers meals that are convenient and simple. Quail is served with exquisite side dishes that may be decorative but not filling. The conversation about quail is itself undesirable to the Marcy cultures around the world, because it excludes them. While individuals from the projects might agree that Jay-Z will more than likely escape jail, they believe that they are doomed to the lifestyle of activities that could put them behind bars. Avoiding jail is not a likely reality for those totally immersed in the hood. Although jail is a likely consequence, they cannot diverge from criminal activities.

Nevertheless, Jay-Z's lyrical dexterity in hits from the *Blueprint 3* like "Real as it Gets" includes language that is only understood by the educated. An average dealer, an eighth-grade dropout, or any functionally illiterate person would not immediately recognize "Braille" as the decoded alphabet for the blind. Uneducated subcultures will not have the patience to decode a line in which Jay-Z describes himself as the musical equivalent to Braille. Such a reference requires an understanding of the denotation of each word, in order to comprehend the entire phrase and the comparison being made. Thus, his language excludes the uneducated and those who will not understand his ambiguities, lending him to the criticism of being lyrically obscure and potentially irrelevant to the hood.

Jay-Z must not turn away from intellectualism and enlightenment, but he must face the consequences that ensue. He understands the pressures of being a Philosopher King because he declares that success is nothing short of a headache because it requires too much stress ("Success"). The stress is the result of trying to conform to the Platonic Philosopher King instead of endorsing self-reliance. It is due to being forced into a role of leadership, and it is caused by bearing the guilt of adjusting to the light, empathizing with the masses still imprisoned, and embracing his new-found knowledge and culture, requiring exclusivity and an entirely new disposition.

Conclusion

Jay-Z, our post-modern Philosopher King, must redefine the role by situating it in an Emersonian context. Critics who dismiss him based on the faulty premise of inauthentic representation ignore his responsibility to the self. His accomplishments mentioned are not exaggerated. They are colossal achievements that would not have been possible without emerging from the cave of darkness to attain enlightenment. Returning to imprisonment suggests that the Philosopher King must revert to oblivion and verisimilitude. By nature, he is disinclined to do this, and he does not want to deliver the prisoners from the void of their existence. In a post-modern perspective, returning to physical darkness exposes the Philosopher King to danger. Because he has done what concerns him — acquire property, stocks, and other investments — he has become a bull's eye to those he once shared shackles with. Emerson may shun envy, but its permanency is undeniable in that people are always aspiring to want more. It is gluttonous, but it is reality. So, in addition to forced leadership and an inevitable culture gap which warrants charges of disingenuousness, the Philosopher King exposes himself to being robbed, literally. Yet, no man could ever rob him of his intellect.

The Philosopher King is at first apprehensive about walking toward the sun and cannot adjust to the light, and so finds himself in a meta-physical state. He finds solace in turning his head toward darkness, but he cannot deny the bliss he has witnessed and will soon embrace. It almost compares to purgatory where the soul must dwell in between the terrestrial and celestial realm, awaiting its entrance into Heaven. The person is dead and must wait for God to come and lead him into Heaven. Similarly, he was caught between the cave and enlightenment. Turning back and being the voice for the voiceless is symbolic of seeking refuge in darkness because of the blinding light, and not being able to adjust immediately. It is a gradual process, which is why those who argue that he embraces this role of leader, and who believe that he does desire to return, using outdated lyrics like the aforementioned as evidence, are mistaken.

As Socrates supposes, if the "chosen one" is led to the light, returns, and notices discordance amongst his former cellmates, they will mock him for having gone toward the light, because they will no longer share the same "realities," in that his realities will have become truths. In this sense, prisoners like Sigel will make the Philosopher King's new milieu feel more like exile than paradise. They are the crabs in the bucket clenching his garments so that he can rejoin them, to borrow a concept from Booker T. Washington. In expecting him to give back, in the interests of nepotism, they do not recognize their own limitations.

Alas, the Philosopher King will endure if he can resist conformity; he cannot be fragile or docile in the face of the consequences of ascending. Jay-Z must not feel compelled to dumb down for his audience to double his dollars ("Moment of Clarity"), because his words are original thought. He must courageously hold true to originality and not fall to the pressures of society or even his audience. He has to believe in both heterogeneity *and* homogeneity. The enlightened individual, after growing "accustomed to the sight of the upper world" (Emerson 388), must be allowed to linger amongst other Philosopher Kings. He must also understand that some must remain in the cave, for intellectualism is mysterious and perhaps designed for a selected few. This characterizes heterogeneity. When Jay-Z understands his role as the "Self-Reliant Philosopher King," he will sing a song of thanks for his moment or period of clarity in which his honesty can come forth as truths that can impact the world ("Moment of Clarity"). I hope he will be exonerated of these charges and escape being demonized for simply embracing the light. The title "phony" will be seen as a misnomer. Maybe then Jay-Z will be applauded for accomplishing this "rags-to-riches-melting-pot story," which is part of the traditional American

Dream. Critics must remember that he cannot exist on another plane and live in the cave simultaneously. In these respects, perhaps Jay-Z is exonerated from all "charges" because he redefines the Platonic Philosopher King: he is the "Self-Reliant Philosopher King."

For Further Consideration

QUESTIONS

1. Beanie Sigel says, "If you had to go through hardships and struggles in your life, and then you get to the point where you are out of that, why let your brother go through that pain too?" (see YouTube, 'Beanie Sigel Addresses His Situation Towards Jay-Z'). Looking at Plato's Allegory of the Cave and the "Talented Tenth," using excerpts from Ralph Waldo Emerson's Essay on Self-Reliance, what responsibility does success mandate to those whom you were "in the cave" with at some point?

2. What exactly does Emerson's phrase "foolish consistency" mean? Is it fair to accuse Jay-Z of misrepresentation or contradicting himself in terms of concepts and statements, or both?

3. The rapper Drake's commercial hit "Successful" and the video highlight an apparently tormented Drake. What is/are his problem(s)? Do the lyrics of "Trey Songz" complement this track or serve as a distraction to what Drake is trying to portray? Is this song is an indictment on images of materialistic success in hip hop? In what ways is Jay-Z's "success" attainable or even conceivable to most of the people to whom Jay-Z claims to speak? In what ways has Jay-Z transcended normalcy in the rap industry? Provide an explanation for each.

Works Cited

Arenas, J.C. "Sell Out: Jay-Z Loses Credibility for a Seat in the White House." *Breitbart.com. Big Hollywood* . 9 March 2010.

Beatty, Paul. *The White Boy Shuffle.* New York. Picador, 1996.

Du Bois, W.E.B. *The Souls of Black Folk: Three Negro Classics.* New York: Avon, 1965.

Emerson, Ralph Waldo. "Self-Reliance." *The American Tradition in Literature.* 11th ed. Ed. Barbara Perkins and George Perkins. Boston: McGraw-Hill, 2007. 419–29.

"Entertainment: Shawn Carter — *Best Life* Interview on Personal Success." *Best Life Magazine Online.* 11 March 2009. TDMG. 2004.

Jones, Preston. "Jay-Z: *Kingdom Come.*" *Slant Magazine Online.* 22 November 2006.

Jay-Z. *American Gangsta.* Roc-A-Fella/Def Jam, 2007.

_____. "Beanie Sigel: The DJ ON&ON Interview." *Jumpturnstyle.com.* 29 November 2009.

_____. *The Black Album.* Roc-A-Fella/Def Jam, 2003.

_____. *The Blueprint.* Uptown/Universal, 2001.

_____. *Blueprint 2: The Gift & the Curse.* Def Jam, 2002.

_____. *Blueprint 3.* Roc Nation/Atlantic, 2009.

_____. *The Dynasty.* Roc La Familia, 2000.

_____. *Kingdom Come.* Roc-A-Fella/Def Jam, 2006.

_____. *Reasonable Doubt.* Roc-A-Fella Records, 1996.

Murfett, Andrew. "Beyond Bentleys and Chains." *The Age*. 26 February 2010. Fairfax Digital, 2008.

Plato. *The Republic* VII. Trans. J. Harward. *Great Books of the Western World*. Ed. Mortimer J. Adler. Chicago: Encyclopedia Britannica, 1990. 388–401.

Sarup, Madan. *An Introductory Guide to Post-Structuralism and Postmodernism*. 2d ed. Athens, GA: University of Georgia Press, 1993.

Sigel, Beanie. "Beanie Sigel Gets Detailed on Why He Went In on Jay-Z!" *Worldstarhiphop.com*. 30 October 2009.

_____. "50 Cent x Beanie Sigel Interview with the Hot Boys in Philadelphia PT 1." *YouTube.com*. 4 November 2009.

About the Contributors

Melina Abdullah is acting chair and an associate professor of pan–African studies at California State University, Los Angeles. She has authored numerous articles and book chapters, with subjects ranging from political coalition building to hip hop womanism and is working on her first book, on hip hop and political mobilization.

Julius Bailey is coordinator of philosophy and religion in the Department of Humanities at Central State University, Wilberforce, Ohio, and is a visiting professor of philosophy at Wittenberg University, Springfield, Ohio. His research interests stretch from Russian literature to hip hop culture, with a common thread being the doings and sufferings of people purposed toward voice and inclusion.

Sha'Dawn Battle is an assistant professor of English at Central State University, Wilberforce, Ohio. She is primary editor for Speaker of the House Publishing and has been accepted into the University of Cincinnati's doctoral program in literature.

Toni Blackman is an award-winning artist, and the U.S. Department of State selected her to work as the first hip hop artist to work as an American cultural specialist and hip hop ambassador. Her first book was *Inner-Course* (2003). She is considered one of the pioneers of hip hop theater.

A.D. Carson is a high school educator whose only aspiration as a high school student was to become a professional rapper. After releasing two albums independently and living out his rap dreams he chose education as a professional career. His work has appeared in *Collage* and *The Alchemist's Review* and *Quiddity International Literary Journal*. He recently published *Cold: A Hip Hop Novel* (2011).

Gil Cook is an assistant professor of English in the Rosary College of Arts and Sciences at Dominican University in Illinois. His research examines diasporic black subjectivity via analyses of global black literatures, hip hop culture, and critical race theory.

Davey D is a hip hop historian, journalist, deejay, community activist and cofounder of the Bay Area Hip Hop Coalition. He sits on the advisory board for civic organizations like Black Youth Vote as well as Rock the Vote. He was the guest curator for the Rock and Roll Hall of Fame "Hip Hop Nation" exhibit when it came to San Francisco's Yerba Buena Center in 2001.

Daylan Dufelmeier is a researcher with Harvard University's Hip Hop Archive and program director for Chicago Hunger. He graduated from Florida A&M University with a degree in philosophy and religion.

G. Jahwara Giddings is a professor of Africana history and chairperson of the Humanities Department at Central State University, Wilberforce, Ohio. His research interests include African American nationalist theory, pan–African cultural history and Afrocentric pedagogy, including service-learning. He is the author of *Contemporary Afrocentric Scholarship: Toward a Functional Cultural Philosophy*.

Nicole Hodges Persley is an assistant professor of theatre at the University of Kansas. Her research and teaching interests include African American theater and performance and hip hop studies. Ms. Hodges Persley is writing a comparative study of hip hop theater and performance artists in the United States, England, and France.

T. Hasan Johnson teaches at California State University, Fresno, in the Africana and American Indian Studies Program. His research focuses on Africana resistance cultures and media within Africana communities.

Bakari Kitwana is a journalist, activist, and political analyst whose commentary on politics and youth culture have been seen on the CNN, Fox News (*The O'Reilly Factor*), C-Span, and PBS (*The Tavis Smiley Show*), and have been heard on NPR. He is senior media fellow at the Harvard Law–based think tank The Jamestown Project and the CEO of Rap Sessions: Community Dialogues on Hip-Hop, which conducts town hall meetings around the country on difficult dialogues facing the hip hop generation.

Stephany Rose is an assistant professor in the Department of Women's and Ethnic Studies in the College of Letters, Arts and Sciences at the University of Colorado at Colorado Springs. Her areas of specialization are 19th and 20th century American literature, critical race theory, and critical whiteness studies.

David Stovall is an associate professor in educational policy studies and African American studies at the University of Illinois, Chicago. His scholarship investigates critical race theory, concepts of social justice in education, the relationship between housing and education, and the relationship between schools and community stakeholders.

Index

Abdul-Rauf, Mahmoud 134
Abdullah, Melina 10, 141–155
Adorno, Theodore 180–183
African(a) Studies 211; *see also* Black studies
Africanist 42, 46, 49–50, 53, 58
Afrika Bambaata 40, 58, 84, 120
Alexander (the Great) 5
Alger, Horatio 134, 137
Allegory of the Cave 192, 197, 200, 209
Ani, Marimba 42
Authenticity 10, 39–40, 48, 74, 120, 134, 155, 189, 191–193, 202

Baldwin, James 2, 125
Baraka, Amiri 28, 39, 43
Baraka, Ras 16
Battle, Sha'Dawn 14, 191–209
Beanie Sigel 44, 59, 193–194, 196, 209–210
Beatty, Paul 209
Bell, Derrick 10
Bennett, Bill 109
Black aesthetics 109
Black bourgeoisie 101–102, 107, 109
Black liberation (pedagogy) 106, 126, 185–186
Black middle class 19, 101, 107, 111–116
Black Power movement 91, 101, 105–106, 113, 120
Black studies 180, 184; *see also* African(a) studies
Black unemployment rates 100
Black Youth Project 111, 115
Blackening up 110
Blackman, Toni 14, 25–38
Blasphemy 195
Blues (music genre) 27–28, 39, 45–46 102, 110, 160
Boyd, Todd 180
Britto, Marvette 6
Brown, Chris 152
Brown, James 10, 12
Bryan, Carmen 150
Buck (personae) 60, 143–145, 154, 185

Capitalism 13, 19, 27, 32, 36, 103, 105–106, 108, 113, 122–123, 126, 128, 144, 204

Capitalist studies 1–2
Carson, A.D 8, 172–179
Charlamagne Tha God 196
Che Guevera 105, 113
Chuck D 2, 25, 56, 58, 134, 136–137, 139, 146, 155
Civil rights movement 31, 91, 99, 101, 115
Clear Channel 146
Clinton, Hillary 3, 53
Cobb, Jelani 31, 143
Cohen, Cathy 115
Cohen, Lyor 46
Common (MC) 18, 33, 43, 59, 87, 93, 126–127, 135, 172
Cone, James H. 46
Consciousness (socially) 4–5, 85–87, 93–94, 119, 126, 138, 144, 148, 153, 160, 186–188, 193
Contemporary politics 1–2
Cook, Gil 14, 180–190
Coon 143, 153
Cooper, Anna J. 2
The Coup 147, 149
Crenshaw, Kimberle 10
Critical analysis 7, 162
Crime and Punishment 12, 21
Crouch, Stanley 31, 110
Cultural consciousness 192, 195, 205
Cultural studies 1–2, 180, 182, 189

Davey D 14–16, 52–65
Dead Prez 27, 49, 58, 137, 147
Def Jam (Records) 5, 136, 163
Delgado, Richard 10
Derrida, Jacques 11, 19, 202
Dionysian 7
Djeli 42, 76, 78; *see also* Griot
Dostoevsky, Fyodor 12, 20–21
Drug game 73, 161
DuBois, W.E.B. 2, 14–15, 46, 101, 105, 199
Dufelmeier, Dylan 6, 12, 132–140
Dyson, Michael Eric 20, 29, 58, 69

Ellington, Duke 10, 50
Ellis, Cose 115

Emcee 26–29, 32–35, 39, 41, 44–49, 52, 54, 69, 72–73, 76, 78, 80, 87–89, 91–94, 159, 169; *see also* M.C.
Emerson, Ralph Waldo 4, 191–193, 199–209
Eminem 44, 49, 80, 172
Eve 149

Fabolous 195
The Fat Boys 143
Female exceptionalism 151
Feminism 150
50 Cent 8, 20, 49, 80, 103, 114, 194, 210
Forman, Murray 187
40/40 Club 21
Franklin, Aretha 39, 48, 50
Frazier, E. Franklin 2, 101–102, 105
Freire, Paulo 186

Gates, Henry Louis 112, 116, 130
George, Nelson 120, 143, 184
Giddings, G .Jahwara 6, 39–51
Glaucon 197
Glaude, Eddie 2
Gordon Gekko 5
Graham, Otis 112, 116
Gramsci, Antonio 169
Grandmaster Flash 2, 31, 40, 58, 62, 70, 82, 120
Griot 27–28, 42, 68, 71–72, 74–78, 80–82, 178, 192; *see also* Djeli

Haiti 4, 44, 139
Hall, Stuart (decoding theory) 182–183
Hare, Nathan 102, 107
Harlem Renaissance 11, 78, 79, 82–83
Healy, Mark 49
Hedonism 19, 87–88, 123
Hefner, Hugh 100, 110, 112
Hermeneutics 195
Heron, Gil Scott 2
Hill, Lauren 120, 149
Hip hop 20, 25–34, 37–53, 56–60, 62, 64–81, 84–104, 109, 111–115, 118, 120–122, 126–128, 130, 134, 136, 138–155, 163–164, 168–174, 179–181, 184; aesthetics 40–42, 48, 103, 110–11, 120, 128; commodification 121, 145, 148; community 59, 122, 125, 143, 146–151; corporate interests 64, 138, 143; generation 6, 30, 49, 105, 109, 113, 148; purists 103, 164
Hodges Persley, Nicole 9, 67–83
Holiday, Billie 39, 45, 50
Hood (existence) 2, 7, 12, 14, 20, 73, 99, 175–176, 185, 187–188, 191–194, 196–198, 201, 203–204, 207
Horkheimer, Max 180–183
Hughes, Langston 11
Hurricane Katrina 4, 34, 108, 128, 138, 198
Hurston, Zora Neale 192

Iguodala, Andre 195
Imitation 13, 15, 33, 72, 86, 90, 125, 168, 200–202, 208

Immortal Technique 147
Individualism 13, 19, 87, 88, 110, 127, 200
Innovation 8, 10, 12, 39
Islam 86; nation 31, 56, 86, 106
Islamic Council of Youth Forums 25

Jamila, Shani 149
Jazz 10, 28, 31, 39, 49, 51, 102, 110, 133
Jeffries, John 187–188
Jezebel 142–144, 150, 155
Jim Crow 2, 11
Johnson, James W. 12, 20
Johnson, Robert 133, 136
Johnson, T. Hasan 9, 16, 84–95

Karenga, Maulana 47
Kitwana, Bakari 9, 10, 49, 95, 99–113, 123, 138 153, 170, 189
Knowles, Beyoncé 41, 44–45, 52, 58, 61, 92, 147, 151–152, 195
Kool Herc 58, 84, 120–121, 142
KRS-One 2, 16, 35, 74, 84, 86, 89–90, 144
Kurtis Blow 58, 143
Kuti, Fela 67
Kuzusa mtima 41
Kweli, Talib 34, 87, 93, 126, 134–135, 173, 179

Last poets 2, 27, 28, 31
Lawndale/Little Village School for Social Justice 167
Lee, Spike 31, 106, 114, 116
Lexical ambiguity 195
Lil Kim 44, 145–146, 149, 153, 155
Lil Wayne 38, 48–49, 52, 80, 103
Lord, Albert 67–68, 71–72, 75
Lupe Fiasco 193

Malcolm X 19–20, 25, 29, 31, 44, 55, 65, 86, 101, 105, 106, 112, 114, 116
Mansback, Adam 10, 127
Marable, Manning 105
Marcy Projects 2, 14, 43–44, 59, 64, 71, 191, 194
Matrifocal 40–41, 47–48
Mayfield, Curtis 2
M.C. 26–29, 32–35, 39, 41, 44–49, 52, 54, 69, 72–73, 76, 78, 80, 87–89, 91–94, 159, 169; *see also* Emcee
McQuail, Denis 182
McLyte 149
Memphis Bleek 44, 54, 151
M.I.A. 102
Misnomer 162, 208
Misogyny 47–48, 93, 126, 142, 148, 160, 169, 184
Monie Love 149
Morgan, Joan 112, 149
Morrison, Toni 2, 15, 39, 40–41, 46 179, 192
Multicultural consciousness 192, 205

Narcissism 87, 147
Nas (Nasir Jones) 25, 61, 76, 80, 91–92, 103, 114, 116, 149–151, 173
National culture 99–100, 102, 109–112
Nationalism: American 124; black 100, 106; cultural 6, 39, 47
Nicks, Stevie 10
Nietzsche, Friedrich 12, 119
Notorious B.I.G 2, 9, 43–44, 55–56, 67, 72–73, 82, 91–92, 148, 201–202
N.W.A 86, 151

Obama, Pres. Barack 3, 25, 30, 44, 49, 53, 58–62, 64, 99–100, 111, 115, 194–195
Oral narrative: African 68–71, 75, 78; Greek 68
Oral tradition 25–26, 29, 34, 41–42, 67–72, 77–79
Orature 41
O'Reilly, Bill 187, 109

Paltrow, Gwyneth 49
Paris 16, 90, 112, 149
Parry, Millman 71–72, 74
Patillo-McCoy, Mary 101
Pedagogy 14; hip hop 7–8, 18; of liberation 185–186
Perry, Imani 67, 142, 168
Peterson, James 116
Pharmakon 11
Philosopher-king 1, 4, 8, 14, 191–193, 195, 197–203, 205, 207–209
Pimp/whore structure 44
Plato 2, 14, 20, 191–193, 197–200, 207, 209–210
Post civil rights 15, 20, 104, 106, 108
Post-structuralism 202, 210
Pough, Gwendolyn 153, 155
Powell, Adam Clayton, Jr. 101
Powell, Kevin 170
Public Enemy 16, 25, 63, 85, 90, 120, 136, 144

Q-Tip 44, 47
Queen Latifah 149

Radio One 16, 146
Rapsessions.org 111–112
Rashad, Phylicia 2
Redding, Otis 48
Remy Ma 149
Reverse racism 107
Rhoden, William (Rhoden's Paradox) 132–136
Rihanna 44, 152
Roc Nation 5, 21, 51, 190, 209
Roc-A-Fella Records 163
Rocawear 5, 164
Rock, Chris 102
Rock and roll 11, 110
Rose, Stephany 6, 13, 117–131

Rose, Tricia 58, 112, 126, 137, 138, 149
Roxanne Shante 142–143
Run D.M.C 143

Sartre, Jean-Paul 106
Scarborough, Joe 3
Schur, Richard 10
Self-reliance 200, 204, 207, 209
Sexism 85, 118, 122, 126, 141–144, 146, 148–150, 153–154
Shakur, Tupac 9, 26, 28, 55, 84, 91–92, 103 149–151, 173–174
Sharpton, Al 26, 38, 202
Shelby, Tommie 112, 116
Sidbury, James 40
Simmons, Russell 13, 16, 31, 49, 57, 60, 65, 105, 134–135, 164
Simone, Nina 2
60 Minutes 4
Snoop Dogg 44, 55, 103, 151
Social justice 57, 84, 86, 102
Socrates 2, 15, 192, 197–199, 203, 205, 208
Spirituality 17, 25, 32–33, 40–41, 44–46, 56, 85–86, 90, 93, 123, 162
Stovall, David 7, 10, 159–171
Street consciousness 65, 105, 113, 116
Street culture 103, 111

Talented Tenth 101, 199, 209
Thurman, Wallace 11
Toms (uncle) 143, 154, 205
Too Short 55–56, 149, 151
Toure 136, 138
Transcendence 44, 104, 195–196, 198
Trina 110, 114–115
Truth, Sojourner 12

United Nations (water for life campaign) 4
Universal Music Group 146

Victorian ideals 9

Walker, Alice 51
Washington, Booker T. 12, 105, 208
West, Cornel 1–2, 6, 10, 15, 17, 19, 29
West, Kanye 44, 80, 88–89, 196
White middle class 110
Williams, Tennessee 6, 19
Williams, Thomas Chatterton 112, 116
Wilson, Elliot 10
Winfrey, Oprah 4, 19, 27, 70, 150, 184, 187
Womanism 47, 141, 150, 211
Womanist masculinity 141, 143, 145, 147, 149, 151–153, 155
Wright, Jaguar 44–45

X-Clan 69, 73, 85, 90, 93

Yo-Yo 149